EBURY PRESS

MADAM SIR

Manjari Jaruhar is a 1976-batch officer of the Indian Police Service (IPS). She has served in Bihar and Jharkhand, at the SVP National Police Academy, and with the Central Industrial Security Force (CISF) and Central Reserve Police Force (CRPF). She retired as special director general, CISF, in 2010. As the very first woman IPS officer in Bihar, she built a reputation as a highly effective, professional yet caring officer. In recognition of her contributions, she has been awarded the Police Medal for Meritorious Service and the President's Police Medal for Distinguished Service. After retiring, Jaruhar headed the anti-piracy wing of the Indian music industry and currently serves as a consultant to TCS on homeland security. She is also an adviser to the FICCI Private Security Industry Committee. Jaruhar is a student of English literature. Besides reading, she enjoys travelling, cooking and spending time with her grandchildren. She lives in Delhi with her husband, Rakesh, a fellow IPS officer.

T0274715

ADVANCE PRAISE FOR THE BOOK

'I have had the good fortune of knowing Manjari Jaruhar for the past forty-five years. I was tasked by Arun Nehru, then minister of state in the Ministry of Home Affairs, GOI, to select a good IPS officer to serve on the faculty of the National Police Academy at Hyderabad.

I first asked Kiran Bedi, who straightaway said 'NO'. There were very few women in the IPS with the experience needed to instruct IPS probationers. I studied their ACRs and hit on the Bihar cadre couple of Manjari and Rakesh Jaruhar. Manjari had an outstanding record in the field. Rakesh was by temperament a scholar. Both would fit in with the NPA's requirements. Its director, A.A. Ali, was consulted. He immediately agreed. Since the couple itself was willing to leave mainstream policing in their native Bihar, every stakeholder was happy.

Manjari is not only a good police officer with the right values and sense of justice but she and Rakesh are both good human beings—a quality the people we serve demand.

Excerpts from her experiences in the service will convince readers about her commitment to the Constitution, the law and to the people she has sworn to serve.

Women IPS officers were a rarity when Manjari qualified and was chosen. In Bihar, she was the very first! So, it does not surprise me that her superiors of the time were uncertain and wary of her utility in difficult times. But she more than proved herself and was much sought after by seniors on the lookout for capable and effective junior leaders. This book will tell you why!'—**Julio Ribeiro, IPS (retd)**

* * *

'This is a rich and moving memoir of a woman's ascent to success. The story of Manjari Jaruhar's life captures her grit and singular dedication to forge an independent identity. In a searingly honest biographical account, Manjari takes us through scenes and spaces of her life. Tracing her aspirations over time, the book is both an inspiring portrait of an individual and a glimpse into the gendered complexities of social and public life in India.

I had the privilege of meeting Manjari as a student at Delhi University. Over the years, I have seen her travel from strength to strength, beginning as a junior police officer, to becoming the special director-general of the Central Industrial Security Force (CISF). This was not an easy road, as the book reveals with insight. *Madam Sir* is a remarkable story of a personal journey that throws light on Manjari Jaruhar's experiences and about what it means to survive and succeed as a professional woman in India'—**Radha Sarma Hegde, professor, media, culture and communication, New York University**

* * *

'There had always been a feeling that there were not enough women officers of the Indian Police Service (IPS) who put down their thoughts on their careers after hanging up their boots. Manjari Jaruhar's beautiful memoir fills in, at least partially, this long-felt need.

This easy read is soaked with sentiment that the fluent pen of Manjari brilliantly captures. There is a positivism that is striking. Bihar of yesteryear always evoked negative responses. Manjari steers clear of the pessimism that marks all the writings on a once-blighted state that is fast shedding its earlier image of a lawless and shoddy place.

There are many situations described by the author which were tricky. Yet Manjari was able to manage them with aplomb. Remember that at the time she entered the service, there were not many women in the higher echelons of the force. So Manjari had no role models to follow. She had to devise her own strategy to handle knotty field issues, which had the potential of dethroning her. She emerges from her memoirs as a bold and enterprising leader who was equal to all the challenges that policing a tough state like Bihar posed.

Amidst all this, she had to raise a family of two children and ensure they were not neglected. Her husband, Rakesh—himself a busy IPS officer—no doubt lent a hand. But which husband can fill the role of a mother? I have the greatest admiration for Manjari for her dignity and courage. She undoubtedly reflected the best in an Indian woman.

This is a book that must be read by policewomen at all levels, who must draw from it the much-needed inspiration to discharge their duties in a hostile environment'—**R.K. Raghavan, IPS (retd) and former diplomat**

MADAM

★★★ || ★★★

SIR

The Story of Bihar's First Woman IPS Officer

Manjari Jaruhar

EBURY
PRESS

An imprint of Penguin Random House

EBURY PRESS

USA | Canada | UK | Ireland | Australia
New Zealand | India | South Africa | China

Ebury Press is part of the Penguin Random House group of companies
whose addresses can be found at global.penguinrandomhouse.com

Published by Penguin Random House India Pvt. Ltd
4th Floor, Capital Tower 1, MG Road,
Gurugram 122 002, Haryana, India

First published in Ebury Press by Penguin Random House India 2022

ISBN 9780143457794

Typeset in Adobe Garamond Pro by Manipal Technologies Limited, Manipal

www.penguin.co.in

*To women who refuse to be fettered and who have the self-belief
that they will find a path, or make one*

Contents

Acknowledgements

I did not want to write this book. That is my honest confession.

Why would anyone be interested in knowing about my life and my struggle?

It was my brother, Pramath, who wanted me to write my story. He was unrelenting in his pursuit and unstinting in his support. My children, Tushar and Anshuman, who have lived my story with me, approved of this idea wholeheartedly and kept reminding me to record my journey.

Even then, it took me a long time to recall all the significant incidents of my life. As I began writing, my husband, Rakesh, was my only reliable source for cross-checking facts spanning over forty years. As in life, he became my go-to person for this book.

I am grateful to have them in my life. I am so glad they forced me to write. I have enjoyed the process, thanks to my editor, Samhita Chakraborty, who painstakingly culled out the full story from my police-report-style writing. I acknowledge Preeti Singh's effort in diligently editing an early draft.

I thank them all.

And most of all, dear reader, thank you for reading my story.

Preface

Anyone can do anything. I often make this claim in my speeches and career advice to young people. For me, it is not merely a catchy one-liner. The first seeds of this were sown early in my life.

When you read *Madam Sir*, you will know why.

Manjari Sinha was the first-ever Bihari and only the fifth 'lady officer' in the country to qualify for the Indian Police Service (IPS) in 1976. This is the story of her remarkable life. For years, I have urged her to pen her story. It is a stunning journey that few people, even those very close to her, know about in any detail. It is a story that will touch you, move you and inspire you, as it has done for me. In my life as an educator, I have met and been inspired by many, many leaders, and their stories have left a lasting impression on me. I have invited many of these leaders to share their stories with students. I witnessed how their authentic and vulnerable narration of their journeys has the power to change someone's life forever. I hope *Madam Sir* will do that for you.

This is a story of tragedy and despair, of courage and hope. Of never giving up. Of standing up for yourself and what you believe in. It is an everyday story. Yet, it has elements of extraordinary grit and resilience, authenticity and dignity, and commitment with purpose. It is the story of millions of girls and women in our country, at home and at work, as they continue to battle against ingrained attitudes and orthodox social norms. It is the story of being human, while maintaining the professionalism of power and authority. At a time, when our bureaucracy is constantly berated and vilified, it is a beacon of hope. It shows that, as long as there are good human beings, there will be good civil servants and good governance. The salutation 'Madam Sir' itself gives a hint of the many contradictions and paradoxes contained in this book.

Madam Sir is also a chronicle of our times. It discusses life in a small town, caste and politics, and a country transforming across generations. It is a valuable account of significant historical events that shaped India, such as the Bhagalpur blindings and the 1984 anti-Sikh riots. For many of us, these are mere newspaper articles or words in a history textbook, but you will live them through the meticulous eyes of a policewoman and an investigating officer.

Manjari Jaruhar, IPS, as my father insisted on addressing her in his letters, is also my didi, the eldest of my three sisters. We were born to four generations of Hindi writers. While my father did write adapted and fictionalized versions of my sister's early life in his short stories, you could say this was a book she was destined to write.

Moreover, every family has a story that defines it and changes its trajectory. *Madam Sir* is that story of my family. We will never know to what extent it transformed us, because who knows how life would have turned out otherwise. My parents were literally left with no choice but to abandon their deeply held beliefs and accept an almost alien new way of life. My sisters all grew up to be highly educated and driven professionals with independent careers spanning the globe. I was exposed to very adult and grown-up issues while I was still a kid, being the last-born and a late child. It brought us all close in ways that can only come from a story like the one you are about to read.

After many years of prodding, followed by an almost abortive false start, I am delighted to present to you *Madam Sir*.

New Delhi   Pramath Raj Sinha
20 October 2020

Student at Patna
Women's College, 1970

Superintendent of Police (SP), 1980

Prologue

It was a cold December morning in 1977. I woke up early and lay in bed in my parents' home in Patna. Was I nervous? Excited? I think a bit of both. It was a fresh new beginning. The beginning of my life on duty.

I put on my new uniform, a smart khaki ensemble that I loved. Shirt tucked into trousers, a sweater, then a cross belt across my uniform, a peaked cap and shoes that shone and winked at me. I looked into the mirror. A young, determined officer looked back at me. My mother came into the room to check on me. She looked surprised, even a little bemused. It was the first time she was seeing her eldest daughter in khaki.

'Very nice,' she smiled.

I smiled back, trying to quell my nervousness. In the distance, the clock tower struck the hour. It was time. This was the day I had been working for so hard. The long hours of study, the gruelling exams, the tough interview, the arduous training, the army attachment—the rigours of the past five years all led to this day. And I was ready.

The Churchill-pattern clock mounted on a tall brick tower is part of the Patna Secretariat. It's one of the city's most recognizable architectural landmarks. The gong of this clock had marked our daily lives in Patna since my childhood. The Secretariat is a sprawling, imposing building.

Back then, there was nothing between the tower and our house. We could see the grand structure and hear its gong every hour. As a child I used to wonder what went on inside this big, busy building. I remember my father taking us to see the Secretariat garden; in winter it was always in full bloom.

Today, that stately building was my destination. I had to report for field training to the office of the inspector general (IG), Bihar police, which was housed in one of the wings of the Secretariat.

As I climbed out of my father's car, I could feel many pairs of eyes on me, following me as I walked up the stairs. I was possibly the only woman in trousers there. The staff in the IG's office stopped their work and stared. I tried to block out the curious glances.

This feeling of being like a fish in a glass bowl was to become my constant companion wherever I went in uniform in the days to come.

I shivered slightly. Was it a cold draught in the building, or was it my own nervousness? I was feeling intimidated by the surroundings and the curiosity I was commanding. But I was also brimming with pride and confidence, having completed the rigorous training.

I was ready for active police duty.

I was first ushered into the office of the deputy inspector-general or DIG (administration), Mr Kailashpati, who gave me some paperwork to complete. He asked me rather curious questions—why had I joined the police, did I know that it was a tough job, would I be able to work night shifts . . .

It surprised me that he seemed to already know everything about me—who I was, who my parents were, my background and even minute details regarding my life. Soon, I would learn that this was the norm in Bihar police. Even before you arrived at any posting, the moment you were notified to join a place, the officers would do a full background check—especially your family, caste, community and personal history.

After waiting for a while, I was asked to go meet the IG, Mr Rajeshwar Lal. I entered his room and executed a sharp salute. I was in awe of him and wanted to make a good impression. After the salute I stood at attention, waiting for his instructions. He said nothing, and the seconds ticked by. He didn't even look up, but continued to write in a file.

After long moments of silence, he finally looked up. He did not ask me who I was. He already knew.

'Oh, you have come?' He took one look at me and went straight back to his file.

'But I don't know what to do with you. I cannot post you until I study Kiran Bedi's file. I have asked for it from Delhi.'

I stood there in silence, wondering why another officer's file was relevant to my posting. She was an IPS officer of the 1972 batch; I was from the 1976 batch.

I would learn soon enough. She was the first woman IPS officer of India, I was the first in the Bihar cadre. The IG went on to express his misgivings about having a 'lady officer' in the force. 'Kiran Bedi is working in Delhi. Bihar is a very, very different place. I don't know where I can post you for your training,' he said, dismissing me.

I was crushed. As I stepped out of his office, I shivered again. This time it was from the frosty welcome I had just received.

So, that was my first day on the job.

But, in your career, as in life, there is always the next day, and then the day after that. I brushed off my initial disappointment like a speck of dust on my new uniform. It is this ability to look past hurdles and hiccups that has held me in good stead throughout my career.

In that moment, I wanted to focus on what an honour it was to be the very first woman IPS officer of Bihar police.

This is my story.

1

A Delicate Daughter

One of my earliest memories is of being in class 1. Twice.

I was a gentle, happy child, growing up under the loving, yet watchful, gaze of my maternal grandparents, my *nana-nani* (maternal grandparents), in their sprawling Patna home. When I turned six, Nani—Mrs Parbati Varma—enrolled me in class 1 at Mount Carmel School. I used to cry every day, possibly because my previous school, Suhas Kanan, was right next to our home. I had felt safe gazing up at the huge, white trunks of the eucalyptus trees that stood between my classroom and my grandparents' veranda, which spanned the front of the house.

A year passed by, and I moved to class 2. There, I cried even more. So, one day, my grandmother marched into the principal's office.

'Manjari is very unhappy in school, she is crying all the time. I don't know what kind of a teacher you have in class 2, but Manjari does not like her at all. Send her back to class 1. She had grown fond of the nun who was her class teacher last year; she will be happy there.'

So back I went to class 1. My parents didn't get to know of this, nor was anyone perturbed by it. No one could have anticipated the impact this loss of a year would have on my life and my career. Possibly because no one imagined I would even have a career. Today, people do these things deliberately, even reducing the age of their children in official documents. But back then, Nani had decided, and that was that.

The principal, despite being a strict disciplinarian nun, could not defy my nani. What an imposing figure she must have cut in her impeccable cotton sari worn the traditional way, the pallu in front. She knew a smattering of English, which she spoke with confidence. She was often seen holding a cigarette or expertly dealing cards at the bridge table. She brooked no nonsense from anyone, be it at home or outside. The poor nuns stood no chance in her formidable presence!

My grandmother was a stickler for discipline and a tough taskmaster. Nothing would escape her notice. Very organized, very sociable, very competent—that is how I remember Nani best.

'You must dress properly, even at home.'

'You must always wash your hands and wipe them on a towel.'

'You must eat a proper breakfast every day, with toast and an egg.'

'You must always eat at the table, with a fork and a knife.'

'No, you cannot go out with friends.'

Nani had never been to school herself. When my grandfather, Dr B.P. Varma, married her, he schooled her himself, having returned from England with a Fellowship of the Royal College of Surgeons (FRCS), a rarity in those days. He had decided to return to India to serve his countrymen, inspired by the words of Mahatma Gandhi.

Amma and Babuji—my parents, Sheela and Udaya Raj Sinha—were not around much in my initial years, often going away to my father's ancestral village, Surajpura, leaving me with my grandparents. Amma was known as Baby at home, and it gave rise to much amusement when my father would call out, 'Baby . . . Baby,' and his wife would respond.

My parents had two more girls after me—my dear sisters, Reshma and Mini. Our little brother, Pramath Raj, or Samir as we call him at home, came along much later, when I was nearly fourteen. The men in my father's family all had two names, including my father, who was also called Shivaji.

Life was lived by the rulebook at my grandparents' house. I grew up with my cousins—my *mausi* (aunt) Leela's son Ranjit and daughter Ranjana—and we accepted the discipline. No movies, no eating ice cream from Patna's famous Golden *thela* wallahs (street vendors), no munching on roasted peanuts from hawkers.

Instead, we were taken out for nice meals at restaurants, while other treats were made for us at home. We got toys and books and were showered with affection. But my abiding memories of my early childhood are of the strict discipline at home. It now seems as if they were preparing me for the regimented life that I would lead as a police officer!

Nothing could be farther from the truth, though.

Despite the emphasis on going to school and doing well in exams, no thought was given to the girls' careers. Nani insisted I know my multiplication tables in Hindi, but it was purely an academic exercise. Career, ambition, independence, self-reliance were not for us. We were supposed to study well, be groomed well and marry well. Of course, to someone *they* would choose for us.

Years later, when I was posted at the Sardar Vallabhbhai Patel National Police Academy in Hyderabad as an assistant director, I attended a counselling session with the famous Dr Gouranga Chattopadhyay of the Indian Institute of Management, Calcutta. He pointed out that many children who are brought up by grandparents or guardians, who are not their parents, remember being under very strict discipline. The guardians feel the pressure of bringing them up in a proper way, and, unknowingly, this pressure is transferred to the children. Parents, in turn, are able to take a more relaxed approach. Looking back, I wonder if my incessant crying in primary school was precipitated by the absence of my parents during those formative years.

Even today, after having retired from the service a decade ago, discipline defines my life. My breakfast of toast, butter and jam must be just so, day after day. My clothes are without a crease, my daily calendar is up to date, and my eye is always on my watch, so I never arrive for an appointment even a minute late. As an officer, I would often arrive too early for a meeting and then wait in my vehicle to kill time.

* * *

My father belonged to a feudal family of zamindars, all highly educated but extremely conservative. Babuji was never interested in the education of his daughters, but my mother insisted the girls be 'convent-educated'. In 1959, when I was in class 3, she enrolled my sisters and me in St Joseph's Convent.

When I was a little older, my parents moved to Patna and built a house near Nana-Nani's and I began to spend more time with my mother and father. But whenever I fell sick, I would be carted off to my grandparents' home, with Nana fussing over me. I fell sick frequently, with diphtheria, whooping cough, mumps. Miserable days that were made bearable by Nana's constant love and care. Being a doctor, Nana would often write his delicate Manjari a note for school and I would happily sit out PT class or any outdoor activity. Little did I know how many gruelling hours of parade awaited me in adulthood.

Nana took a lot of interest in teaching me at home. He inculcated in me the habit of reading, bringing me *The Adventures of Sherlock Holmes* by Sir Arthur Conan Doyle, humorous tales by P.G. Wodehouse or the detective stories of Perry Mason by Erle Stanley Gardner. But he would read them first, and only allow me those books that he thought were appropriate for me.

Nana was a very good doctor, and from him I developed an interest in learning about human physiology. I excelled in the subject, even dreamt of becoming a doctor for a brief while. I was terrible at mathematics, although I always ranked within the first five or six in class, with needlework pulling up my overall score.

The German nuns who taught us needlework were very meticulous. I was one of the favourites of Sister Agnes— otherwise a very strict nun—because of my needlework skills, which we three sisters had picked up from our mother.

In school, I was known as a good organizer, and always took the lead in organizing programmes, exhibitions and fêtes. I loved being a part of these group activities, and, of course, they got you out of many a boring class as well. My mother always attended the programmes in our school. My father had neither the interest nor the time.

I was proud of my needlework as well, which occupied pride of place in the annual needlework exhibition at school when I was in class 10. After the show was over, my mother gathered up every item I had made and my teachers said to me, beaming, 'They will go as part of your wedding trousseau.'

I was sixteen, yet marriage felt right around the corner. It had been like this ever since I could remember. On the subject of marriage, my mother's side and father's side of the family—otherwise so very different in outlook and lifestyle—were on the same page.

When I was in class 6, my sisters and I had just come back from a birthday party, and one of us bumped against the maid, who was carrying a big *dekchi* (pot) of hot milk. The maid lost her balance and the steaming liquid spilled on my legs. I was wearing ballerina shoes and long nylon socks, which got plastered to my skin. My parents were not home, so I ran to the bathroom myself and frantically ran water over my scalded skin, wailing in agony. I tried to peel away the socks but bits of nylon remained stuck to my skin.

Within minutes my legs were covered in angry red blisters. Hearing about the accident, my grandparents immediately rushed over. Nana prescribed egg whites be applied on the affected area. I can still remember the sting of the raw, red skin stretched taut by the drying egg whites. I cried through the night in pain and also because I would miss my half-yearly exam the following day. I was competitive; I did not want to lose out on my class rank because of a missed exam.

Late that night, when my father came home, he was most concerned. His words are still etched in my memory: 'Oh, this is going to leave marks on her legs; it will become a problem when we are fixing her marriage.'

I had once fallen off the bed as a toddler and broken a couple of my front teeth. My parents had been extremely worried that I would end up with crooked teeth and, therefore, with poor marriage prospects. Later, I was taken to a Chinese doctor in Calcutta, who put their fears to rest. Well, the hot milk did not scar my legs, and my teeth are indeed set a little unevenly. Neither made me a good wife, or a bad one at that!

Odd as it may sound now, I never despaired over this obsession with my marriage, and was unaffected by it. Today, most girls will rebel at any talk of an early marriage, but it was different in those days. I just went about my life. School was great fun and, when I look back, my happiest years. St Joseph's Convent laid the foundation of my character. Our education was comprehensive. Along with learning history, geography, science, mathematics and languages, our school encouraged sports and cultural activities. Great emphasis was laid on developing our overall personality and character, which is the hallmark of India's famed 'convent education'.

School began with moral science every day, and Bible studies twice a week. During Easter, we would have a two-day Retreat, when we couldn't speak in school. We had to read prayer books in silence and go to the church to pray quietly. At the time, we were too young to understand the real significance of 'Retreat', but later in life, I learnt to appreciate the power of prayer and meditation. When we were taking the Senior Cambridge exams, we were all ceremoniously taken to the church to pray. Even though we practised a different religion at home, no one minded our being taken to church. I feel people are too quick to take offence over such matters nowadays.

The moral science classes gave us a sense of wrong and right, the value of being truthful and honest, of having integrity. I still

don't know why moral science is not included in the curriculum
of all schools today.

* * *

We were three girls at home, but my parents never yearned for
a boy. They were quite content to bring up their daughters, our
marriage being their topmost concern. Even my grandparents
on both sides didn't seem to mind the lack of a 'male heir'.
But there was constant pressure on my parents from the wider
family, especially from my several aunts. They would drop hints
about the importance of having a boy. One of my aunts, Maya,
even took my mother to a famous Shiv temple to pray for a
son. And the old maid who lovingly brought us up would be
constantly doing one *mannat* (special prayer) or another so that
my parents could be blessed with a son.

The entire clan rejoiced when our brother, Samir, was
born. Our family pandit charted his horoscope, which said he
would become an engineer and his wife would have a wheatish
complexion. This came as a great relief to Nani, because that
meant he would not marry a foreigner. Two of her grandsons
who had gone abroad for studies had ended up marrying
foreigners and moved away from the family. Clearly, 'foreigner'
back then meant only white people.

My father came from a family with a strong literary
tradition; his own father, grandfather and great-grandfather
were men of poetry and literature. Babuji, too, was a writer
and journalist. Given his literary legacy, stalwarts like Acharya
Shivpujan Sahay, Rambriksh Benipuri and Ramdhari Singh
'Dinkar' impressed upon Babuji the need for a Hindi literary
publication. Thus was born *Nayi Dhara,* with Rambriksh

Benipuri as the editor. The first issue came out in April 1950, six months before my birth.

Many writers would come to our house for literary discussions. Poet Mahadevi Verma, writer Gaura Pant (better known as Shivani), Raja Rao (who wrote in English), Ramdhari Singh 'Dinkar', Phanishwar Nath 'Renu' . . . they all visited our home. The famous Hindi writer Kamleshwar stayed in our house for two to three months to take out a special edition of *Nayi Dhara*. Our father was deeply embedded in the political, social and intellectual fabric of those times.

Staying true to its name, Babuji would encourage young writers by giving them space in *Nayi Dhara*, which means 'new stream'. Promising writers, fledgling poets, young thinkers—they would get published in *Nayi Dhara*, along with literary pieces by established writers and commentators. Nowadays, many writers and poets who receive awards and recognition often recall that their first essay or poem was published in *Nayi Dhara* way back in the 1950s and 1960s.

Nayi Dhara continued to be published without a break during his lifetime. Babuji used to worry about its fate after him; he would have been pleased that Samir continues to publish *Nayi Dhara* as a bi-monthly. In late 2019, we all gathered in Patna to celebrate the start of its seventieth year.

Babuji's works were appreciated across the country and included in many college and university syllabi. Researchers did their PhD on his books. His book *Bhoodaani Sonia* was taught in Rajasthan University, while *Andhere Ke Viruddh* was included in the Hindi syllabus at Magadh University.

Throughout his career, Babuji received numerous awards and recognitions, including a special award from the Uttar

Pradesh government in 1972 and the Dr Rajendra Prasad Shikhar Samman by the Bihar government in 2002.

My paternal grandfather, Raja Radhikaraman Prasad Singh—whom we called Baba—was also a highly respected writer of Hindi literature. In 1962, he was conferred the Padma Bhushan, one of the top civilian awards in India. My paternal grandmother, Lalita Devi, passed away when I was a baby and I have no memory of her.

Baba—or Rajaji as he was called in literary circles—was best known for his Hindi novel *Ram-Rahim*. The story goes that one day, one of Baba's best friends declared that there was nothing in Hindi literature to rival William Makepeace Thackeray's *Vanity Fair*, and challenged him to write India's answer to this English masterpiece. Baba took up the challenge and wrote *Ram-Rahim*, a voluminous novel, which was very well received and for which he is remembered in Hindi literature even today. Some of his other novels are *Purab Aur Paschim* and *Chumban Aur Chanta*, while his story *Kaano Mein Kangana* is considered the first short story in Hindi.

Although he held the title of 'Raja', people called him 'fakir raja', because he never succumbed to the trappings of being a feudal landlord. Baba had spent his childhood with Rabindranath Tagore in Santiniketan and had gone on to receive a gold medal in English literature from Allahabad University. Throughout the day, students would visit him at our home; they would all gather on our front veranda, discussing literature, poetry and all kinds of intellectual pursuits. As we kids silently observed these comings and goings, they led to a certain engagement with the wider world, and a kind of intellectual maturity that belied our cloistered upbringing.

This was ably complemented by Nani and my mother's active involvement in social work, especially with the All India Women's Conference (AIWC) and the Bihar Council of Women (BCW). They started a small-crafts school for the local women, to teach them embroidery and stitching to help them earn a livelihood. My mother would stitch frocks for the children of friends and neighbours, and the proceeds would fund the crafts centre. Every year, the members of the AIWC and the BCW organized small fêtes called Anand Mela, and we children would get involved in putting up little stalls, making and selling food items and donating the proceeds to charity.

When the 1962 war broke out, our army was ill-equipped to fight a war in the bitter cold. Every day, huge bales of wool would come to our house, to be distributed among the members of the AIWC and BCW. They would knit socks, sweaters, mufflers and gloves for our jawans and hand them over when trains headed for the battlefront passed through Patna. We children were a part of all this.

This had a profound impact on my career. When I gained some seniority, the welfare of my men and their families became one of my top priorities. It stems from watching Amma and Nani from childhood. I feel children today are underexposed to many forms of community activity. They often remain confined to their screens, which does little to develop their overall personalities.

As busy as my parents must have been with the late arrival of a son, and their myriad social and literary activities, their focus never shifted from the pressing matter of my marriage.

2

It's Your Turn Next

Ever since I was in class 9, my mother had made sure I was learning how to cook and embroider. In fact, between my mother and my grandmother, there wasn't a single skill that I wasn't taught to make me an eligible bride. I was sent for painting classes, I learnt batik, I learnt baking and Chinese cooking, I even learnt shorthand and typewriting. My cousin Ranjana and I were made to learn singing as well, which we did not enjoy because the teacher would come home just after school. The lessons stopped after five long years, when the teacher got fed up with our indifference and quit. I also learnt dancing for some time.

In my late teens, the household acquired a 'gas stove' and an old aunt was summoned to come and teach me fancy recipes. I enjoyed these lessons with my great-aunt and till date I love cooking for my family. Strangely, although my mother supervised my grooming very closely, she herself never taught me to cook any dishes. I picked up some recipes from her only after my marriage.

My parents felt I should acquire all these 'life skills' before being married off. For some reason, driving a car or travelling alone or making important decisions were not considered core skills for a girl. In fact, I was so sheltered that, if the driver failed to pick me up from college, I would keep waiting outside the gates. I did not have the courage to hail a rickshaw and get home on my own.

Even as I was learning to cook, sew and paint like a good girl, I was being exposed to an eclectic atmosphere at home. My father's elder brother, Rajendra Pratap Sinha alias Balaji, was a member of Parliament in the Rajya Sabha for twenty years. He was the patriarch of the family. Another uncle contested several assembly elections in Bihar. Babuji was always their campaign manager. Political discussions, ideological debates, news of the world and national developments swirled around us from childhood, and we children absorbed it all.

We got a taste of how campaigns were conducted in rural Bihar. I saw elections from close quarters as a child—there would be crowds milling about, my father and uncles would be out canvassing for votes the whole day, and then returning to our village home in Surajpura at night to discuss the strategy for the next day. I remember there was no electricity, and they would gather around a lamp to talk about the campaign. People would come home and ask them to visit areas they had not yet covered, raising electoral issues that they needed to address. Then, of course, there were discussions over caste combinations, and how critical they were in Bihar.

All this came back to me years later when, as an SP or a DIG, I had to supervise elections. One stark difference between the elections I saw as a child and the ones that were conducted under my watch was the prevalence of violence. Back in the 1950s, when Indian democracy was still in its infancy, elections were still a people-to-people exercise where personal equations played a big role. And although money did play a part, elections weren't as commercial as they have become now.

* * *

As I did very well in my Senior Cambridge exams, my parents agreed to send me to Lady Irwin College in New Delhi to study domestic science. My results had made me eager to pursue higher studies, and this was a highly rated college for this subject. My parents, on the other hand, had always been impressed by my *bua*'s (aunt) daughters who had studied there and then married into the elite circle of Delhi. They thought this would be the best grooming opportunity for me.

The fees for the first semester paid, I started packing for Delhi with a happy heart. My friends were also excited for me. 'You are so lucky to get this opportunity to study in Delhi,' they said. I couldn't wait for college!

As my departure neared, my father started fretting in earnest. On the day I was to board the train to Delhi, he went to Nana-Nani and confessed that he did not want me to go. 'If she leaves now, it will be like her *bidai* (a ceremony where a daughter bids farewell to her family after marriage). She will get married after college, she will never come back to this home. I am not ready.'

So, my ticket was cancelled, it was decided that I would go to college in Patna. When my parents broke the news to me, I was shattered. I sat in silence amid a sea of open suitcases and new clothes in my room, while a storm of disappointment raged within me. But I did not say a word in protest. No angry scenes, no rebellion, no tantrums.

'*Babuji bhej nahin rahe hain* (My father is not sending me),' I told my friends. My father was the custodian of my life, he had decided for me. End of story.

I had my heart set on studying at Lady Irwin College and being in Delhi. I felt sad, disheartened, dejected. Only girls with a science background were allowed to enrol for domestic science at Lady Irwin College, but I had made it despite coming from the humanities stream, because of my high marks. It had felt like such an achievement. But for what?

The best option available in Patna was Patna Women's College, where my mother had studied. Run by nuns, the campus was the archetype of routine, discipline and rules. The college was essentially an extension of a convent school, minus the uniform. It was an all-girls institution and close to our home, so my father was happy to send me there.

As soon as I reconciled to staying back in Patna, I wanted to study for an honours (specialization) in geography, a subject I was interested in, and which I was good at. But geography, history and political science honours courses were only offered by Patna College, and the classes were held at the Patna University campus, which was co-educational.

That meant studying with boys. And my father would have none of it. I would have a good laugh about it a few years later, while training at the National Police Academy. Not just classes, I was training shoulder-to-shoulder with men in everything from parade to unarmed combat to rock climbing. I was the only woman in my squad.

But during my college days, my father's word prevailed, and the only two choices I was left with were English literature and domestic science. I couldn't bring myself to take up domestic science in Patna. So, I ended up studying for an honours in English literature, even though I had no interest in the subject. For me, the only attraction was that my closest friends, Shubha and Alpana, were studying English literature too.

In life, no kind of education goes to waste. I may not have wanted to pursue English but reading great works of literature must have honed my language and writing skills. For, throughout my career in the police, I was repeatedly appreciated for my meticulous, articulate and precise reports—a trait that is invaluable in a young officer. They paid me rich dividends too: my research and report-writing skills brought me some landmark cases, including the investigation into the infamous Bhagalpur blindings of 1980.

* * *

My aunts had always lamented that, unlike my siblings, I had not inherited my grandmother and mother's regal peaches-and-cream complexion. In colour-obsessed India, this is considered a great drawback in matrimonial matters. 'She has nice features, though,' my aunts ceded, hoping that my complexion would not dim my matrimonial prospects. I do not remember my mother getting stressed about my skin tone, so neither did I.

In fact, I did not bother with this entire exercise but, by the time I reached Senior Cambridge, there was constant talk of finding a suitable groom. I was neither consulted, nor did I question it. I don't think they wanted a teenager's opinion in the serious matter of husband-hunting.

And serious it was. Grooms from the civil services were the new princes of India. My father and uncle would scan the Union Public Service Commission (UPSC) results and mark out the Kayastha boys, the caste we belong to. My uncle, who was an MP and lived in Delhi, through his friends in the home ministry and other high-level connections, would find out the addresses of these promising boys. Then my father would start a correspondence with those families.

The search acquired a sense of urgency when my elder cousin Kanchan's marriage was fixed right after she completed her Senior Cambridge. We all came to Delhi to attend the wedding, which was a grand affair, befitting the stature of her father, my parliamentarian uncle. The reception at Hyderabad House was graced by Mrs Indira Gandhi, the then prime minister of India, and several cabinet ministers. More than the fine clothes we wore or the fancy things we ate or the famous people milling about the reception, I remember the constant quips of 'Manjari, it's your turn next'.

In 1969, my nana fell very sick with cancer. He had repeated surgeries, and seeing him lying on his sickbed was devastating for me. When he came back home after his second surgery, my mausi, my mother, cousin Ranjana and I turned the home into a hospital and nursed him round the clock.

One day, I decided to come home from college abruptly—I cannot explain why—to find that Nana was sinking. He passed away in front of me. Watching him go was one of the hardest things that had happened to me up until then. I felt I had lost an emotional anchor.

* * *

A while later, in October 1969, my mother came to my room. 'We are going to Delhi, and you are coming with us.' No one told me why, but I knew. It was not as if the marriage talk was discreet. The new clothes that suddenly arrived for me were another dead giveaway. For the first time I began to wonder exactly who it was they had found for me. Would I like him? What was the family like? I hoped I could finish college at least.

All these questions silently swirling in my mind, our overnight train rolled into Delhi and we went straight to my aunt's house. Two of my buas lived in Delhi at that time, and they got busy sprucing up the house for the guests, applying *ubtan* (home-made mask) on my face to make me look fairer and dressing me up. In the evening the boy came with his parents to 'see' me. He was in the highly prized Indian foreign service and I felt rather nervous as I got ready for this all-important 'interview'.

Life had far more important interviews in store for me, but that is another story.

After the elders exchanged pleasantries, the two of us were allowed to speak privately. What does one say in five minutes before making a life-changing decision? I think he asked me, 'Where are you studying?' and 'What do you read?' I answered him shyly but did not ask any questions in return. I don't think I was expected to either.

Later that night, I was told that the marriage had been finalized. My parents were so happy that I was overwhelmed and started crying. My aunts were especially thrilled because they themselves were married to Indian Administrative Service (IAS) and Indian Civil Service (ICS) officers, and they felt happy and relieved with what the family had now achieved for me. Our family has always valued alliances with academically and intellectually sound families, and not necessarily with rich ones.

The next day I was engaged. The day after, I was back in Patna, and back in college. When the engagement was announced in Patna, everybody congratulated us. It was, after all, a groom in the foreign service and a father-in-law in the CBI.

That was a big deal in Patna back in the day. I suspect it still is. Other families with young girls started consulting my parents on how to find a similarly good boy and family.

My impending marriage was now the talk of the town.

A few years later, my impending divorce would also become the talk of the town.

3

Taking Charge

If you ask me what went wrong in the marriage, I will not be able to give you a straight answer even now. All these years later, it still remains an inexplicable mystery to me.

Ours had been a rather long engagement, of nearly a year and a half, with ample time for the families to get to know each other. I had come to think of them as a loving family, and of my fiancé as a very warm person. He was in Delhi, I was in Patna. He would occasionally write to me—nice, affectionate letters—and I would write back. He came down to Patna once for his birthday, and my family threw a big party in his honour. He was always courteous with my parents and pleasant to my sisters. Nothing seemed amiss.

In the spring of 1971, when I was in my BA final year, we got married with much fanfare. My parents, who had been planning for this day my entire life, went all out with the preparations—the wedding finery, the gifts, the guest list, the feast and the hospitality. They made it a spectacular and memorable celebration—a big affair in our small city.

It had been decided that I would complete my final examinations and join my husband later that year, by when he too would have finished his foreign-service training. I went to Delhi right after the wedding but returned within a fortnight because my college was still going on. My in-laws gave a lot of importance to my education. I was delighted that I had married into such an understanding family.

It turned out I had rejoiced too soon. That summer, as India fought another war with Pakistan, this time over what would become Bangladesh, a silent war tore my life apart. I had a long study break before the exams, so I went to Delhi for a few weeks, with a head full of dreams and a bag full of books and notes.

My husband was undergoing training, so I planned to study while he was away during the day. However, within a few days I realized that the dynamics of the relationship had changed. The husband had become uninterested in me, the in-laws controlling and critical. I did not feel like I was a part of the family, but rather like an unwelcome guest. In fact, I was asked to stay in the guest room on the ground floor, while their bedrooms were on the first floor. I had no access to the husband's room.

I also noticed that the husband and his mother had a very close relationship, and she did not adjust well to my presence. While I was out of sight, away in Patna, perhaps she could wish away my existence, but my physical presence in his life made her resentful. This, of course, is my deduction now, but back then I was a clueless young girl, unaccustomed to the ways of other families.

The house had peculiar rules. I could not go out anywhere, neither could I have anyone visit me. One day, a cousin came to see me. I was so uncomfortable that I didn't even invite him in, but exchanged a few words and bade him goodbye at the door.

They had very few visitors themselves, nor did they visit anyone as a family. The three of them just kept to themselves. They had another son, a few years younger than my husband, who was kept in a special home outside Delhi. In all the months that I was a part of that family, I never saw the younger son. But his absent presence hung heavy over their lives. Looking back, I feel that perhaps having a child with special needs made the mother cling to her older son even more and she found it harder to share him with another woman.

I don't remember going out for a movie or to a restaurant with the husband, like any newly married couple usually does. He would be immersed in his training and any conversation he had at home would be with his mother. I had never really interacted with boys my age and therefore, had no clue about how to deal with this complex man who was suddenly in my life. Even when he came to sleep in the guest room at night, we led separate lives, like two islands in a soundless ocean of stillness.

What I remember most about that house is the silence. It made me think of Miss Havisham's dismal house from *Great Expectations*. Coming from a bustling household like ours back in Patna, it was very isolating to be confined to that one room all day long, with only my study notes for company. Often, they did not even acknowledge my existence. On most days, I only met the others at the dining table.

One day, when the husband was away, suddenly the in-laws summoned me to the drawing room and asked me to sit down before them, which was quite intimidating. They had sent the orderlies and household help away. It was just me and them. For about an hour and a half, they railed against my family and me. Nothing about me seemed good enough for them, be it my looks, my complexion, my education or my dowry. The silver given was not enough, the clothes I had brought were too ordinary for Delhi, my family was too feudal—the allegations went on and on. But I did not know what they expected of me. They were not asking me to go back to my parents, they were just hurling a series of accusations my way.

'You are not fit to tie my son's shoelaces,' the father-in-law raged. Those words are seared into my brain to date. But I was a meek, timid girl. I said nothing in response and just wept quietly the entire time.

They warned me against saying anything to their son and, given my nature back then, I did not breathe a word when he returned that night. Not that he welcomed any conversation with me. He was not really concerned about me or my life.

Confused, scared and alone, I kept crying, and reading my notes through my tears. I could not eat properly and felt sick inside, but there was nothing else to do.

After six weeks, I returned to Patna. There was a lot of excitement; the family's eldest girl was coming home for the first time after marriage. When I arrived, my sisters and parents crowded around me, eager to hear all about Delhi and my new family. Sitting on my parents' bed, the dam burst. Sobbing and sniffing, I told them everything—the indifference, the humiliation, the allegations.

Amma and Babuji started crying too. It was a big shock for us to see our father in tears, we had never seen him cry; my sisters still remember that fateful day. Our old maid, who had raised us like a second mother, came running into the room. The household was thrown into chaos, lunch forgotten. By the afternoon, my father calmed down. 'Enough is enough. There is no question of your going back,' he said firmly.

I was stunned.

Today, I realize the enormity of his decision. Back then, I was not prepared to take such a bold step. Despite his feudal moorings and conservative outlook, my father's heart ached for his suffering child and he was ready to face the social consequences of a broken marriage, two other unmarried daughters notwithstanding.

In the next few days, close relatives came to the house to comfort us, as if there had been a bereavement in the family. It did feel like something in me had died.

There was no communication from the husband or his parents either. When I called, he would hang up the moment he heard my voice. When I wrote him letters, he never replied. My aunt and uncle who had fixed this alliance were stumped. They could not imagine that such a good family could be so dysfunctional in private. 'Give it some time, things are bound to settle down,' my buas advised us with misplaced optimism. They told me stories of Sita's sacrifices and perseverance. A mythological standard is difficult to live up to!

Those were some of my worst days. My self-esteem hit rock-bottom, the stress took a toll on my mental and physical health. I withdrew into a shell, refusing to go anywhere, meet anybody, lest they ask me about my life as a newly-wed. Weak to my bones, I would throw up often, and it was a struggle just to keep myself together so I could write my BA exams.

Through this traumatic period, my two school friends, Shubha and Alpana, stood by me like rocks. They kept me calm and helped me study. What I loved most about them was that they never probed; they knew things were not right in my marriage, but they were neither inquisitive nor judgemental. Their friendship was very soothing, it was my safe space.

It took ten long months to finish all my exams, instead of the usual three, with constant cancellations, postponements and walkouts being the order of the day. This was the time when the 'total revolution' agitations led by Jayaprakash Narayan raged across Bihar, and college campuses had also got caught up in the *jan andolan* (popular agitation). The boys of Patna University would often walk out of an exam and then instigate those of us who were writing the examination in Patna Women's College to do so as well. Thus, the paper would need to be cancelled and rescheduled.

In those anguished months, I missed my nana and nani the most. We had lost Nana while I was in my first year of college. Losing him felt like losing my greatest pillar of strength. Nani passed away just two days after my wedding. When I returned to Patna a fortnight after my bidai, I headed straight for Nani's house. But she was gone, and my parents had not even informed me because they did not want to bring bad news to a new bride.

I felt that, had my guardian angels been around, this misfortune would not have befallen me, and without them I felt totally lost. Maybe there is no logic to this—what could two old grandparents sitting in Patna have done to save a crumbling marriage in Delhi? But that is the power of unconditional love. It makes you strong.

After my exams, my father sent me to Bombay via Delhi for a holiday to stay with one of my buas. I consulted my Delhi bua and *phuphaji* (uncle), and went over to the in-laws' place to try and salvage the marriage once more. It was probably the first time in my life I was doing something without telling my parents. The past ten months, I had watched my family suffer on my account. The impact of my failed marriage on my parents and siblings had been heartbreaking.

Emboldened by my desperation to make the marriage work, I went and pleaded with the husband to allow me back into his life. He seemed to thaw a bit. He said that if I wanted to, I could come and live with them in Delhi. A few days later, he announced that he had been posted to Moscow and that he would be taking me with him. A small window had opened and a tiny ray of light had been let in. I hoped that being away from family and familiar surroundings might allow the two of us to form a bond and forge a new beginning.

Before leaving for Moscow, they said I could go visit my parents in Patna. Also, the in-laws handed me a long list of things I should buy—household items like bedsheets, a dinner set, wine glasses, cutlery. This surprised me somewhat, since my parents had gifted us all this and more during the wedding. I had not even opened those boxes.

But it was a small blip in the face of the odds this marriage was facing, so I went to Patna and spent the next few days shopping by the list. Although my parents had not insisted on this reconciliation, when they realized that I was going to Moscow, they too got involved in getting everything ready for me. I flew to Russia in July 1972.

A month later, the father-in-law came to visit us in Moscow. There had been no change in the husband's behaviour, and it was left to his father to inform me that the marriage was not working out. He wanted me to return to India with him. Although I did not return with him then, by the end of autumn it was abundantly clear to me that I was as unwanted in Moscow as I had been in Delhi, although I was none the closer to understanding what had gone wrong.

The marriage was dead. And I was done with it. I accepted that there was nothing more I could do to resuscitate this relationship. I returned to Delhi and my parents came to take me back to Patna. But I refused—my first act of defiance in life.

I went to Rao's Study Circle in Connaught Place instead, and enrolled myself to prepare for the UPSC examinations. I had made up my mind that, from then on, I would decide what I had to do. It was time to take charge of my life.

4

Daroga's Job

Why did I decide to join Rao's Study Circle in Delhi when I returned from Moscow? I think there were two reasons.

Although Nana-Nani had brought me up very conservatively, because I was a good student, Nana would sometimes casually say that I should try for the ICS. His words had remained with me, so when I was looking to reboot my life, I thought of joining the IAS—the most elite of the civil services. I doubt he meant it seriously, for he might not have imagined or approved of his granddaughter taking up a profession.

The other reason was that, since some of my relatives were top bureaucrats and senior police officers, I had seen from close quarters how highly the civil services were valued in society. They were perceived to bring stability and prestige to the family. I thought that I should give it a try. Yet, I did not want to put all my hopes in one basket, so I prepared for the State Bank of India and Reserve Bank of India exams as well and also enrolled for a master's degree so that I could become a lecturer. I did not want to miss out on any opportunity that was available to me to take up a career.

My parents were very apprehensive about my staying in Delhi. Babuji was paranoid that I might come to some harm from the in-laws. He implored me to return to Patna and do my master's there. I could become a lecturer at Patna University, he said. I did not listen to my father. My life was *my* life now. I also wanted to escape the gloom and doom that had descended upon our household.

Babuji wrote a letter to all our relatives and friends, making it clear that he was not sending me back, and that the marriage was over. That scotched any possibility of rumours and speculation, but the impact of my failed marriage on my family was tremendous. My mother was always crying, my father was marshalling his resources to fight the divorce case, my sisters were rebelling and refusing to get married until they had a career. Even our baby brother, Samir, who was barely eight years old at the time, was having dreams where he was shooting my ex-husband.

Almost forty-eight years later, when I was confined to our Patna home for many weeks during the COVID-19 pandemic in April 2020, I started looking through my late father's papers. I discovered three stories that he had written during this time, all of them with a striking resonance with my situation. My heart ached. I only remember him being consumed by anger at that time. Reading these stories made me realize all over again just how much he must have been hurting inside because of the misfortune that had befallen his first-born child.

* * *

When I joined Rao's Study Circle, Mr Rao had a detailed interview with me, curious to know why I was taking the exams. After I frankly shared my story, he was very encouraging and gave me a long list of books to read—on Gandhi, the Indian Constitution and Hindu culture, among others. He insisted that I read at least two newspapers every day, the *Times of India* and the *Statesman*, especially the editorial sections, so as to get a balanced view of every issue. The UPSC exams had never been on my radar, so he wanted me to first lay the groundwork and then approach the subject papers.

I remember having to write a précis for the general English paper. The first time round, it took me six hours to write a small piece of 150 words. I had been trained in the art of becoming a housewife my whole life, so I found studying for the competitive exams extremely challenging. It required a lot of mental discipline. Mr Rao, a tough taskmaster, kept a close eye on my progress. I worked extremely hard. Now, when I speak to young aspirants, I always advise them to enrol in a coaching institute, if possible. The guidance and structured approach that I learnt at Rao's proved invaluable to me.

In July 1973, I joined Indraprastha College for Women for a master's in English literature under Delhi University (DU). Although my father was not happy about this, when my youngest sister Mini also enrolled in the same college—popularly called IP College and considered more conservative than Miranda House or Lady Shri Ram College—my father felt somewhat relieved that the two of us would be there together and look after each other.

I stayed with our uncle in Hauz Khas, and my 'overprotective' father sent a car with a driver all the way from Patna to ferry me to college. Yes, it was *that* crazy! Mini would have none of this mollycoddling. She went straight to hostel. After a few months I realized I was wasting too much time commuting, and also missing out on a lot—group studies, friendships and fun. I moved into the hostel in the second semester—it was a big, bold step for me.

Hostel was a whole new world: of carefree, confident young women who wore what they wanted to, went where they liked, smoked, drank and partied and studied hard, and didn't let anybody tell them how to live their life. Our PG hostel overlooked the back gate of Miranda House. I used to observe with amusement and shock all the comings and goings of the Miranda House girls: the boys waiting for them and the free intermingling of boys and girls.

This was the 1970s, when bell-bottoms, polka dots, pantsuits and oversized shades were all the rage. In the midst of all this, there I was, sari-clad and suffering from acute culture shock. My father had insisted that I wear only saris after marriage. I never even questioned it.

Overcoming my shyness, I made two very good friends in IP College—Bharoti Pande from Kolkata (then Calcutta) and Radha Sarma from Chennai (then Madras). One of the reasons we bonded was because we were outsiders, and not graduates from Delhi University. I felt the DU girls went about life with their noses in the air, looking superciliously down upon those who had come from other universities.

On her first day at DU, Radha recalls looking for 'a girl with very long hair, elegantly dressed in a sari'. This is how Radha's sister Sudha, whom I had first met by chance in the corridors of the university's arts faculty, had described me. 'I still remember your old-world charm and elegance in everything you did and still do,' Radha often tells me.

Radha, Bharoti and I came from somewhat privileged backgrounds. Away from our protected cocoons for the first time, learning the ropes of living in a hostel and fending for ourselves, our shared experiences forged a lifelong friendship that has survived both time and distance.

With them, I grew more confident of travelling on a bus, shopping at Janpath, roaming around Connaught Place, eating out and doing all the things I had never done before. I even started commuting by train between Delhi and Patna all by myself.

We began to explore the city and travelling on our own. Bharoti even taught us how to hitch a ride from strangers. Harassment and eve-teasing were rampant on the roads of Delhi even then. One day, we boarded a very crowded bus and stood in the aisle holding on to the overhead rod, chatting away without a care in the world. When our stop came, Radha shouldered her way towards the door, but I could not move.

I realized that a man standing behind me was holding me by my long, thick plait. Everyone in the bus was sniggering. Radha was horrified.

I turned around and said in a stern, calm voice, 'Let go of my *choti* (plait)!'

The man was so stunned that he silently released his grip on my hair, and I walked out. Years later, Radha says, 'I can now see that the cop in you was already there.'

One day, Radha fell very ill with kidney stones, and I carefully nursed her until her mother arrived. Radha's mother was a lovely, warm lady who would often come and stay in the hostel and look after her. We all had a very warm bond with Radha's mother and sister. My sister Mini would come over sometimes too, and we all spent very good times together.

I was happy, even though life in Delhi piled a lot on my plate, especially since I was sitting for various exams. I had to get up early, finish all my chores, take a bus to Rao's Study Circle at 6 a.m., come back and go for my MA classes, prepare for the semester exams, cover the UPSC syllabus *and* handle my divorce case. I was juggling so many new things simultaneously in those days that I had lost count.

A new defiance was building up within me.

'What's the worst that can happen?' I thought. From this defiance was born a determination, that I *would* take control of my life and *would* make something of it.

Radha and Bharoti were struck by how focused I was even at that young age, about having a career and standing on my own feet. Both of them had wanted to take up small jobs, but seeing me, they were inspired to pursue their careers more seriously. After her marriage, Radha ended up going to the US, where she did a PhD. She is now a professor at New York University, while Bharoti moved around with her husband and finally settled down in Singapore, where she teaches at the Singapore Management University.

A few months into the separation, my family received a notice that the husband had moved court in Delhi, bringing a barrage of allegations against me, ranging from a bad character to lack of education to mental instability. Babuji dug in his heels and said he would fight the case tooth and nail. 'I earn money only for two things: my family and my honour,' he declared.

Our lawyer explained to us that their inability to prove the charges in court would mean that we would not get a divorce. So, we filed a counter-case against them in Patna, alleging infliction of mental cruelty. Back then, there was no divorce by mutual consent. You had to file a case and win it to be able to secure a divorce. So, I had to deal with two divorce cases to get legally free of the husband.

The cases dragged on, cutting into my study time. Eventually, the charges brought against me by the in-laws were thrown out by the Delhi court, and the divorce was granted on the basis of our counter-case which we won in the Patna court. But that came after nearly five years, by which time I had almost completed my training at the National Police Academy.

Radha and Bharoti say they were amazed at my maturity, my detachment from the divorce proceedings and my single-minded devotion to my new path. Radha was the first one who pointed out, with awe and incredulity, that I held no bitterness in my heart towards my ex. I think she was right. It was only because I was truly able to leave my past behind that I could move towards a better future.

* * *

I had been preparing for the UPSC exams in earnest, but Mr Rao did not think I was ready to take the exams in 1974, he wanted me to try the following year lest I get demotivated by the results. But my ICS phuphaji pointed out to me that there was a definite age limit in the UPSC exams and I should not miss any attempt within that prescribed age limit. I calculated that if I did not take the exams in 1974, I would not be able to avail of the proviso of three attempts until the age limit of twenty-six years. As DU did not have compulsory attendance, that very day I left for Patna to prepare with total dedication for the UPSC exams of October 1974.

I found out that my neighbour in Patna, Neeraj Kumar, was also sitting for the UPSC exams that year. My family knew his family very well, and I was happy there was someone with whom I could discuss the preparations for the exams.

It was almost a shock when I cleared the UPSC exam in my very first attempt! It was a booster shot of confidence—not just for me but for my family too, who had become very supportive of my career choice by then. However, I did not qualify in the interview. Although I was disappointed, I was also greatly enthused to have cracked the exams and started preparing for the following year with renewed vigour.

I got my master's degree in 1975, appeared for a few interviews for lectureship in Delhi University, and left for Patna to continue the preparations for my next attempt at the UPSC examinations.

Then the floods came.

In September 1975, about a month before I was to take the UPSC exam for the second time, Patna witnessed devastating floods. We had to abandon our home on the ground floor and take up residence with my cousin, Ranjana's family on the first floor of the house. There was no electricity, no water, no space for me to study. I wrote to the UPSC to request a change of exam centre from Patna to Delhi, which was granted.

On the day of my departure, we had to hire a boat which took me, along with my study books, to the train station. My younger sister Reshma was studying at the Indian Institute of Mass Communication in Delhi by then. She was a tower of strength to me during those days, helping me with notes, motivating me, even coming to the exam centre with food and fruit juice in between papers.

I cleared the exam in my second attempt as well, despite all the drama and disruption. The day of the interview dawned on a summer morning in 1976. I was nervous, but also confident and far better prepared.

At the interview, they asked me questions on history, geography and issues relating to Bihar. I thought it was going quite well. Then Amita Malik, the famous journalist and food columnist, who was on the panel, asked me, 'You have listed cooking as one of your hobbies. What do you like to cook?'

'I like to make Continental dishes, ma'am.'

'Name a dish that you can make.'

'I can make a Russian salad, ma'am.'

'Tell us the recipe step by step.'

Now, for a girl who had been groomed in the culinary arts since she was in middle school by her mother, grandmother and grand-aunt, this question was almost too easy. I replied with confidence, clarity and flair.

But Ms Malik was wanted to know more about one of the ingredients. 'Now tell us, how do you make mayonnaise?'

In the break between my Senior Cambridge and college, my mother had sent me to Delhi for better grooming. My bua had admitted me to Mrs Balbir Singh's famous cookery classes, where I had learnt to make mayonnaise. I explained to the panel, drop by drop, the entire process. The panel, including Ms Malik, seemed satisfied with my answer.

As I like to say, no education in life ever goes to waste!

Just as I was thanking the panel and leaving the room with a sigh of relief, a big, burly gentleman, who seemed to be a police officer, suddenly shouted in a booming voice, 'Stop, stop . . . I have another question.' I stopped in my tracks and turned around.

'If I ask you to shoot a person, will you shoot him?' he asked me.

I was stumped.

'A criminal is running away and I ask you to shoot him, will you?' he asked again, more aggressively.

I thought about my answer for a second, my heart thumping. 'If the law permits me, I will shoot him,' I replied in a calm voice.

They said I could leave.

The results were announced; I had cleared the interview! But I had qualified for the Indian Police Service (IPS), not the IAS, which was what we had all wanted for me. Perhaps that last question had been the clincher. Later, I was to learn that officers do not have a blanket licence to shoot, but the law allows an officer to shoot under certain extreme circumstances. So, my answer must have left its mark on the panel.

I had another attempt left to try and make it into the IAS, so I took the UPSC examinations again in 1976. This time, I did not even clear the exam, let alone reach the interview.

But I still had the IPS offer.

It is curious how some predictions come true. When I was a child, a palmist had read my future and said, '*Iske haathon mein bahut* power *hai* (She will wield a lot of power).' Our old maid was convinced I would marry into a rich zamindar family. When I was studying for the UPSC exams, my sister Reshma's then boss had also predicted that I would get to a position of power, although not as an IAS officer. He was sure I would make it to the income tax service.

Little did anyone ever imagine that shy, delicate Manjari was destined for a service that wielded 'power' in the most literal sense.

My father found it hard to accept the idea of me joining the police force. '*Yeh daroga ka naukri hai, tum kaise karogi* (How will you do the job of a police sub-inspector)?' he asked incredulously, all his protective hackles raised as he imagined his delicate daughter roughing it out among cops and criminals. He wanted me to stay in the safe confines of our Patna home and become a lecturer.

But all I wanted was to seize this opportunity that I had worked so hard for. My friend Neeraj Kumar, who had also qualified only for the IPS, said he was taking it up. I felt that if he could become an IPS officer, why couldn't I?

My father was finally persuaded to let me go by his uncle Mr R.A.P. Sinha, who was a former IG of Bihar police. I remember that evening vividly. There was a power cut, and his uncle was pacing up and down the veranda in the dark, giving my father a lecture.

'Shivaji, *kya bewakoofi kar rahe ho* (What is this stupidity)! Look at Kiran Bedi, she is marching on the Rajpath. Why are you holding Manjari back? She has done so well, she must go.'

His words made a strong impression on my father. I wonder whether he would have allowed me to go if Kiran Bedi ma'am had not become the first woman IPS officer in 1972. I have always said that because she joined the IPS, I could join too.

Another person who helped sway my father's decision in my favour was the wife of former IG Mr Suchit Akhauri, also a relative. She came home and spoke to my parents, assuring them that there was a lot of safety in the police service because all police officers are always provided with manpower to protect them. It was the power of these simple and practical words that tilted the balance in my favour.

My parents came to Delhi to see me off and it became an emotional parting. Wracked by second thoughts, my father started crying and I couldn't hold back my tears either. It was like another bidai. '*Bas dekh ke waapas aa jana, haan?*' my worried father tearfully suggested that I just look around the academy's campus and then promptly return home.

By then, even I had begun to doubt my ability survive in the IPS, although I was still excited about going 'just to see'.

Rumours were rife in those days that even though one or two girls had qualified for the IPS they did not join it because the training was just too arduous. I must admit that I was rather apprehensive of this hard life that awaited me. I was also worried that I would be the only girl in my batch.

I arrived in Nagpur at the National Civil Defence College and sent a jubilant message to my father—there were six girls in my batch.

Six! I was not going anywhere.

5

Born Again

'You are not fit to tie my son's shoelaces.'

There was a time when the mere memory of those words would reduce me to tears. But, as I laced up my heavy, brown, ankle boots in my room at the National Police Academy, that bitter episode only brought a smile to my face. I was an IPS officer now, considered a higher rank than the state police service to which my former father-in-law belonged. How strange, unpredictable and beautiful can life be, if only we allow ourselves to take a few chances.

It *was* a bit of chance, coupled with many months of hard work, that had brought me to the academy. The Sardar Vallabhbhai Patel National Police Academy in Hyderabad is very special to me because this is where I was born again.

Before that, on 13 November 1976, I had arrived at the National Civil Defence College in Nagpur, where we had to train for about two weeks before proceeding to Hyderabad.

My roommate was Letika Dhar from Kerala. She was athletic, confident and outgoing—having lived all her life in a hostel, unlike me. Yet, we bonded easily. The friendship grew stronger when she contracted malaria and I took care of her. I also became very friendly with Asha Gopal from Bhopal. Then there was O. Chhaya from Andhra Pradesh, Renuka Bhatia from Delhi and G. Tilkavathi from Tamil Nadu. We girls would always be together, except Tilkavathi, who had her own group of friends among the men from Tamil Nadu. I found Tilkavathi to be an exceptional woman who was not only married but a mother of two.

In Nagpur we learnt about civil defence, home guards, first-aid and the police's interface with civilian authorities. After two weeks, our entire batch of 106 probationers was put on a passenger train to Secunderabad. It was a very slow train and the journey seemed interminably long. Perhaps it was only my excitement to finally see the academy that made it seem so.

We arrived in Secunderabad late in the evening, and were received by havildar Mishra, a tall, hefty policeman. Our luggage was piled on top of police buses and we started our journey for the academy in Shivaramapalli. How beautiful Secunderabad and Hyderabad looked, all lit up, as we drove through the twin cities. Then we seemed to plunge into the dark for miles on the Hyderabad–Bangalore highway, before we saw the lights of the academy twinkling in the distance. We crossed the famous Mir Alam Tank, which became a landmark for us, and entered the hallowed gates.

Disembarking from the bus, we got our first taste of police discipline. Chief drill instructor (CDI) Misra gave us sharp instructions, commanding us to fall in line. Our luggage was unloaded, identified and swiftly despatched to our rooms by the support staff. I found their efficiency quite remarkable.

The IPS mess was impressive and inviting, with wall-to-wall carpeting and a huge portrait of Sardar Vallabhbhai Patel. Setting up a training academy for the IPS officers of independent India was his brainchild, and when the academy shifted to Hyderabad from Mount Abu in 1974, the academy was named after the Iron Man of India.

* * *

We had individual rooms at NPA, with en suite bathrooms—a luxury after the common toilets in the DU hostel. I was allotted room no. 4.

The following day, we were taken on a tour of the sprawling premises. The weather was beautiful, the campus seemed even more so. Spread over 227 acres of undulating landscape, rock clusters typical to the Hyderabad topography and open spaces dotted with trees and flowering shrubs, I loved the vibe of the place. I had never lived in a place like this. I was glad that I had stood my ground and taken the opportunity to get here.

From Nagpur itself, we had been treated as officers and not as students. Bed tea was served every morning, our uniforms were laundered and ironed, and meals laid out efficiently for us in the IPS officers' mess.

From 1972 to 1975, there had been only one lady probationer in each batch. Ours had six. So, a woman orderly was engaged for the first time for us. Ganeshi, who came from Mt Abu, was an efficient woman who would clean our rooms and ensure that several sets of our uniforms were always ready, besides looking after our small personal needs. It was such an indulgence after the hard life in a hostel!

Our regimented life started in earnest a day later, when we were asked to 'fall in' by 6.15 a.m. We marched to the parade ground and were expected to start the morning by running six rounds of the ground. My eyeballs almost popped out at the size of the ground—it was larger than a football field! CDI Misra ordered us to start with two rounds and work our way up to six.

Our PT uniforms had not arrived yet, so we were asked to wear civilian workout clothes. I didn't own any such thing. All I had were saris. Luckily, I had packed a pair of jeans and a top, and I had to make do with that. The arrival of our uniforms later caused tremendous excitement. Donning the khaki trousers and shirt, the beret and the boots, was a matter of great pride. It made me feel good. The uniform was also an equalizer, it made me feel the same as everybody else.

Our squad's junior *ustaad* (trainer), Joseph Christopher, was extremely strict and a stickler for detail. I realized that keeping my hair up was a challenge during PT and parade; my long, heavy locks would always come undone, and he would point it out to me sternly, asking me to fix my hair. I used to get quite stressed out about keeping my hair in place; I felt he was always picking on me. Later, I realized he was a kind man and only wanted to make sure that I looked neat and clean.

Police training seeks to impart various skills that help us do our policing job well. One of the fundamentals of this training is to develop stamina and strength to protect yourself and others. The academy kept us on our toes from 5.30 a.m. to 10.30 p.m. to prepare us for the demands of our new life. While the UPSC had deemed me medically fit, I was acutely aware that I was incapable of strenuous physical work. I now had to do every kind of PT exercise that I had studiously avoided as a child, and so much more—parade, apparatus work, rope climbing, rock climbing . . . .the list was endless.

My feet were swollen, my calves were sore, my shoulders were throbbing . . . it was physical agony like I had never known. But I kept trying my best, and our ustaads appreciated the effort. It was also a solace to see that some of the male probationers were struggling too. Bit by bit, my fitness started improving.

Mentally I was fine. In fact, I was flourishing. Despite being out of my depth in the outdoors, I never gave up. In the academy, I never felt low or lamented about where I had landed myself. I was enthused, I felt I was learning or achieving something new every day.

Parade with a rifle was a revelation. Until I picked up a .303 rifle, I had no idea how heavy it was! I could barely lift it, and marching with it was even harder. My arms would feel like they would pop out of my sockets and drop to the ground. But, by the end of our training, the rifle did not feel heavy at all, it almost felt like an extension of my arm.

In our batch, we were six women and over a hundred men. Sequestered with only girls from school right up to university, I was quite unnerved by the constant proximity with men. But I had to shed my diffidence immediately. The six girls of our batch were assigned to different squads, and we had to do everything with our squad. So, whether it was marching shoulder to shoulder or practising unarmed combat or getting into the pool for swimming lessons, I had to work with my squad mates, all of whom were men. All our instructors were men too.

Swimming lessons posed a double challenge. Not only did I have to conquer my reluctance to swim with so many men, but I also had to conquer my fear of water. We were also taught driving, which all of us were very keen to master. But our training did not stop at just learning how to drive. We had to learn about each and every part of the vehicle, as well as how to change a tyre and fix minor malfunctions.

As IPS officers, it was not likely that we would need to do these jobs later in life, but the academy believes in all-round training and development. An officer may have many subordinates to do these jobs, but a leader must be able to fend for himself or herself. I wholeheartedly agree with this philosophy. It enables an officer to lead from the front if the need arises and helps instil a sense of respect within the rank and file.

Musketry or shooting skill is a sine qua non of police training. Handling all kinds of firearms—rifles, light machine guns, Sten guns, pistols and revolvers—was a novel experience, a far cry from my early life of sewing, knitting and cooking. We learnt to dismantle, assemble, clean and maintain the firearms.

Firing a rifle for the first time was nothing short of thrilling. When I managed to hit the bullseye with all five bullets in my very first attempt and the ustaads praised me, I felt like I was on top of the world. At night, I discovered my collarbone and shoulder had turned black and blue from the recoil, but I didn't care; I was a good shot. That's all that mattered.

People on horseback is a common enough sight. What is not so common is knowing how difficult it is to ride a horse. Here is an animal being forced to respond to your command—one wrong move and the horse may throw the rider off its back. A horse is several times stronger than a human being, it has to be won over to accept you as its rider. This requires extraordinary skills of courage, patience, gentleness and grit. When I finally mastered riding, it was such a confidence booster!

Even now there is a debate in police circles as to why probationers need to learn riding; this skill is hardly ever needed in the field. Some of my batchmates were always trying to get out of riding classes. But being able to ride well and passing my equestrian exams made me feel like a whole new person. It gave me tremendous confidence. I could not imagine riding a horse in Patna or even being allowed to by my father. In fact, during those days, I often thought of Babuji with a smile, wondering what he would have to say if he saw me jostling with my male colleagues, riding a horse or driving a car, let alone shooting a gun.

The IPS training made me acutely aware of the gaps in my upbringing. Why do we not encourage our girls to take up a sport, to build muscle, to build stamina? Why do we protect them from the outdoors for fear of 'ruining' their complexion? Surely, a strong body and fit mind are more to be coveted than fair skin! I did not have daughters of my own, but now, as the granny of two little girls, I hope to ensure that they pursue at least one sport seriously that will stand them in good stead in life.

* * *

Reputed police officers, administrators, journalists, political leaders and scientists would come and address us on various subjects, ranging from the need to create a scientific temper to protecting the vulnerable sections of our society to issues relating to national security. It opened new vistas for me, exposing me to topics of vital importance to our country. It was a world where things were happening and I was expected to contribute my bit.

I slowly began to realize that I was equal to most men. The opposite had been drilled into me since childhood. In indoor subjects like the Indian Penal Code or forensic medicine, I knew as much as most of my male colleagues. From lifting fingerprints to labelling blood stains, I was as good as any other probationer. Police work brought out a new facet of my personality. By the time our training finished, I was prepared to work with men in a predominantly male police department. I felt I was fully capable of directing large groups of men under my command.

As the months went by at the academy, from being objects of curiosity and interest, the men too began to accept us girls as one of them. I think the novelty wore off. That did not stop them, though, from playing pranks. I became the target of one such prank during Mess Night.

A senior SP—rumoured to be a 'confirmed bachelor'—was visiting the academy for a course, and apparently, he had his eye on me. I had no clue. Some of my batchmates fed him a story that I too liked him and advised him to wear a red tie to impress me during Mess Night. The unsuspecting gentleman turned up in a flaming red tie and kept following me around the party. He just wouldn't leave my side, as much as I tried to dodge him! I can imagine how much my batchmates must have enjoyed this.

While I was a reserved person by nature, more comfortable with the other lady officers, I did eventually become friendly with some of the boys. Neeraj Kumar continued to be a trusted friend, and I became friends with B.V. Wanchoo, who was very meticulous and reliable, Praveen Mahendru, Chittaranjan Singh, A.S. Bedi, U.S. Dutt, A.C. Uppal, Y.J.K. Singh and my squad mates V. Rajagopal, R.C. Prasad and Yashovardhan Azad. Y.J.K. Singh and V. Rajagopal were inseparable during those days, while A.C. Uppal tried to confuse our law instructors by asking convoluted questions in class. I also fondly remember Deepak Swarup and R.K. Shukla, who were always up to some tricks, providing us much entertainment amidst our regimented days.

Another time my batchmates had fun at my expense was when I had a riding accident while executing a jump. My right palm got stuck inside the pommel, which is the protruding front portion of the saddle. It broke the last bone connecting my palm to my little finger. The pain was excruciating and my hand had to be put in plaster. It became very difficult to ride or march with the rifle.

My batchmates teased me mercilessly about being so 'delicate' that my cap had fallen on my hand and had broken my bone. It was a far cry from the reaction that such an accident would have elicited back home, where my parents' and grandparents' households would have ground to a halt. It would have been quite a tamasha. And here I was, shaking my head at the silly joke about being injured by a falling cap! I feel these experiences really toughened me up for life in the force.

Despite my hand being in a cast, I managed to clear my riding exams, which was a huge relief. By then, I felt I could do anything. At the academy, I was truly born again.

Every campus and era has its own lingo, code words and acronyms. We had ours too. One acronym that was particularly used for me and some of my friends was 'KTP'. It stood for 'keen type probationer'. 'She is a real KTP,' they would say as we were the sincere ones, the proverbial first-benchers. It was all in good humour. This epithet followed me to the foundation course in Mussoorie as well.

Then there was the dreaded 'love letter'. A love letter is coveted on most campuses, but not in the academy. If any probationer was late for class or an official dinner or failed to turn up at any of the training sessions, or if there was any misbehaviour or tardiness, the very next morning you received a memo from the deputy director (training) and had to explain yourself in writing. We called these memos love letters, which affected our final assessment. So, we had to very assiduously avoid getting a love letter.

Just like in school, I was very involved with cultural activities at the academy. Even after a gruelling day, I would make time for rehearsals. I became the go-to compère for many of the events at the academy. I often struggled to fit everything into twenty-four hours, wishing that I could, somehow, stretch time!

But I was having too much fun even racing against the clock.

* * *

My younger sister Reshma got married during my training, in January 1977. I was granted three days' leave to go for the wedding. I was keen to attend because I had been very involved in finding a 'suitable boy' for my sister. My parents would fret about Reshma's wedding. They felt she was 'too rebellious', and worried that my disastrous experience had put her off marriage.

I was thrilled to learn that Reshma's marriage had been fixed with Anil Nigam, whom I had met with our uncle when he had come down to Delhi from the University of California, Berkeley, USA.

Reshma had completed her course in mass communication at IIMC, topping her class and receiving a gold medal. She then worked for *Searchlight* in Bihar and moved to the *Statesman* in Delhi. So, she was rather frustrated that, while her colleagues were covering the biggest stories of their lives during the Emergency declared by Prime Minister Indira Gandhi, she was getting mehndi (henna) on her palms and jetting off to California.

As a probationer, I used to get a monthly pay of Rs 1017, which allowed me to arrive at our uncle's home in Delhi carrying a few small gifts. Buying something for my sister with my own money was yet another empowering feeling.

Our whole clan was present at the wedding, and everyone kept asking me about life in the academy. 'How are you managing all this, Manjari?' they asked me in awe. I felt quite good about myself, to be honest. It was a far cry from the recluse I might have become as a soon-to-be divorcee, had the IPS not happened to me.

At the wedding, I was up at 5 a.m. out of force of habit, and the officer in me took over. Before I knew it, I had taken charge of various things to help out with the wedding arrangements. The wedding went off smoothly and it was heart-warming to see my parents looking happy after ages.

Little did we know there would be another wedding in the family in just over a year.

6

An Officer and a Wife

Initially, Neeraj was the only boy in my batch with whom I was comfortable chatting. He used to joke that it was only because *he* joined the IPS that my father even considered allowing me to go for IPS training. Decades later, I was extremely happy when Neeraj became the police commissioner of Delhi.

Right from Nagpur, I had noticed someone—a tall, fair-skinned, good-looking boy full of confidence who stood out from others. He had a hearty laugh. I didn't know who he was, nor was I going to find out. I was not interested in men anymore, one traumatic encounter being enough to put me off men for a lifetime. Or so I had felt then.

If my parents even broached the subject of remarriage or mentioned some proposal that had come for me, I would get very upset. It had never occurred to me that I, a divorced woman, could ever get married again. It was also surprising for me to see that people were interested in me. For me, the end of my marriage had signalled the end of the world.

But fate, of course, had other plans.

A few days after we settled in at the academy, Neeraj introduced me to Rakesh Jaruhar, a fellow Bihari and his college mate from St Stephen's College in Delhi. It was *that* boy. I was very aware of his presence but, consciously and deliberately, I would block him from my mind. There were a number of boys who showed more than a passing interest in me at the NPA, but I kept everyone at arm's length.

I never realized when Rakesh's gentleness and friendly nature broke through my defences. He was from Jamshedpur, and we discovered many common acquaintances within our extended families. We often exchanged news about them. Like me, Rakesh had also had a Jesuit education, at Loyola School, Jamshedpur. All this made it very easy to relate to and talk to him.

Maybe it was his quiet presence that was never overbearing, or that he was such a caring person. Or maybe it was simply because I was attracted to him, but we started getting close.

About halfway through our training, I realized that he was fond of me. By then, I had begun to like him as well. But I was still extremely wary of allowing myself to fall in love. Besides, my court case was still going on; I was not a free person yet.

All my life, I have always wanted to be fair to people. Who knew when my divorce would come through or whether it would come through at all! I did not want take advantage of his feelings or disappoint his parents, who must have had so many expectations of their only son. Was it right of me to shackle him to a lame relationship with a divorcee? But Rakesh now says he thought nothing of it.

Throughout our training, we would try not to be seen in each other's company too often, lest we set tongues wagging. My former father-in-law's being a very high-profile police officer meant that everyone knew whose daughter-in-law I was, and also that I was going through divorce proceedings.

'When I think back to our courtship, all I remember is us being careful and restrained,' Rakesh now recalls.

Once in a while, I found myself wondering whether it was possible for me to be married again, and to a *nice* man. I didn't even know if his parents would agree to the match. We belonged to a conservative era, after all, and I was a divorcee. It was only later I realized that divorce was not the end of the world.

What I want to reiterate is that any relationship or marriage may end because of any number of reasons. That is life; both good and bad things happen to good and bad people. We can always rebuild our life and make better choices. We should not be so hard on ourselves.

Around May–June 1977, we had to undertake a tour in batches of around twenty. It was called Bharat Darshan, during which we visited one part of the country to see the cultural, social and political life and also get acquainted with the police practices of those states. I opted for south-west India. For fifteen days, we set off on a tour of Bombay, Goa, Bangalore, Ooty and Chennai. But this was no paid holiday. We were on a very tight schedule, and I felt we were always running from one appointment to the next—meeting the director-general (DG) and other officers of the headquarters, attending a cultural event, interacting with the subordinate ranks, visiting a Police Training College (PTC) then getting back on the train for the next stop. In between, we were taken to some historical sites and places of interest as well.

Rakesh and I were on the same Bharat Darshan tour. It was here that I saw him up close for a fortnight outside the regimen of the academy. He was full of warmth, with an infectious laugh, gentle to a fault, helpful without being demanding and, above all, very understanding of others. The more time I spent in his company, the more I was convinced that he did not have a crooked bone in him. He brought me out of the shell of depression and anxiety in which I had buried myself after the break-up of my marriage. While my achievement of competing for the IPS propelled my life in a new direction, it had only glossed over my emotional scars.

Rakesh set me free.

* * *

Midway through our course, around July 1977, we were allotted our cadres. We had to fill in a form before we joined the academy, listing two preferences of state cadres if we did not get our home state. After Bihar, I had opted for Himachal Pradesh and Punjab. In fact, I didn't really want to go back to Bihar. I had heard that Himachal Pradesh was a very peaceful cadre. My next choice was Punjab because I had occasionally visited my school friend Shubha and her husband, Piyush Kant Verma, in Chandigarh and liked the place.

My UPSC rank was third among candidates from Bihar. When the cadre allotment was announced, six people got Bihar—three from the state and three from outside, according to the rules. But my name was not on this list. Anil Kumar, who was first, and Rakesh, who was second, had gotten Bihar, followed by R.C. Prasad, who was much below me in the ranking.

I was rather upset, and my parents were doubly so. We had taken the Bihar cadre for granted because of my rank. But I was also in two minds, as I had been allotted Himachal Pradesh and wondered whether I should just go there and see what happened. But my parents would have none of it. They couldn't bear to think of their daughter being denied her rightful cadre. I suspect it had less to do with justice and more to do with wanting me close to them.

After being advised by friends, my parents asked me to file a petition with the ministry of home affairs. I did so, and to my immense surprise, a letter arrived for me at the academy, fixing a date in early August for me to meet Union Home Secretary Srinivas Vardhan in Delhi. Many probationers would not have had the courage to walk up to the home secretary, but the defiance that had propelled me into this new life now gave me the confidence to boldly go to Delhi by myself and meet him.

When I walked into his office, I found it to be a large and forbidding room. Srinivasan Vardhan appeared to be a commanding, no-nonsense officer. He did not offer me a seat, so I remained standing. Before going in, I had learnt that Ashwini Kumar, the DG of the Border Security Force (BSF), was also inside.

The home secretary had my file before him. 'Oh, you must be domiciled outside Bihar, that is why you have not been allotted Bihar,' he said.

'No, Sir, I was born in Bihar and I have lived there all my life.'

'Maybe you opted out of Bihar?'

'No, Sir, I did not.'

'Maybe you are mistaken about your rank.'

'Sir, as far as I know, my position is third in Bihar. I would be grateful if you could have it re-examined.'

The exchange took less than five minutes. I thanked him and left. As I was speaking, Ashwini Kumar, who was sitting with his back to me, turned around and looked at me, his expression clearly spoke volumes: 'Who is this chit of a girl speaking so boldly with the home secretary?' it said.

Of course I was nervous, but I was amazed at my clarity of thought and poise.

After a month, a letter arrived at the academy, changing the cadre for a few of us. I had gotten Bihar, while R.C. Prasad was moved to the Punjab cadre. Later, he and I resolved the sticky matter of cadre allotment between us and remained good friends. But that did not prevent others from gossiping that I had 'managed' a cadre change only because I was a woman.

There was a large contingent of officers from Bihar in our batch, and when many of them didn't get their state, they were initially very disappointed. After nearly thirty-five years in the service, however, I feel those officers had it better, in states like Gujarat, Maharashtra, Tamil Nadu or Andhra Pradesh. They hardly ever thought of going out on deputation, whereas the officers in the Bihar cadre had to constantly think of going to work for the government of India for various reasons—be it for our children's education or medical facilities or just better working conditions. My batchmate U.S. Dutt moved to the CBI on deputation for many years, while Sital Das preferred to move to the Punjab cadre after his marriage.

Working in Bihar meant working under very difficult conditions. Rakesh and I were not so concerned with the trappings of the service, but sometimes I would notice wistfully how IPS officers in other states had good housing and better living conditions, or how seats were reserved for their children in medical or engineering colleges by the state.

But all this is hindsight. When the reallotment happened, my parents and I were very relieved that I had gotten Bihar. In our time, cadre allotment used to happen midway through the

NPA training; now it happens even before training begins, so you can decide straightaway whether you want to join at all if you don't get the state cadre you want.

Rakesh was talking seriously about marriage by now, but I wanted to be a free woman first. Reserved as I was by nature, I found myself sharing my dilemmas with him. I found him to be very supportive, cogent and logical in his suggestions. I realized that he was somebody I could turn to for genuine advice. His quiet presence in my life gave me the confidence to deal with everything else that was going on in my life. Five years after we filed the case, my divorce finally came through, just before our passing out parade (POP).

* * *

A fortnight before our POP was to be held on 7 November 1977, I was asked to command my platoon. It was a big honour and I was excited to do it, but crestfallen when I learnt that my parents were not going to be there to witness it.

So many of my batchmates' parents came to see their children; even Rakesh's parents came, but mine didn't. They sent my sister Mini, cousin Ranjana and her family as proxy. It really hurt and infuriated me. My father was refusing to travel anywhere by then, blaming his failing health. I knew it was an imagined illness and not a real one, which made me angrier still.

The days leading up to the POP were spent in a tizzy. After our batch joined the NPA in November 1976, within two months the director S.M. Diaz left, and we did not have a regular director for seven to eight months. Looking back, I feel things were rather lax at the academy during our time. We, of course, did not feel it then; we thought the discipline was strict enough, who wanted more of it?

The then home minister, Charan Singh, was supposed to be the guest of honour at our POP. Just two weeks before the parade, R.D. Singh came in as our director. We got a taste of his discipline right from Day 1, when he dismissed our parade routine out of hand. 'Make them practise a hundred times,' he boomed at the assistant director-outdoors (AD-OD).

Mr Singh tried a complete overhaul of the academy in those few days. He was very keen that we put up a very good show for the home minister. He also announced that everything in the academy must now be bilingual. All the signboards in the academy were painted in Hindi and English almost overnight. Even our badges worn on the shoulders had to have 'IPS' written in Hindi as 'Bha. Pu. Se.', meaning Bhartiya Police Seva. We were all made to buy these new badges. But the boys from the south rebelled, citing the IPS rules, which did not mention bilingual badges anywhere. Suddenly, language politics entered our campus. In the end, because the IPS rules were sacrosanct, R.D. Singh realized his mistake. The order was retracted but the bilingual signboards remained.

I enjoyed commanding my platoon at the POP as well as participating in the play we put up. After the play, we all lined up on stage to meet Charan Singh. He was walking down the line, shaking hands with all the officers and congratulating them. When my turn came, I put out my hand. In convent school we had been taught that a man should not ask to shake a woman's hand; she must offer it first. However, the home minister did not shake my extended hand but folded his hands in a namaste. I was a little taken aback and disappointed. I was later told that as per government protocol, a man doesn't shake hands with a woman.

But, I thought, when in uniform, am I not an officer first and a woman later?

While the winds of change were blowing, with a handful of women entering the police service during our time, accepting this change was still a far cry. Before our batch, which had six women officers, there had been just one woman in each batch, starting with Kiran Bedi in 1972. It took many years for the numbers to reach double digits. Now there are thirty, often forty women in each IPS batch, which is very heartening.

On the day of the POP, I met Rakesh's parents and two sisters for the first time. The Jaruhars were very friendly and warm towards me at our POP. My parents had already been to Jamshedpur and met them, so this meeting was extremely significant. But it was a busy day for me, I barely had time to interact with anyone. Later that night, before falling asleep exhausted, I wondered what my future in-laws thought of me. I wished I could have spoken to them for some more time. Now, I know I needn't have fretted at all. Rakesh's family turned out to be just the kind of supportive family a working woman needs.

* * *

The very next day, we had to leave for our army attachment, which was an extension of our training. I was attached with the 17th Mountain Division in Mongpong, Assam. The army camp was in the interiors of the jungle. Every morning, we had to fall in for PT and parade. During the day, we had exercises on strategy and long hours of firing practice. At night, they would take us deep into jungle terrain to show us jungle warfare tactics.

Brigadiers and captains addressed us. They looked after us well, but we saw how arduous life was in the army. The sense of isolation was all-pervading and the conditions extremely hard. There was no electricity, so petromax lamps had to be used after dark. Sundown also meant 'sleeves down' because of the swarms of mosquitoes.

Very often in the night, I would be startled by the sound of drums. This meant we had to stay indoors. The men would beat drums loudly because elephant herds were moving in the vicinity and they would often attack the camps.

We also visited Nathu La Pass in Sikkim. It was bitterly cold, and we saw how our army jawans were living under extreme conditions. We visited them in their bunkers and had lunch with them. The officers briefed us about the deployment there. The air was extremely rarefied, many of us were breathless. I found it difficult to climb even twenty steps to the look-out post. The Chinese were just across the border. Seeing our large presence, they came out and waved at us, watching us through binoculars the entire time.

The army attachment was a good experience, it gave us an exposure to army life. We learnt how army battalions moved, how every item was numbered, marked and accounted for before and after movement. We also saw how swiftly and efficiently camps are set up in the army. Later in my career, when I came to the Central Reserve Police Force (CRPF), I noticed that their battalions also followed procedures similar to the army's.

After our army attachment, I went back to Patna. It had been several months since I had come home, so my parents were delighted. On his way home to Jamshedpur, Rakesh came and met my parents for the first time. It warmed my heart to see how well they got along. I was surprised and secretly pleased when my father came and did a tika (a religious mark on the forehead) for Rakesh to give his approval and formalize our engagement.

On New Year's Eve, Rakesh and I announced our impending nuptials to our batchmates, which took most of them by surprise.

For every girl, marriage is an unknown journey. For me, it was even more so. Rakesh and I got married on 5 March 1978. Our district training and wedding preparations kept us all busy that spring. The baraat was to come from Jamshedpur, gifts were being readied, wedding songs were being sung by the ladies of the family every day, the house was being decorated. A festive atmosphere prevailed.

My father's happiness was a great source of hope and solace. I couldn't help but wonder, though, what my life would be like after the guests had gone, the notes of the *shehnai* (Indian oboe) had faded and the shamiana (marquee) had been folded. Before I could even sort out my myriad emotions, I was being called to perform the *jaimala* (exchange of garlands). Rakesh looked splendid in his sherwani (ceremonial coat), flashing that disarming smile upon seeing me walk over to him.

I instinctively knew this man would love me and take care of me.

Within a couple of days after our wedding reception in Jamshedpur, we left for Mussoorie to begin our foundation course at the Lal Bahadur Shastri National Academy of Administration on 13 March 1978. It would be a 'honeymoon to remember', the two of us completing our course and stealing some moments of togetherness against the majestic backdrop of the Himalayas.

It was memorable all right, but for reasons that I could hardly have imagined. Even now when I look back, I wonder how I managed to survive that ordeal.

Soon after we arrived, I started feeling sick and low on energy, I lost my appetite and didn't want to get out of bed.

But there were drills to be done, horses to be ridden, classes to be completed and dinners to be attended. Yet I was sick, miserable and anxious all the time. Six weeks later I found out why.

I was pregnant.

The unplanned pregnancy came as a shock to us. I didn't know how I would complete my foundation course. Despite being a beautiful campus, the living conditions were quite basic and not at all suited for my condition. Morning PT became difficult for me, and often I would just lie in bed, not sure what I should do. The damp, cold weather added to my woes, as did the odour of horse dung, which left me nauseous all day. Rakesh was very concerned, but he couldn't sit by my bed all day, holding my hand, as he had to complete the course himself.

I was also quite embarrassed—of falling pregnant so soon, of being sick, of asking to be excused from rigorous exercises and of people finding out. Somehow, I completed the course, passed the exam and returned to Patna to continue my district training.

Our son Tushar was born on 29 November 1978.

7

Fish in a Glass Bowl

After returning from our army attachment, those of us allotted to the Bihar cadre reported to the Patna headquarters. We were supposed to be attached to the headquarters for about two weeks, and then proceed to our respective districts.

This is when I reported to the IG of Bihar police, Rajeshwar Lal, brimming with enthusiasm. But he asked me to wait until he had read Kiran Bedi's file to help him decide 'what to do with a lady officer'. Although I was disheartened, I later saw that I had been posted to Patna, which was considered a very good district. Rakesh went off to Ranchi for his district training while I reported to the senior superintendent of police (SSP), Patna.

The Patna district was traditionally reserved for the topper from Bihar in the IPS batch. I was third in rank, yet I was given Patna. Naturally, the topper, Anil Kumar, was not happy. He would often taunt me, saying that I had been given Patna only because I was a woman. It may have been true—the senior officers possibly felt that a city posting was more suited for a 'lady officer' rather than field training in a rural district, especially in a 'difficult' and 'sensitive' state like Bihar. But I hadn't asked for it and had been prepared to take up any posting I was given.

SSP Patna S.K. Sinha was a competent officer and a gentleman. He contributed much to my training, even though I had my share of problems with him, but that came later. During this time, I also had to work with SP (city) Balmiki Sharma and additional SP (rural) R.N. Prasad. Although they didn't seem too pleased with my presence, they took it in their stride.

At this point, my job was mainly to observe—and absorb— everything that was happening in the offices of the SPs. I particularly remember sitting in the office of the SSP, watching him deal with a steady stream of visitors, most of whom came to him with minor grievances. He laid great importance on officers taking the time out to sit in their offices for the public to come and meet them.

One of the most novel experiences during my field training was going on night rounds, which meant visiting different localities of the city and keeping an eye out for criminal activities. We also checked up on 'history-sheeters' or 'dossierists', as people with a criminal record or dossier are called in police parlance.

I had to do five night rounds a month, accompanying my immediate senior, Assistant Superintendent of Police (ASP) town A.P. Singh, who later became director, CBI. He would visit the lock-up of police stations during night rounds and interrogate suspects who had been brought in during the day on various charges. Sometimes this would carry on into the wee hours of the morning. I was surprised and impressed to notice that even at those odd hours, the officer-in-charge of Pirbahore police station, inspector L.P. Tiwari, would always be in uniform.

Back in those days, there were some officers who would never be seen in civvies (civilian attire) on duty, whatever be the time of day or night. As a young girl, I used to look at them in wonder: When do they go home? When do they wear normal clothes? When do they even relax? They seemed to be always on duty. But that was the culture. It has changed now, with officers often being spotted sporting jeans and jackets while on duty.

Throughout my career, I have always been an advocate of officers on duty wearing the uniform in the right way. Looking back, I think this was unwittingly instilled in me during my field training, observing officers like inspector Tiwari and others.

Another thing that had a profound impact on me were my first few night rounds, not least because of the cold, misty, desolate streets we roamed. What shocked me most was the condition of our lock-ups. Coming from a sheltered home where my parents and grandparents took care of my every need and luxury, I was quite horrified to see these suspects in lock-ups, huddled against the bitter cold, their clothes threadbare. They all crowded together on the floor, as if trying to find a shred of warmth in numbers. But such is the nature of our job that, over time, even this unnerving experience became mundane.

The ASP, A.P. Singh, was not from Bihar. He had been brought up and educated in Delhi and I always felt his outlook towards me was different from other seniors. He wasn't wary of me, nor did he keep me at arm's length or made me feel like an outsider invading the boys' club. In fact, he was always willing to take me around to all the police stations he visited, and on his night rounds. He took my training as seriously as I did.

Visiting police stations was a new experience for me, as well as for those I visited. Everywhere I went, I found the staff curious to know who I was. But after the initial curiosity abated, the constables and police officials were quite willing to explain the nitty-gritties of the job to me.

Even visitors to the police station would often stand and stare in wonder at a woman in uniform—a sight they had clearly never seen before. They settled down soon enough. Many of them were eager to tell me their grievances and wanted me to look into their cases. I think they felt I would be more compassionate and help them.

Pirbahore police station was in the heart of the city, it handled all the law-and-order matters of Patna. It was one of the first police stations the ASP took me to. Inspector Tiwari—the one who was always in uniform—was a very seasoned police officer. For every question the ASP asked him, his standard reply was '*Huzoor bahadur* (Respected Sir)'.

'Has that file arrived?'

'Huzoor bahadur.'

'The constable still hasn't returned from leave?'

'Huzoor bahadur.'

'This case must be wrapped up in a week.'

'Huzoor bahadur.'

What is he really trying to tell the ASP, I wondered. Much later, I realized the beauty of the phrase. It conveyed everything—from 'yes' and 'no' all the way to 'I have heard what you have said'.

What I remember most about those exchanges is how Inspector Tiwari offered his views and advice on cases to the ASP. Despite being senior in rank, Mr Singh would listen. I realized that while rank may appear paramount in the police force, one must recognize the value of experience.

I would visit the police lines with SSP Sinha. There he would ask me to update the service books, which was a tedious job but helped me become conversant with police procedures. Of course, my way to those service books was lined with wide-eyed stares from the men present in the police lines.

The first time I had visited the police lines, a crowd had gathered to watch me. I was painfully embarrassed. A shy, reserved person by nature, becoming a spectacle was extremely distressing for me. I really wanted the earth to open up and swallow me.

Even at the Secretariat, drivers, constables, clerical staff— they all came out to get a good look at a woman in a police uniform. More so than when I entered the Secretariat, this happened when I was leaving. By then, word would spread about my presence. The first time this happened, I had just gotten into my jeep; I casually glanced up and cringed at the furtive, sidelong glances being thrown at me. I looked away immediately, only to espy many more pairs of eyes boring into me from the anonymity of their little windows above.

I think one of the reasons for this odd behaviour was not just seeing a woman in trousers, but the novelty of a woman in an officer's uniform. Back then, officers were supposed to be men, without exception. Even among the constabulary, there were just a handful of lady constables, mostly widows of policemen who had been given the job on compassionate grounds. They wore saris and salwar kameez, not trousers. Gradually all that changed; now all women constables wear shirts and trousers, with a few exceptions.

* * *

As a part of my induction and training programme, I also worked in different offices of the police department, like accounts or the confidential section of the SP's office.

As anyone in the force will tell you, police work involves mounds of paperwork. Going from office to office, I realized this indubitable fact in the police system; furthermore, no document exists in isolation and is invariably a part of a long paper trail. The filing system is thorough, to allow for cross-checking, so that no one can easily fudge documents. I also realized that in the police department, rules were paramount. Everything—even the minutest paperwork—had to be done in a particular manner. I had a lot to learn about processes and procedures, and I had some of the best teachers a young officer could have asked for.

My teachers in those initial, unsure and nervous days were not just senior officers but also members of the subordinate ranks, who were often more experienced. There was one very senior head clerk, Radha Babu, in traditional kurta-dhoti, and then a head moharrir (head of crime statistics), Talha Sahib, always in kurta-pyjama and a white cap. I remember them fondly, they were the only civilians amidst policemen in uniform, engaged in office work.

They never said, '*Yeh* lady *hain, inko kya sikhaye* (She is a lady, what to teach her)?' They were eager to teach me everything. I soon figured out that they were my allies, and did my best to learn from their wealth of knowledge distilled through years of experience.

As an ASP probationer, we had to undergo one month of thana training attachment in a rural police station, and one month in an urban police station. This was followed by three months of holding independent charge of a police station.

For my rural attachment, I was sent to Phulwari Sharif police station. Unlike the city, where something or the other was happening almost every hour, this was a small, sleepy post.

Occasionally there would be land disputes or some petty crimes. Here, I got a taste of rural India, and it reminded me of my village home in Surajpura.

I learnt that the backbone of rural policing in Bihar was the *chowkidari* (watchmen) system. Every village had a chowkidar, who functioned as the eyes and ears of the police. And every few chowkidars were grouped under a *daffadar* (head watchman). They were loyal representatives of the police who faithfully reported all happenings of their villages to the thana. They had a uniform, which they wore proudly. They felt it enhanced their status. It is unfortunate that the chowkidar-daffadar system has now collapsed, having been neglected by many officers.

For my urban-police-station training, I was attached to the Kotwali thana, which was the nerve centre of policing in Patna. The officer-in-charge (OIC) was inspector Radheshyam Singh, a competent officer. But he was wary of me. Although he made sure my training was completed on schedule, it was obvious to me that my presence made him uncomfortable.

One day, a strange incident occurred. It was my first brush with the underbelly of policing.

A man approached me when I was the acting OIC at Kotwali thana. He said he had set up a small ironing shed on the pavement in front of a shop selling coffee. The shopkeeper was objecting to this because he said it was blocking his entrance. A dispute ensued and the shed owner humbly requested our help. I asked Inspector Singh to look into it. Although he agreed, he was visibly displeased. I think he felt the matter was beneath his rank.

That evening, the owner of the ironing shed returned to the police station. Thanking me profusely for helping him, he suddenly dived under the table to touch my feet. Horrified, I protested, assuring him that this was not necessary.

As the man left my room, I felt something rustling near the folds of my sari; officers were allowed to be in civvies in the evening. I bent down and discovered four crisp ten-rupee notes on the floor. I immediately called him back to return the money, but he was almost in tears, refusing to take it back. I didn't know how to convey to him that he needn't do this. Finally, I got up and put the money in his hand and he left. Outside my room, all the policemen of the thana had gathered to watch the commotion.

It was a strange experience, my first time being offered a bribe. It got me thinking—this man was giving us money for helping him. But we hadn't done anything extraordinary except our duty.

Inspector Singh was not happy about the whole incident, although it was unsaid. But there were others who made up for such difficult colleagues. Like assistant sub-inspector (ASI) Kameshwar Mishra, who took me under his wing and taught me many things about investigating a crime scene. A wizened police officer, he was hard-working and loyal to a fault. When I was posted as SP Bokaro, he sent feelers that he would like to come and work under me, and I managed to get him transferred to my district. We have kept in touch all these years; he even came all the way to Delhi when my older son Tushar got married in 2008.

* * *

I learnt about people management from the SSP, especially how to deal with the constabulary. The issue of leave causes much heartburn in the force. Constables are not allowed to keep their families with them, so they are always hankering for leave to go home. The idea behind not giving too many constables permission to keep families is that, when there is an emergency, they must be available in the barracks so they can be immediately mobilized and dispatched for law-and-order duty.

There is a tendency among the constables to go home and overstay, besides a tendency to make up excuses to get the leave sanctioned. And then I learnt that famous expression, 'death *kar gaye*' to imply that someone in the family had died. This expression is common throughout Bihar police. Invariably, we could make out when this death '*kar jana*' was false. The sergeant major would often say, '*Yeh teesri baar inke* father death *kar gaye hain* (This is the third time his father has died).' Some of them would indeed be false claims. If leave was due, it would be regularized against that or they would be given extra drill or censure or a pay cut.

I also learnt an important leadership trait—balance. You can be neither too harsh with the constabulary nor too lenient. I also discovered that the harshest punishment was to assign a constable extra drill. I absorbed all this because soon I was expected to take up independent charge.

I was also attached to the office of the DIG central range, Patna. Known to be a tough taskmaster, L.V. Singh took my training very seriously and checked on my progress almost on a daily basis. One day, he asked me to inquire into a land dispute petition under Bihta police station, a rural part of Patna district. There were also allegations about the officer-in-charge being partisan in this case.

I went to the spot, held a detailed inquiry and submitted my report. But the DIG was not satisfied. 'You have not given a conclusive opinion in your report about who you think is right, who is wrong and about the role played by the OIC. An IPS officer is always expected to lead. You must give an opinion about every case you handle. In your career, there will be many times when you will be asked to adjudicate or to brief seniors. Being decisive is a requisite for leadership.'

He added that, as an officer, I could not be ambivalent in my report, and that I should record my clear opinion without worrying about whether my superior officer would agree with my conclusion or not.

It was an important learning. Yes, we were taught about leadership in the academy, but I didn't realize that even in a matter like this inquiry, an IPS officer must display leadership qualities. This helped me when I started conducting independent inquiries later in my career.

DIG Singh was a stickler for inspections and took me along, even for the outstation ones. He took particular interest in the training of IPS officers, he would often say they are the future of the force. In the midst of an inspection, he would suddenly ask me a question and test my knowledge. One had to always be alert when DIG L.V. Singh was around. He took his role as mentor very seriously, a quality I often find lacking in the officers today.

I must admit I found the training demanding at times, but I am grateful for the rigours the DIG put me through. The SSP too would take me along for inspections; those were like practical classes where every day I learnt something valuable.

Looking back, although my presence as the first lady IPS officer in Bihar evoked an unnerving amount of curiosity and some wariness within the force, my field training did not lag, thanks to the SSP and the DIG. They treated me on a par with my male colleagues and made me do everything that an officer is expected to undergo at this stage.

The presence of a woman officer, however, had given rise to a peculiar confusion within the subordinate ranks.

What to call me?

Officers were always addressed with utmost respect by their juniors, as sir, sahib or huzoor. But what should they call a woman officer? The constabulary came up with a unique coinage, and soon everyone, from junior officers and constables to clerks and drivers, were using it—Madam Sir.

8

My Career Will Be Finished

Getting an independent charge of a subdivision as an ASP felt like going back to square one. The same doubts that were raised before my field posting were aired again. Where can we post a lady officer? What kind of work can she do? What will be safe for her?

All my batchmates were given charge of a subdivision; my husband, Rakesh, was posted as ASP Town, Patna. But I was all but told to be happy that I had done a field training. IG Rajeshwar Lal posted me as ASP, CID (Criminal Investigation Department). It was essentially a desk job.

In our time, IPS officers in Bihar used to be promoted to the rank of SP within four years of joining service. As I belonged to the 1976 batch, at the end of 1980, I would be promoted as SP. But without a field posting as ASP, I knew I would find it hard to get a district charge as SP. I would end up pushing files and making reports for a lifetime. After undergoing the rigorous NPA and district training just like my colleagues, I felt cheated. What was it that I lacked, after all?

There was no precedent of an IPS officer getting posted as ASP in the CID. But here I was, sitting in a dingy little cubicle made of wooden partitions, crammed into a tiny space next to the noisy CID control room. It was quite demoralizing.

One of my jobs was to read special report (SR) files. It was mandatory for SPs and SDPOs (sub-divisional police officers) of every district to personally supervise important cases like murder, dacoity or atrocities against 'lower castes', etc., and send their supervision notes to the CID for analysis and comments. I had to read all these SR files and offer comments on the investigation, which were then presented to senior CID officers for their perusal and direction.

Supervision notes would pour in from all the districts of Bihar, sometimes as many as thirty a day. Although I was dejected at being stuck in the CID, I would read the cases diligently and record my comments.

The weeks rolled into months, I kept sitting at my desk. 'Why have I been banished here?' I kept asking myself; there was nobody I could turn to for help. It had been nearly six months since our field training, in another six months we would become SPs. I was getting quite desperate when, as luck would have it, Rajeshwar Lal retired and S.K. Chatterjee took over as IG, Bihar police. He had four daughters, one of whom, Palash, had been with me in school and college. I gathered my courage and went to Mr Chatterjee's office.

'Sir, my career will be finished,' I said without preamble. I had his attention. I could be a bit frank with him because he was mild-mannered and I had known him all my life as Palash's father; I used to call him 'uncle'. I told him how, despite having completed my field training, I was not awarded a district posting.

He was quite taken aback to learn that I was languishing in the CID. 'Why, why?' he asked me in surprise. He promised to post me to a subdivision.

True to his word, within a couple of days, Mr Chatterjee passed an order posting me as ASP Danapur without waiting for a government notification. I heaved a sigh of relief. Finally, I would be doing the work for which I had joined the force.

* * *

Located just outside Patna, Danapur is a large subdivision with both semi-urban and rural areas. As soon as I was posted as ASP Danapur in January 1980, I knew I would have to quickly prove myself to my seniors, the local thanas as well as the subordinate ranks that I was as capable of doing a field job as any male IPS officer.

I think I managed that through some meticulous casework, a thick skin and a woman's intuition.

The day I arrived in Danapur, that very afternoon, a murder was reported from Rampur Nagwa village under Paliganj police station. There had always been caste tension between the Bhumihars and Yadavs. Naxalism was just raising its head in those parts. As soon as I took charge, I had to leave with a team to supervise the case.

The victim was an aged landlord. The body lay in a field rippling with crops, arms and legs splayed out. His throat had been slit. After studying the crime scene, we started looking for clues around the field. Amid the stalks of wheat, we spotted a large footprint in the soft soil.

An elderly circle inspector, K.R.P. Sinha, was part of my team. I discussed with him that we should lift that footprint properly as a vital piece of evidence. Fresh from training, I showed my team how to collect footprint evidence, the right way of labelling an exhibit and the correct procedure for dispatching it. The other officers watched me curiously, appearing impressed that I knew so much about scientific methods of investigation.

Finding a footprint was very well, but we needed a suspect. I decided to check whether the victim was embroiled in a land dispute or had enmity with anybody in the village. We started collecting intelligence from the local chowkidars. We found out that there were some people working in the field with the victim who were witness to the crime. But they had fled, too scared to talk to the police. We took the villagers into confidence and painstakingly convinced some of them to give us eyewitness accounts. They provided names of the people they had recognized. After verifying their whereabouts, we were able to connect them to the case.

The caste rivalry between the Bhumihars and the Yadavs added another dimension to the case, but I decided I would not bother about caste equations. We conducted massive raids, checking every household in that village irrespective of caste. We finally managed to arrest the people involved and chargesheet the accused.

When the murder happened, the old-timers in the police station told me, 'Madam Sir, *yeh toh aapko salaami de rahein hain* (They are giving you a salute).' It was a common notion that when a police officer is posted to an area, this is how the criminals welcome you, with a message. Hopefully, the raids and the chargesheet were understood by those criminals as my 'salaami' to them too.

Of course I wanted to bring the guilty to book, but I also wanted to send a message to the local population that I was not one to go easy on criminals; that I would not tolerate a breach of law and order; that I would not be partisan. The message I wanted to send to my men was that I expected them not to get involved in the caste politics of the area.

Going into the villages in my uniform, conducting raids, leading my men from the front and taking charge from Day 1 were all valuable experiences that did much to bolster my confidence, besides building my image as a tough cop. Thankfully, I could feel my team beginning to look up to me and accepting me as an officer and a leader. Sentiments that my superiors didn't quite share.

Yet.

* * *

Around this time, some parts of Bihar were becoming notorious for bus dacoities. None of the cases were getting detected. Just before the Holi festival, there is a lot of movement across Bihar, as in many parts of India. People go home, often buying new clothes and other gifts to celebrate the festival of colours with their families.

In 1980, Holi was celebrated on 25 February. A day or two before the festival, there was a bus dacoity in the Bihta police station area and a young man was killed. This was a case of dacoity and murder, considered one of the most heinous crimes under Section 396 of the Indian Penal Code.

The criminals had boarded the bus in the guise of passengers at Patna. As the bus arrived at a secluded spot in the middle of the night, they whipped out their countrymade pistols and threatened the passengers, forcing them to hand over jewellery, watches, wallets and other possessions. All the passengers surrendered their valuables and fled the bus, except one young man who resisted. He was stabbed.

We received the information early in the morning and rushed to the place of occurrence, known as PO in police parlance. We found the floor of the bus covered in blood. The victim had a small but very deep cut on his thigh. The blade must have sliced an artery, causing him to bleed to death.

What moved me about this particular case was that the deceased was a young man, newly married. We learnt that he ran a cloth shop in Palamu, for which he was carrying dress materials and bolts of cloth. Although there were over fifty eyewitnesses, the passengers could not identify the gang because they had taken care to mask their faces with cloth. They said, apart from the countrymade pistols and *chaku*s (knives), the dacoits also had a gun. They had fired at the passengers with the gun to intimidate them, before melting away into the night.

That morning, as I was hurriedly getting ready to leave for the PO, there was a call for me. It was my senior SP, S.K. Sinha, sounding upset—upset not because I had done something wrong, but because he had been saddled with a 'lady officer'.

'I don't know what to do about this; a lady officer has been placed in such a difficult subdivision. How will I control crime like this?' he yelled into the telephone. He said my predecessor had been a tough officer who had always been on the move. 'He would sleep out in the open field, on the embankments, to check crime. But how can a lady officer do all this? What is the use of having a lady officer, I really don't know,' he mourned bitterly.

I clutched the handset and stood there like a statue, listening to his insults.

'We had a murder that day and today we have a bus dacoity with murder. How can I manage?' he lamented.

I must confess that a little bit of my resolve broke that day, his words piercing the hard shell I had built around me. Tears of humiliation and anger overwhelmed me. Yes, I am a woman—what can I do about that? The SSP told me that even the local MLA, Kanhai Singh, had been opposed to my posting and had taken up the matter with the IG.

The SSP nearly succeeded in breaking my spirit that day. But he also made me realize I was made of sterner stuff. Not one to wallow in self-pity for long, I wiped my tears, washed my face and left for work.

The SP rural and the OIC of Bihta police station didn't make my job any easier either. The OIC would often report things directly to the SP, excluding me from the chain of information. My ally was Circle Inspector K.R.P. Sinha, who would keep me apprised of such petty politics.

I tried to block out all this white noise as I investigated the bus dacoity case with single-minded focus. There were standing crops around the spot where the bus was abandoned, and we found the crops flattened in a clear route of retreat. We followed the trail and combed the area, managing to find a train ticket from Tarengana station under Masaurhi police station.

We went to the station and asked around. This line of inquiry eventually didn't yield much, but I wanted to follow every lead, every clue and cover as much ground as possible. Since the passengers had reported firing from a gun, I decided to look into every person who had a licensed firearm in the villages along the road where the bus was found. We also looked up the crime directory to locate all the history-sheeters in those villages.

We zeroed in on a petty criminal in Kanchanpur village, which was close to the PO, and discovered that his father had a licensed firearm. We conducted raids in the village and went to his house, but only the women of the house were present. They denied any knowledge about the whereabouts of the menfolk or when they would be back.

While searching the house, I noticed a stack of boxes against the wall, full of new saris. I asked the women why there were so many new saris. 'There was a wedding in our family. We have to bring home the bride now, so we have bought these as gifts for her family,' they said.

The women seemed genuine enough, so I did not probe further. But something did not seem right. As we were returning from the raid, I kept mulling over the presence of the saris and wondering why it was bothering me. Then it struck me. All the saris were of the same print, in different colours.

Now, as any woman will tell you, when we buy saris for our relatives or friends, we never buy the same print for all the women, do we? Where's the fun in that?

I remembered that the young man who had been stabbed was carrying material for his cloth shop. I had a hunch that the saris could be part of the loot from the bus and shared my suspicion with Inspector Sinha. We decided to mount another raid that night. Collecting all the manpower we had, we surrounded the village and went to that house again to search it thoroughly.

Near the house, we came upon a dry well. Flashing our torches into its depths, we noticed that many items had been dumped inside, including several pieces of luggage and bales of cloth. We hauled them up, recovering the entire loot from the bus dacoity.

We knew we had identified the right house. This was the breakthrough we needed. One by one, we identified everybody involved with the bus dacoity over the next few days. We arrested eight members of the gang, seized the licensed gun and countrymade pistols, and chargesheeted all of them.

Bus dacoities had become a huge menace in Bihar by then, the murder of the young man had made this case even more sensational, with a lot of attention in the media and pressure from the top to take action. It became the first bus-dacoity case in Bihar to be solved—a huge success for my team and me.

This incident taught me something important about human nature. When a crime happens and the family is questioned, a father will turn his son in, a brother or sister too, but a mother will always protect her son, no matter what. Throughout my career, I noted this repeatedly.

After this case was wrapped up, both IG S.K. Chatterjee and DIG (admin.) K.C. Sinha called me to the headquarters and asked me in detail how I had solved the case. Because of the rampant bus dacoities, many officers were interested in knowing how I had worked the case.

Because this was the first bus-dacoity case we had managed to crack, I received an unusual amount of praise from senior police officers. IG S.K. Chatterjee sent me a letter of approbation, saying,

'I must record my appreciation too for the flair that you had displayed and the dedication that you had shown in achieving this task. You have exhibited all the qualities that are required of you for leading your officers and men to sustained performance and final accomplishment of the requisite task.'

My training DIG, L.V. Singh also wrote me a letter to commend me on a job well done. These notes were a huge source of encouragement for me, especially since I had been hankering after a field posting for so long.

A few days later, SSP Sinha summoned me. I braced myself for some more barbs. You can't win over everyone, I reminded myself. I had a good mind to call his bluff. My driver and bodyguard had told me that the previous ASP had never spent a single night outside his home in all his time as in-charge!

I was in for a surprise. The SSP wanted to share something he heard. MLA Kanhai Singh had apparently asked IG Chatterjee, 'Don't you have any more lady officers in the force? You should only post lady officers in my district.'

I was grateful to the SSP for telling me this, although I wondered why he had said all those humiliating things to me on the day after the bus dacoity. I put it down to a good senior who was having a bad day.

When a senior person is under pressure, he or she may invariably take it out on a subordinate. While it is unfair, especially because a junior does not have the authority to retaliate, over the years I have learnt that this is a part and parcel of professional life. A junior has to take it in the right spirit and not be overly sensitive, while not putting up with bullying, of course. A calm demeanour, especially before an unreasonable boss, has always held me in good stead.

After the bus-dacoity case, both seniors and the subordinate ranks started accepting me as part of the force. People started seeing me not just as the only woman officer of Bihar police but as an efficient, no-nonsense and hardworking cop. That November, at the annual crime-prevention mela in Sonepur, I was awarded a wristwatch for successfully investigating and solving the bus-dacoity case. I felt things were finally falling into place.

There was a particular case during my ASP Danapur days that tested my presence of mind; one that required me to take a very tough and split-second decision. This case became known in the media as the 'mandir *kaand*' (incident) and occupied a lot of column space for days.

We had a new senior SP, Anil Kumar Pandey. A fine officer, he was non-interfering and supportive of his juniors. Since Danapur subdivision had both urban and rural areas, for the rural area I reported to SP (rural), and for the urban areas of Danapur and Khagaul, I reported to SP (city). I found the SP (city) a little difficult to work with. He was not really a team player, always believing he knew best.

One Monday morning, an altercation broke out in a small temple in Khagaul, in a railway colony in the Patna district. The temple stood in the heart of the town, in a crowded marketplace. Some antisocial elements had taken control of the temple premises, drinking, smoking ganja, pilfering from the temple collections and being a nuisance.

That morning, they had misbehaved with some local women who had gone to pour holy water on the *shivling* (the statue of Lord Shiva), as was their practice on Mondays in the auspicious month of *Sawan* (July–August). That was the last straw. Hundreds of local residents gathered in front of the temple, blocked the road and demanded that the police flush out these antisocial elements from their temple.

Circle Inspector Ramanand Prasad rushed to the spot with a small contingent from Danapur police station. I followed within a few minutes.

The miscreants had invaded the sanctum sanctorum of the temple and taken up position behind the shivling. The priest, a frail, old man, did not know how to handle the situation.

'*Agar koi andar aya toh goli chala denge*,' the ruffians screamed in a frenzy from within, threatening to shoot anyone who approached the temple.

The agitated crowd was swelling by the minute, demanding police action. The shops in the marketplace were opening, traffic was increasing and the roads were choked. Time was running out for us. It was a veritable powder keg.

As the crowd grew restive, I kept trying to reach the SP (city) to brief him and take directions. But he was not available, nor was he responding to my wireless messages. Khagaul was under his jurisdiction, he knew this area well. He should have been there with us, helping us control the situation.

I realized I had to take charge. We had to keep the control room informed, negotiate with the crowd, keep an eye on the armed hoodlums and ensure that no one stormed the temple.

'I think we should enter the temple now, we can handle whatever the miscreants are planning to do,' Inspector Ramanand Prasad suggested. I was concerned about the safety of the crowd, as well as my men. But I also agreed with the inspector. If we didn't act now, things could spin out of control very fast.

'Let us go in,' I agreed. 'If we need to fire, we will fire.' Inspector Prasad started walking up the steps of the temple; I and the rest of the force followed a few steps behind him.

All of a sudden, two of the gang members, with long, flowing hair, picked up swords and charged towards us. Bellowing a cry of rage, one of them came alarmingly close to the inspector. The inspector also let out a cry and fired his revolver. The bullet hit the man on his forehead; he fell to the ground and started rolling down the steps.

Within seconds of the gunshot, the entire crowd dispersed. I don't think I have seen five hundred people vanish from a scene any faster. We entered the temple, arrested the gang and freed the priest. We found stashes of ganja, countrymade liquor, firearms and bullets inside.

We were concerned about our firing attracting censure. Thankfully, opinion within the police department and the media was all in our favour because we had acted in good faith. It turned out that the deceased was a dossierist in the police station. He had formed his own gang and had captured the temple to collect donations.

The SP city was, of course, unhappy that such an incident had taken place in his jurisdiction and that a lady officer had ordered the firing, but our senior SP was unfazed. All he said was, 'You did what you had to . . .' and laughingly added what he would always say when something untoward happened, '*naukri toh nahin jayegi na* (we won't lose our jobs, right)?'

There is a fine line between 'acting in good faith' and 'jumping the gun'. As officers, we are often called upon to make a split-second decision, that too in a tense situation. When to order 'action' and when to exercise 'restraint' is a critical judgement call which speaks volumes of your leadership qualities. This is probably what the board member had intended to find out when he asked me if I would fire at someone during my UPSC interview.

* * *

If some cases inspired us to go out and do our best to serve the people day after day, others pitted us against the stark realities of our country and caused much heartbreak.

Early one morning, I received a message that a body was being taken towards the Sone river under Bihta police station.

A girl had died in her in-laws' home and they were taking the body to the river to dispose of it, either by cremating it or dumping it in the water. I immediately headed for Bihta, giving instructions over the wireless to the OIC to immediately proceed towards the river. We had to stop them before they got rid of the body, thereby destroying the most crucial evidence.

The OIC arrived at the riverbank just in time to intercept the funeral procession. Abandoning the body, everyone ran away. When we inspected the body, we saw the girl had suffered severe burns, so we sent the body for a post-mortem.

But now we had another problem. Even though some people had been alleging that the girl was killed by her in-laws, there was no one to lodge an FIR.

The girl was originally from Gaya district. I sent a team to Gaya to meet her parents and bring them to Bihta. The parents came, bringing with them letters from their daughter written over the past few months—letters that revealed that her husband and in-laws had been constantly pressurizing her to ask her father for more money. She had written about how they would taunt and torture her. The letters spoke of a young woman's dashed dreams, of the depths of human greed and the harsh reality awaiting many girls in our country who are married off with neither education nor economic independence.

The girl came from a very poor family. 'They have murdered our daughter because we could not satisfy their greed for more dowry,' the parents wept bitterly. They lodged an FIR and we proceeded with the case.

Throughout my career, the plight of women, especially when they have fallen victim to our patriarchal society and cruel practices, have had a profound impact on me. It was as if the eyes of those girls haunted me, spurring me to seek justice on their behalf.

Acting on the parents' FIR, I arrested everybody in the husband's family. They said the girl had committed suicide; alternatively, that her clothes had accidentally caught fire while cooking. Based on the evidence collected, I slapped a murder case against all of them.

By then, I had already started acquiring the reputation of being tough, and this case further reinforced that image. I tried to make sure that we built a strong case so that the accused could not exploit a loophole and go scot-free. I was busy preparing to fight the case on behalf of a girl whom I did not know when she was alive, but who had become so important to me in her untimely death. Little did I know that in our country, waging a legal battle is not always enough.

One day, the girl's parents came to me with folded hands and started pleading with me to close the case. I suspected the family of the accused was threatening them into submission. Or, being poor and old, they were too scared to pursue the case. I told them that their daughter's memory deserved justice and assured them that no harm would come to them.

What they said left me stunned to my very core.

'*Nahin* (No), we have come to withdraw our complaint because they have agreed to marry their son to our second daughter. So, we want to put this case behind us and take them out of jail.'

Of course, as a professional, I could not allow the course of justice to be derailed by the devious scheme of the accused to escape punishment. I told them we could not withdraw the case as it was a case of murder.

All these decades later, I still remember that old man standing before me with his palms folded, tears streaming down his face, begging me not to prosecute his murderous son-in-law because he had agreed to marry another of his daughters.

Always full of fiery talk about seeking justice for the downtrodden, I was numbed into silence that day. In the face of the abject poverty of this old couple with unmarried daughters, I had no words.

In that moment the IPS uniform felt meaningless, I wanted to take it off and throw it away.

9

Behind a Desk, Again

After my stint as ASP Danapur, where I was appreciated for my work, I was feeling confident about assuming charge of a district as SP.

Even before we got our promotion, Rakesh was sent to Nalanda to function as SP in July 1980 because the SP there had to go on medical leave. In a few months, one by one all my batchmates were posted to different districts as SPs, but when the orders came for me, I was crestfallen. I had been posted to the CID again, as SP anti-dowry cell.

Back to the desk, back to pushing files, back to doing very little active fieldwork. How much more did I need to do to prove myself? Over the years, I have heard from several women IPS officers in other states how difficult it was for them, too, to get their initial field postings.

Back then, the Dowry Prohibition Act had no teeth, therefore there was little we could do, even though dowry was a huge problem in Bihar and continues to be a menace even today. What was most frustrating was that, although the law was being broken with impunity, it was very difficult to prove that dowry had been demanded 'in consideration of marriage'. This meant that the marriage would take place *only* if money and gifts were given to the groom and his family. So, barely one or two cases would get registered. The two to three members of my tiny team lacked motivation; they felt they had been 'dumped' in a useless branch.

Although dejected and frustrated with my posting, I decided we should rigorously pursue even the trickle of cases that were coming to us. Gradually, the number of cases being registered started going up. After some time, Chief Minister (CM) Dr Jagannath Mishra passed an order converting the anti-dowry cell to a Mahila Apradh Koshang or crimes against women cell. This was the time when many state governments across India were taking steps to address crimes against women as a separate category and creating such specialized cells to pursue these cases. CM Mishra could have ordered the setting up of a new cell, but I feel that seeing our work in the anti-dowry cell, he felt this team could handle more.

Suddenly, the scope of our work increased manifold. Every case concerning women that was taken over by the CID— be it murder, rape, molestation or dowry harassment—was transferred to our cell for investigation. One such case, under Biraul police station in the Darbhanga district, brought me in direct confrontation with my boss and taught me an important lesson in self-respect.

A woman had died in her in-laws' house soon after marriage and the girl's parents had filed a case accusing them of torture and murder. Our cell took over the investigation and I decided to supervise the case at the spot. I travelled to Biraul to try and get witnesses. Cases come to the CID after a delay, so the initial evidence is usually lost. In this case, even a post-mortem had not been done before disposing of the body, so there was very little evidence to go by. However, I could sense that something was amiss. All the men in the accused family were missing, including the husband. The women were there, but everyone was tight-lipped and taciturn; even the villagers would not speak.

The deceased girl's parents had letters where she had confided in them about how she was being harassed and tortured for more dowry. I decided, on the basis of the letters, that there was a case. I made her husband, father-in-law and other male members of the family the co-accused in the case and filed the chargesheet on the basis of circumstantial evidence.

Late one evening, I was in my office when my assistant, Mr Quddus, came hurrying in. 'Madam Sir, DIG Sahib is asking for the file and your supervision note of the Biraul case.'

I sighed.

This was the DIG, CID—my boss and the bane of my existence. The moment I had joined as SP in the CID, my colleagues had warned me about him. He had a very shady reputation, no one liked him or wanted to give him any significant posting. But he managed well enough through political connections. When I think back, the only word that comes to mind to describe him is 'weasel'.

Now, the Weasel was trying to get his hands on my supervision note. Mr Quddus informed me that the bail application was about to come up for hearing and the accused family was standing in the veranda outside the DIG's office. Perhaps they had contacted him to get a copy of my supervision note, which the accused is not supposed to have access to. There were whispers of wrongdoing, but I never had any evidence to prove this.

The Weasel had questioned me a number of times earlier about why I had chargesheeted the family, making his displeasure very clear. Therefore, I did not want to give him my supervision note. But he was my boss, I could not defy him either.

I told Mr Quddus, 'If the DIG wants the file, let him ask for it in writing.' I also warned my assistant that the file was his responsibility, and that if any document went missing, it would go into his performance record. As a subordinate, that was all that I could do to safeguard the case from my boss.

Well into the evening, the DIG kept sending messages through orderlies and over the intercom that I should come to his office. I refused. Now, this *is* insubordination, but by then I had had enough of the Weasel. Ever since I had joined, he had been tracking my movements. Almost every evening, a short while after I left the office, he would call up my home and ask, 'Madam *aa gayi?*' All he wanted to know from the orderly was whether I was back home, he never asked to speak with me. I was then living with my husband in the additional SP's house near Gandhi Maidan and both of us were very annoyed and harassed by this behaviour. But Rakesh and I didn't really know what to do about the Weasel.

So, when he kept summoning me, I decided I would not go. I had nothing to say to the accused party in the Biraul case, nor to my boss. The next morning, he repeated the summons. Again, I didn't budge.

Suddenly, the Weasel appeared in the doorway of my office. I was stunned beyond belief. In a disciplined and hierarchical force like the police, it is extremely unusual for a senior officer to come to a junior's office, and a DIG striding into the office of the most junior SP in the branch was unheard of. It could well be seen as a form of intimidation.

'I have been calling you since yesterday, but you have not come,' he said, walking in nonchalantly and sitting down opposite me at my desk.

Something snapped inside me. 'Please leave my office,' I told him, my voice rising. A moment of tense silence followed. I was really angry. I stood up, pushed my chair back as if to leave and in an even louder voice I said, 'If you do not leave my office immediately, I am going to leave.' Without a word, the Weasel got up and walked out.

I slumped into my chair in relief and despair. My office was actually only half an office—a cubicle really—and the other half was occupied by another SP. He must have heard it all. When I stepped out, I saw the corridor was lined with CID staff. The entire department had witnessed this unpleasant episode.

Fretting over the possible repercussions, I reported the entire matter to IG CID, N.N. Singh. He was perplexed by the DIG's behaviour too, but he backed me. 'Never mind, you need not report to him anymore, I will make sure of that,' he said, much to my relief.

For the next few days, my face-off with the Weasel was all everyone could talk about. I was worried that he could still harm my career, especially as he had political connections.

Surprisingly—and thankfully—despite being the lone woman officer, all the other men in the department were very supportive of me. SP (special branch) A.N. Singh advised me that I should put everything on record. He even helped me draft that letter, others vetted it and I submitted it to the IG. The support of my colleagues was extremely heartening. The way the department rallied around me and the respect I received for standing up for myself reinforced in me the determination to always do the correct thing.

I am a great believer in letting one's work speak for itself and ignoring negative comments. But I also believe that unless you stand up for yourself in certain decisive moments, you risk losing not only the respect of others, but your own as well. Confronting my boss was a bold move, a daring move, but I did what I had to because I truly believed that I had done nothing wrong. It was he who had been out of line.

This incident had also sent out a message that Manjari was not one to be messed with, that she would not tolerate any misbehaviour of seniors or peers silently.

Another challenging case during this posting was an alleged rape case. I had never handled a rape case before that. A woman functionary at the block level in a village in Munger district had accused fifteen to twenty men of gang-raping her. All the accused were from the block office or associated with it, including the block development officer (BDO).

While recording the victim's testimony, I was taken aback by her body language, tone, demeanour and words. Something did not sit right with me. She described the repeated assaults on her in great detail, her allegations getting more graphic and gory as she continued her animated narration. She appeared very eager to take me through the horrific acts. Even though as IPS officers we are schooled to always approach a case with an open mind, I came away quite sure that there was more to the case than what met the eye.

Rakesh was back in Patna as SP rural. I discussed the case with him as he had earlier investigated a rape case. He said that usually rape victims are so traumatized that they find it extremely difficult to talk about it. I was beginning to suspect the woman's testimony. When I investigated some more, a can of worms spilled out. According to some witnesses, the woman was married and had been found with another man. She had cried rape to save herself. It became a sensational political case in the district because the entire block office had been named.

There was pressure from some quarters to proceed against the accused, but I turned the case false.

Being a woman officer, it was automatically assumed that I would side with the 'victim' in a rape case. But the evidence collected, as well as her testimony, had convinced me that she was concocting the charges.

I often faced such situations later in my career as well, where women petitioners—even if they were in the wrong—expected me to take their side. My fellow officers would also assume that I would always be on the side of the so-called 'victim'. But a woman, too, can make false allegations, as much as any man. It is for the police to be fair and just in dealing with every case, whatever be the gender of the accuser or accused.

* * *

On the family front, there was yet another upheaval. Even as my parents were just about putting my traumatic past behind them, heaving a sigh of relief that their eldest daughter was now happily married and a new mother, they were confronted with a new challenge. My youngest sister, Mini, announced that she wanted to marry her best friend's brother, a Catholic.

Six years younger to me, Mini was the brightest among us; she had been the head girl of her school. She had a somewhat different upbringing because of all that was happening in the family in those years. It had made her independent and headstrong, and she was also allowed many freedoms that Reshma and I had been denied. Mini went to study in Delhi right after her Senior Cambridge, and was allowed to stay in the IP College hostel and not our uncle's house, after which she went on to pursue an MBA at the prestigious XLRI in Jamshedpur.

Founded in 1949 and run by Jesuits, Xavier School of Management, formerly Xavier Labour Relations Institute (XLRI), is the oldest business school in India, where women students were initially barred. When it was finally opened to women, barely one or two would make the cut. Mini had to work extremely hard to get into XLRI; she was among only two or three girls in her batch. XLRI made her a strong, confident young woman who was firmly the master of her own life.

It was here that Mini met Marie Pinto and, later, Marie's brother John. Marie's father had retired from the railway board and joined the Tatas, settling down in Jamshedpur. John Pinto was a young, successful chartered accountant. Love blossomed, and the two decided to marry.

After completing her MBA, Mini got a job with the planning commission in Delhi and started living with our uncle in Hauz Khas. When she announced her wish to marry John to the family, all hell broke loose. Babuji was horrified. He wouldn't even look at the boy's qualifications or family background, or take into consideration the fact that they were in love.

'Will Mini convert to Christianity? What will become of their children? Mini will never be happy in such a marriage,' our father declared.

Not one to be cowed down by parental pressure, in April 1981, Mini went ahead with a registered marriage with John in Bombay. Those were tumultuous times for our family; we did not know how to make Mini 'see sense'. When I look back, I am surprised at my own conduct. You would assume that given all my life experiences, I would have stood by Mini, but I sided with our father instead. I was confused about the future of an interfaith marriage and whether Mini would be accepted by John's devoutly Catholic family. We all, in fact, supported our father and not Mini. How alone she must have felt; I regret my behaviour now.

Today, we are all so very glad that our feisty little sister did not listen to the family. After they registered their marriage and came to Patna, Babuji had no option but to reconcile with the reality. They had an Arya Samaj wedding and we organized a formal reception for the newly-weds.

Over the years, we, including my parents, have all become very fond of John. His good-natured personality and kind heart won us over. From the biggest roadblock, religion became a non-issue in our family. It is also good to see that both of them continue to follow their own faiths and respect each other's religion; there was no conversion, which my father had been worried about.

We are usually so rigid when it comes to religion in matrimonial matters, but Mini's marriage showed me how a difference in religion is not the end of the world. There are good people everywhere and ultimately that is all that matters.

* * *

Back at the CID, as we were sincerely investigating cases of crimes against women, people started sending petitions directly addressed to me. I felt a sense of accomplishment—from being a cell with barely anything to do, we had started getting a lot of work. The members of my cell were also motivated, they no longer felt they were languishing in an unimportant branch. I would often remember the words of my training DIG, L.V. Singh, 'The chair is not important, the person occupying it is.'

I have always felt that you can make a difference wherever you are posted if you put your mind to it.

Around this time, I became the joint secretary of the IPS association and got involved in many police department events. It came naturally to me because I had experience of organizing cultural activities right from school to my NPA days. At the CID, timings were more or less regular, and the evenings were free. I could devote more time to bringing up my son. Rakesh and I were building a house in Patna, and I was able to oversee its construction.

All this was practically and domestically very helpful, but my heart lay in a district posting. I kept trying; I felt that I was being denied something important. I would mull over this problem even as I went around chargesheeting dowry cases, or teaching Tushar the alphabet, or arguing with the builders at our new house.

This struggle to get a district posting was exhausting. Every day I felt my frustration mounting, of repeatedly having to prove myself capable of a field job and being as good as the men. I decided I would have to push harder to get what I wanted. I went to meet the head of Bihar police, DG Gyanendra Narayan. The post of IG police had recently been upgraded to DG police. I pleaded with him to post me to a district. He said he would 'see', without offering any assurances.

A senior officer advised me to appeal to the then CM, Dr Jagannath Mishra. But how could I meet him being such a junior officer? Even if I managed to get an appointment, I could not directly approach the CM without going through my seniors. It would be considered out of order and an act of indiscipline.

The senior colleague then reminded me that an IPS association delegation was going to meet the CM soon. As its joint secretary, I would be a part of it. 'See if you get a chance to speak to the CM after the delegation has met him,' he suggested.

So, after our points were placed before Dr Mishra and the other members of the delegation left the room, I lingered for a few seconds. The CM looked up at me quizzically.

I said, 'Sir, I wanted to make a request.'

'Yes, what is it?'

'Sir, my career is very important to me. I have done a subdivision, but I am not getting posted to a district as SP. I would like to go to a district,' I blurted out.

He looked surprised. 'Oh! I was told that you do not want to go outside Patna.'

'No, no, Sir, I want to go to a district.'

'*Theek hai* (All right), I will post you to a district.'

I came away feeling very happy, although I kept wondering about the false information that had been fed to the CM.

After about fifteen to twenty days, DG Gyanendra Narayan told me that he was proposing my name for the Vaishali district. This was a new district on the outskirts of Patna. A bridge had recently opened over the Ganga to reach Vaishali directly from Patna. 'Your husband is in Patna, so I am posting you to Vaishali,' Mr Narayan said. I was delighted.

But after the state cabinet meeting, a good friend of mine was posted as SP Vaishali, on his first promotion, although he was a year junior to me. No order had come for me, I was to continue where I was.

I later learnt that when my name was proposed, the local MLA had opposed it, saying he did not want a lady officer and 'that they are very uncompromising'. He was a powerful minister and the CM had listened to him, overruling the DG. Bihar's infamous caste equations had scuttled my chances even further. Apparently, I did not belong to the 'right' caste for Vaishali politics and my junior colleague did; I was thus expected to be more useful to the political bosses.

Not getting Vaishali was a huge disappointment for me. I had already finished a year and a half as an SP in the CID. I decided to stop making any effort to get posted to a district. Soon after, I started expecting my second child. I thought I might as well stay in Patna, look after my personal needs and continue to do whatever I could at the crimes against women cell.

I had my younger son on 31 December 1982. We named him Anshuman.

It may seem that I spent much of my time fretting about a district posting, and I cannot deny that I was constantly worried about its repercussions on my career—but while all this was going on, my posting in the CID allowed me to be part of an inquiry that was making national headlines and shaking up Bihar police like never before. I was selected to be a part the inquiry team only because I was in the CID, with not much work to do.

When I was picked for this case, little did I realize the far-reaching implications of the job at hand, how it would forever shape my understanding of police work and nearly make me a pawn in an unsavoury political power play.

This was the inquiry into the infamous Bhagalpur blindings of 1980.

10

Operation Gangajal

Early in 1981, as the state government plane circled in the air preparing for descent, I looked out of the tiny window. All I could see was a sea of heads. Huge crowds had gathered to watch us land in Bhagalpur, a place that had stormed into the national consciousness with its reports of undertrials being brutally blinded by policemen meting out 'swift justice'. And we were descending right into the eye of the storm.

In November–December 1980, the country had been jolted by a series of media reports that thirty-one undertrials—and possibly many more—had had their eyes gouged out and acid poured into their eye sockets while they were in police custody in the district of Bhagalpur in Bihar. The men were permanently blinded, and the blame was pinned on Bihar police.

It was later revealed that these extra-legal blindings had possibly started sometime in 1979, but the first time it was reported in the national media was on 11 October 1980, when the *Indian Express* carried a small report that a supreme-court lawyer had moved a habeas corpus petition on behalf of ten undertrials in Bhagalpur jail.

'The police deprived them of their eyesight by using acid,' the newspaper said.

That first news report went largely unnoticed. A few days later, a journalist working with the *Sunday* magazine in Calcutta got wind of the story. He arrived in Bhagalpur to investigate and managed to gain access to many of the victims lodged in Bhagalpur Central Jail. He interviewed them at length and even got some photographs of their burnt and bandaged eyes.

In the meanwhile, Arun Sinha, the Patna correspondent of the *Indian Express*, started probing the alleged blindings and, on 22 November 1980, wrote a front-page story with a headline that caught everyone's attention, including the prime minister's: 'Eyes punctured twice to ensure total blindness'. The report also carried a picture.

The executive editor of the *Indian Express* at the time, Arun Shourie, started writing a series of exposés on the Bhagalpur blindings. Other newspapers and magazines followed suit. Images of poor villagers with eyes gouged out and the flesh dissolved with acid shook the country.

Pressure started mounting on the Bihar government to take action. The common refrain was, 'This could not have happened without the knowledge and sanction of senior police officers and political leaders in Bihar.' Even the prime minister, Indira Gandhi, referred to the scandal in Parliament, saying that it made her 'feel physically sick'. According to some media reports, Mrs Gandhi personally called up Bihar CM Jagannath Mishra and asked him to take action. CM Mishra ordered an inquiry into the blindings, and on 30 November 1980, fifteen policemen were suspended.

The inquiry team was headed by DIG CID (anti-dacoity) L.V. Singh, who was my former boss as DIG central range.

With him on the team was SP CID (anti-dacoity) R.R. Prasad, an upright and meticulous officer. Because there was a large number of records and documents that had to be sifted through, the head of the CID, additional IG M.K. Jha, issued an order attaching several other officers to this team, including me. I presumed I was selected because of my report-writing skills, much of which I owe to my reluctant degrees in English literature.

That is how I found myself on a special plane, descending into a sea of people in Bhagalpur. Only that the people had not gathered to welcome us, they were there to protest *against* us.

They did not want the policemen to be investigated for the blindings, they were in full support of the 'punishment' meted out to the undertrials.

As we made our way to the circuit house, a bandh-like situation prevailed in the town. It was a 'police bandh', an unofficial shutdown declared by the local police to protest against the suspensions. Shopkeepers had willingly downed shutters in solidarity with the cops. Agitators were gathered in clusters, raising slogans against us. The air was rife with distrust and animosity. It felt like a case of the CID versus the people and police of Bhagalpur.

To understand why the public was in full support of something as barbaric as blinding someone with acid, it is important to look at the ground realities of Bhagalpur, which was like the badlands of Bihar at the time. Crime ruled with an iron grip, and constant fear was a way of life.

Criminals roamed around openly with weapons, looting, maiming, raping and murdering people. Even if the victims went to the police and the criminals were arrested, they would be out on bail in no time, back to their terrorizing ways. Cases would drag on, as the murderous gangs continued unimpeded with their plundering and pillaging.

Frustrated with the delays in the judicial system, some policemen took the law into their own hands. The blindings had an immediate effect on the crime rate. The people were happy; they felt the criminals had gotten what they deserved.

One excerpt from an article in *India Today* dated 31 December 1980, explains the otherwise puzzling public support very well:

Bhagalpur breeds crime like corpses breed maggots. Bully boys with criminal records as long as their muscular arms, swagger through Bhagalpur's grimy streets, secure in the knowledge that political patronage cloaks them with immunity. Daylight hold-ups, Chicago-style, and caste wars are as commonplace as the dust and the flies. Last July, seven villagers of Telaiya in the Bhagalpur district were savagely bludgeoned to death in broad daylight.

Barely a month earlier, the Patel Sao gang, responsible for a series of robberies and rapes in the district, had stormed into Dhawani in broad daylight, robbed the villagers, and gang-raped 15 teenage girls. The ravines and river-beds that criss-cross the district offer ideal terrain for criminal activities. Fear wears a familiar face in Bhagalpur.

Against that backdrop, it is perhaps easier to understand why the local populace, irrespective of caste and class, took to the streets in support of the barbaric blindings. To them, it was merely poetic justice. 'There will be bloodshed if the policemen are punished,' screamed a female processionist in Bhagalpur last fortnight. She had only one breast. The

other had been hacked off by a member of a gang that had
repeatedly raped her in front of her family.[**]

The blindings had even acquired a title—Operation Gangajal—
in an oblique reference to the acid that was cleansing society of
criminals, just like the holy waters of the Ganga river cleanses
our sins. This was also referenced by film-maker Prakash Jha
in 2003, who made a film titled *Gangaajal* on the blindings,
starring Ajay Devgn as an upright SP.

* * *

DIG Singh was an extremely methodical officer and knew the
nitty-gritties of how the police functioned, so the first thing he
did was to ask us to seize all police records. There were eight or
nine police stations from where these allegations had surfaced.
We took possession of all the station diaries, case diaries,
personal diaries, injury reports, jail reports and court records,
among other things.

Then began the interminable hours of poring over these
documents, matching records from one diary with another,
trying to piece together the chain of events and plot the
movement of police personnel. R.R. Prasad and I would be
up till 1 or 2 a.m., reading, cross-checking and making notes.
We often found discrepancies. For example, an FIR had been
registered but there was no mention of it in the station diary. Or
an attempt had been made to pass off blinded undertrials with no
criminal history as hardened criminals by making them suspects
in cases of old, unsolved dacoities and heinous crimes. Several

---

[*] 'Bhagalpur: An area of darkness', *India Today*, 31 December 1980.

such cases were pending in these police stations. We noted that most of these undertrials had neither been chargesheeted nor convicted, it was evident that their names had been added as suspects only subsequently.

While information on the arrests was sketchy in some cases, in a few high-profile ones it was meticulous. The case of Anil Yadav comes to mind. He was a dreaded criminal of the Sudama Mandal gang, notorious for kidnappings and murders. He struck terror in the hearts of the villagers by hacking his victims into pieces and throwing their body parts in the Ganga. For Anil Yadav's arrest, we found a detailed record in the FIR of when the raid had been carried out, of all those who had been in the raiding party, the time he was brought to the thana— everything. From the drivers and constables to the officers and their bodyguards, everyone's name was included—perhaps in the hope of receiving gallantry awards and commendation letters for arresting such a notorious gangster.

We also noticed that, in some cases, policemen had crucified themselves by not matching their statements with entries in case diaries and station diaries. For instance, nothing was mentioned in the police records about injuries to an arrested person at the time of arrest. The law requires that within twenty-four hours of an arrest, an accused must be presented before a magistrate. Often when they were brought before the magistrate, it was recorded that there were already grievous injuries in the eyes. Sometimes the jail doctor had recorded there were deep gashes akin to acid burns. If the case diaries did not mention any injury at the time of arrest, and the magistrate or jail doctor's report mentioned acid burns, it could only mean one thing—the injuries had been inflicted while the undertrial was at the police station.

Bit by bit we began to piece together what had happened.

The newspapers reported that bicycle spokes or screwdrivers were used to gouge out the eyes. In fact, what was actually used in most of the cases was a *takua*, a long, thick needle found in every police station. It is used to bore a hole through a sheaf of papers to thread them together with string.

We discovered that while the blindings started with dreaded criminals, which immediately brought down the crime rate and enjoyed great public sympathy, not long afterwards, *gangajal* started being used against even small-time thieves and petty criminals, and then simply to settle scores.

There was a Sikh youth who was like a local dada (leader) in the market area. He was picked up for eve-teasing, and later blinded. Then there was a group of labourers who were agitating against the zamindar for minimum wages. The landlord paid off the OIC of the local police station and said, '*Inko* settle *karo* (fix these people).' The leader of the farm labourers was picked up and blinded. In one case of bus dacoity under Rajaun police station, nine people were blinded in a single night. That incident blew the lid off this macabre practice.

Under the guidance and watchful eye of DIG L.V. Singh, we recorded everything, including the testimony of all the victims. An attempt was being made in the police and political circles to give the story a different spin—that the blindings had been carried out by angry mobs of villagers, but all the victims we questioned named the police as perpetrators.

The district police were on tenterhooks; they were behaving like the CID was mounting a witch hunt against them. While we officers remained tight-lipped about our inquiry, we knew the district police constables and sub-inspectors (SI) were trying to get information out of the CID constables and staff. So, we had to be very careful about which constables, typists, secretaries and other personnel we included in our team.

Our inquiry went on for a couple of months, and I had to visit Bhagalpur a number of times. It used to be a long, arduous journey of eight hours by road from Patna, sitting squashed between the driver and another officer, shivering in the bitter cold. In those days, we did not have the luxury of travelling in cars; we had to travel even long distances in extremely uncomfortable police jeeps. But there was a sense of purpose, a challenge, and I was very much up to the task.

What I had not bargained for was the politics that were playing out in the corridors of power in Patna. Officers of the rank of IG and DIG began to turn against one another, fighting bitterly, fearing that their chances of getting to top positions would be jeopardized by this inquiry. Some of them had been posted in Bhagalpur in the recent past and were now afraid of being named in the inquiry report for collusion, if not active involvement. The national media was still hungry for heads to roll, and the Bihar government was under tremendous pressure to show results.

I faced a lot of pressure to omit certain names from the list of accused, especially some senior officers. Being the most junior officer on the investigating team, people began to use all kinds of methods to try and influence me.

One day, the head of CID suddenly suggested that I should proceed on leave so that I didn't continue with the inquiry. I had not been keeping well for a few days, and he seized this as an opportunity to make his suggestion. He knew that I would not fudge my reports, so he wanted me out of the inquiry team. I was stunned at his suggestion.

'How can I just go on leave, Sir?' I asked incredulously.

Very early on, I had decided that I would not bow to any kind of pressure. It was a question of my integrity. I was horrified at what had been done to those men—be it known criminals or first-time offenders or innocent villagers—and felt extremely disturbed that men in uniform could inflict such suffering upon another human being. I was also very aware that when the cases would be opened, I alone would be responsible for whatever I had written. No one was going to come and speak on my behalf if my reports were found to be factually incorrect.

When I refused to be influenced in any way, people dragged my parents into it. My family was quite well known in Patna and everyone knew who my parents were and where they lived. One day, my father was at a petrol station in our neighbourhood when a senior officer who knew my father came up to him.

'*Aap* Manjari *ko samjhaiye; woh toh hum logon ko hathkadi lagwa degi* (Please talk to Manjari, she is out to get us handcuffed).'

My father was quite upset and spoke to me rather sharply. 'Why are you doing this? People are complaining to me about you. Be careful.' He was still protective of me and had started worrying that someone might try to harm me if I did not change my stance.

He was also feeling awkward socially. 'We have to live in this society, and people are saying your daughter is out to get us. This is not good at all,' he said. '*Soch samajh ke kaam karna; soch samajh ke likhna* (Be careful at work; be careful about what you write).'

The pressure put on my family made me even more determined to stick to my decision. My father did not know the nuances of the case nor my exact role in the inquiry. My job was to read the documents diligently and prepare reports, recording everything truthfully and fairly. I also let it be known that I was a young officer who was not going to get her hands dirty trying to cover up for others. I was going to do whatever was right.

But the pressure did not always come from above. The brother of my own assistant in the CID, Mr Acharya, was involved in the blinding of suspects in the Rajaun bus dacoity case. Mr Acharya would plead with me to help save his brother, who was a young sub-inspector. But nine people had been blinded in one night in his jurisdiction; there was no way I could help him.

We completed the inquiry and submitted our report. On the basis of our report, several criminal cases were registered and investigated. The court cases, as we had feared, dragged on for a long time. Later, I learnt that many police officers had been indicted and several victims started receiving monthly compensation. However, by then I had left the CID and moved on to another posting.

This is a peculiarity of police life. Once a posting is over, you have to drop everything you spent days and nights working on and move on to your next job immediately. Often there would be no closure, and I would not even know the fate of my cases. This used to bother me initially. Being a meticulous person, I would have liked to see a case or an inquiry to its logical end, but that was hardly ever possible because frequently inquiries and court cases would drag on for years on end.

* * *

The Bhagalpur blindings showed me how important it is in the police to follow the correct path and not resort to extra-constitutional ways. Many officers feel that encounters are the only way to deal with hardened criminals, but the Bhagalpur incidents taught me a salutary lesson that, although such behaviour might bring quick results and commendations in the short term, it invariably leads you down a dangerous path.

This experience also strengthened my resolve to be extremely meticulous in my own case work and make sure that all records were properly maintained, lest anything be challenged later. It is always better to be on the right side of the law rather than resorting to distorting the truth.

The plight of some of the junior policemen named in our inquiry also showed me that when things get tough, you are on your own. Many of the accused were first-time OICs, painfully young and woefully inexperienced, who got caught up in a horrible affair at the behest of seniors who abandoned them later and only tried to save their own skin. You may work in a team, but ultimately you will be alone in defending your actions. So, you should be able to stand scrutiny at all times.

Being on this inquiry team also taught me a lot about police work. Even though I had not done a district posting as SP yet, I read many police station records, case diaries, injury reports, dossiers, jail reports and court records. All this truly deepened my understanding of the workings of the police, which was earlier restricted to work in a subdivision. I got a glimpse of the bigger picture. It was an opportunity that, luckily, came very early in my career and contributed to shaping the officer in me.

Long after I had moved on from the inquiry and the horrors of the blindings had faded from public memory, I would sometimes look at the mighty Ganga as it flowed by Patna and remember Bhagalpur. The quiet flow of river would take me back to the shocking travesty of justice that was carried out in the name of the holy gangajal. The only solace that I can draw today—after thirty-four years in service—is that this unspeakable brutality was an aberration in the police, not the norm.

11

Hunterwali

After my younger son Anshuman was born in December 1982, I contracted severe jaundice. Barely a few weeks old, my child was separated from me, and I would constantly worry about how it might affect him in the future. As I lay in bed, weak from my difficult pregnancy and pale from the jaundice, I also fretted over my district posting. Every week I would hope for some news, but there was nothing.

Little did I know then—bedridden and miserable as I was—that within a couple of months I would acquire the tag 'Hunterwali'.

When I got a little better and resumed work in the CID, suddenly orders were issued that I should take charge as SP Bokaro. My doctor was vehemently opposed to this.

'Do you know how badly jaundice affects the liver? If you leave Patna now and work yourself to exhaustion in Bokaro, your liver will never recover,' he warned me. But I had been handed this posting after so many months of waiting, there was no way I was going to let it go.

I was asked to take charge immediately because the previous SP had been hastily transferred out. When I ran into Mr Kailashpati, one of my seniors, he cautioned me: 'Look, there has been a major incident in the police lines in Bokaro: the constables misbehaved with the previous SP. My advice is, be careful, don't go to the police lines. You are a lady, they may misbehave with you.'

In every district, there is a district police office and a police lines. Barracks for constables and havildars are situated in the police lines, besides the quarter guard and the armoury. The regular PT and parade in addition to the shared accommodations foster camaraderie and discipline in the force.

I was quite confused. How could I not go to the police lines as an SP? How could I be afraid of my own men yet hope to lead them? I was hearing many stories of indiscipline within the ranks of the Bokaro district police. Nonetheless, I was excited about my posting. It was also a challenge as I had an infant to care for in addition to the residual postnatal weakness and the aftermath of jaundice. We decided that I would go to Bokaro with my elder son, Tushar, who was now four years old and needed to be enrolled in a school. Sadly, I had no option but to leave little Anshuman with my mother for a couple of weeks, until I settled down.

We left for Bokaro by train in the night and arrived in the early hours of the morning. As the train pulled in, I could see the blaze of lights of the Bokaro Steel Plant. It lifted my spirits.

Bokaro Steel Plant was a marvel of engineering and the human spirit. It had started taking shape as a government of India public sector unit (PSU) in the late 1960s, with assistance from the then Soviet Union—a massive steel plant in the wilderness of Chhotanagpur. Soon, an entire township came to life around it with a planned city, modern amenities, a decent standard of living and very good educational facilities. As our first prime minister, Jawaharlal Nehru, had envisioned, our public sector undertakings (PSUs) were truly the temples of modern India.

I found the Bokaro SP's office to be small and compact, compared to the senior SP's office in Patna. This seemed quite manageable. Funnily enough, a lot of people were jealous of my Bokaro posting because it was the only SP's office in Bihar at the time that had an air-conditioner!

I learnt that there was a lot of excitement in town that a lady SP had been posted. Y.N. Srivastava was my DIG; I had worked with him when I was briefly posted in Ranchi as ASP. When our son Tushar was born, Rakesh was in Ranchi, so I had been allowed to continue my training in Ranchi for a few months after my maternity leave. When I called on DIG Srivastava in Bokaro, he brought me up to speed on the problem of indiscipline in the force, which had led to the transfer of the previous SP.

The incident had started as an altercation between two constables and a trekker driver at Naya More, a major transport hub in the town. The driver had asked the constables for their fare, which they refused to pay, and a scuffle broke out. Agitated, the constables returned to their barracks and came out in a gang, armed with hockey sticks and lathis, some in uniform, others in civilian clothes. A free-for-all ensued between the cops, the drivers and *khalasi*s (helpers). When the SP intervened, the constables misbehaved with him as well. The relationship between the SP and his men came to such a head that by the time his transfer orders came, they did not even give him a farewell.

The DIG informed me that there were six known troublemakers among the constabulary, and the first thing

I should do was to discipline them. 'Start departmental proceedings against them for misbehaviour, and show no leniency,' he advised me. I was a little perplexed about how it might play out if my first action in a new posting was to take action against my own men.

But the DIG also suggested a ploy to rein them in. 'Start the proceedings but don't close them, don't pass an order. Keep them on tenterhooks until they calm down and start behaving themselves.' I quite liked the idea of a departmental inquiry hanging over these wayward men like the sword of Damocles.

I soon realized that one reason for this indiscipline—and the DIG concurred—was that Bokaro did not have a separate police lines.

Instead, in Bokaro, life revolved around the steel plant. Everything was provided by the plant management. Some old, dilapidated buildings had been allocated by them to the police, which functioned as barracks; these were dwellings that were originally meant for labourers who had been hired during the construction period of the plant.

Bokaro steel plant had a workers' union and the policemen tended to behave as if they were also a union. The SP rarely visited the police lines and there was no system of regular PT or parade.

In spite of Mr Kailashpati's warnings, I decided that the first thing I would do was go and inspect the police lines. I called a police *sabha* (congregation). In Bihar, police associations had already been recognized and SPs were expected to hold police sabhas regularly to address the men and listen to their grievances.

Everybody was supposed to come in uniform to the sabha. But in defiance of orders, the leaders of the police association had gotten into the habit of coming in kurta-pyjamas, as if they were netas (political leaders). At the police sabha, just as I was about to address the eighty to ninety men gathered there—all in uniform—I noticed five or six men enter through a rear door in civilian clothes. They were the police association netas. On the spur of the moment, I decided to take them on. It was a moment of reckoning.

'*Jo log* uniform *mein nahin hain, woh nikal jayenge. Yeh mera aadesh hai* (Those who are not in uniform should leave. This is my order),' I announced firmly. Twice.

For a few moments, there was a hushed silence. The men were watching me, unblinking, waiting for my next move. I, too, was watching them, an implacable expression on my face, wondering what they would do. I had placed myself between a rock and a hard place. I could neither get up and walk away, nor could I stay and be insulted in the presence of my men. And then, the men in civvies got up and quietly exited through the back door. Phew!

In that moment, I felt something shift in the minds of the men at the sabha. There was an immediate recognition of my authority. They realized that this lady SP would brook no nonsense. In the days that followed, I noticed a new kind of acceptance within the constabulary. They too must have been harassed by these self-styled netas. The thing about bullies is that they make trouble everywhere, even within their own people.

* * *

After addressing the matter of indiscipline within the force, I turned my attention to understanding the problems in the town. There were petty crimes in the urban areas which would spike in the evenings. Snatching, eve-teasing and theft were rampant in the shopping centres and markets. I insisted that from 6 p.m. onwards, all the officers of the police stations would have to be in uniform. The men had gotten into the habit of being in casuals in the evenings. I decreed that everybody in the police station would have to be on duty, in uniform and available on the wireless between 6 p.m. and 9 p.m.

I reorganized the teams to conduct regular night patrolling, going on night rounds myself to set an example. And I would always be in uniform. Those days, I made myself omnipresent. I started driving the jeep myself. To keep the force alert, I would often spring a surprise on them. People didn't know where I would turn up next. I needed them to accept that I was as good as them. I felt I had to send out a very strong message so that they did not underestimate me just because I was a woman.

Next, I discovered that incidents of road accidents were very high. Bokaro Steel City was a planned township, built with Russian assistance. Everything was neatly laid out, in straight lines. The roads were excellent—very unlike in Bihar at that time—broad and well-paved, turning at 90-degree angles at the crossings.

In the township, shift timings of the plant were very important. People often speeded on their two-wheelers to get to the gate on time, and very often skidded and crashed. There was no sense of road discipline. The plant had issued helmets to all their employees, but no one bothered to wear them while driving.

The speed limit was routinely flouted, buses and trekkers would ply with dozens of people on the roof and more hanging out of the doors.

I decided to enforce traffic rules very strictly. Whenever we spotted a violation, we stopped the people and handed out challans (traffic violation tickets) without exception. Soon, the number of accidents started coming down.

One day, a plant employee was hit by a trekker and had to be hospitalized. When I arrived at Bokaro Steel Hospital, the accident victim's wife clung to me and sobbed, 'You have saved my husband's life.' It turned out that the man was on his scooter when he was hit by the trekker, and the doctors had told his wife that he had escaped death only because he was wearing a helmet. 'I would always tell my husband, but he would never wear a helmet. Only because you made it mandatory was he saved today,' she said.

The women of Bokaro were generally very supportive of me, especially because of the helmet rule. They always felt their sons and husbands didn't listen to them, but now here I was—a lady SP who was making them adhere to road rules, ensuring their safety.

All this had a real impact in the town. People suddenly started feeling that the police were being very active and were there for them. Within the first two months, all kinds of stories started floating around about me. This is when I got this moniker—Hunterwali.

Alpana, my good friend from school and college, was in Bokaro at that time as her husband, Pradeep, was working with Bharat Heavy Electricals Limited (BHEL). She would be quite distressed by these stories. 'Manjari, *yeh kya ho raha hai* (What is happening)? They are calling you Hunterwali!' This image of me as a woman wielding a riding whip seemed to have caught on.

She told me some strange tales that were doing the rounds. Apparently, I was not allowing any wife or girlfriend to ride pillion with a man, that I was against couples riding on two-wheelers. One allegation was even more bizarre, that I would not allow any woman on a scooter to wear a sleeveless blouse.

One day, the DIG himself told me another story. 'People are saying that the new SP is so *tagdi* (strong) that when she pushes a truck with her bare hands, it starts moving. Clearly, they have not seen you up close,' he laughed.

Stories of how the lady SP had caught this person or raided that place were indeed everywhere. I did not discount the stories; I just let them float around, although I was quite horrified at this nonsense about my forbidding women from wearing sleeveless blouses or banning couples from riding together!

When I first heard they were calling me 'Hunterwali', I couldn't help laughing, but I was also quite shocked. But later, I thought about it very carefully and said to myself, 'Why should I change my ways?' If this image is having a salutary effect on discipline within the force and in the township, so be it. Personally, I found this tag rather idiotic. Obviously, I was not going around wielding a *hunter*, or a whip. But I thought, theek hai, if this means they see me as a tough cop, by all means, so be it.

* * *

Although Bokaro was considered a comfortable posting, being an industrial area, it had its own law-and-order challenges—labour and union problems, industrial disputes, dharnas, et cetera. And while it was generally peaceful, when a problem occurred, being a township concentrated in large colonies, things flared up very quickly. We would see the worst of it the following year.

By the 1980s, the Bokaro township had grown, with new housing colonies coming up to cater to the increased staff strength at the plant and its ancillary industries. The town had expanded in all directions. It was necessary to secure these new sectors and ensure that the public could reach the police easily. To improve police presence, I decided to open a few subsidiary police stations in the new sectors. These were linked to the main police stations.

When I arrived in Bokaro, I realized that the police and the plant management were always at loggerheads. But why, I wondered. I believed in working in close cooperation with them because, if we were there to secure the town, it was also in the management's best interest to ensure a safe and peaceful township so that their employees could work without worrying about their families. I completely changed this confrontational attitude and received tremendous cooperation from the plant's managing director (MD) and general managers (GM).

There was always a shortage of infrastructure in the police stations those days. The lack of vehicles was especially crippling. Consequently, criminals were faster than us. I asked the MD to allocate some buildings to us so we could establish subsidiary police stations and also asked for a few vehicles along with fuel allowance. They came to our support gladly.

During those days, the menace of dacoity hung like a pall over the township, especially in the Cooperative Colony, because it housed the thekedars (contractors)—moneyed people who ran ancillary services. This private colony stood next to the river Garga, a tributary of the Damodar. The criminals would come via the river route and escape the same way.

Late one evening, a row of houses at the edge of the colony was targeted. Valuables and household goods were looted. Music systems were a rage then and were routinely stolen during dacoities. The residents said the criminals looked like 'local boys'. There were two young girls among those who had been robbed, and they tearfully showed me how their house had been ransacked.

I decided we would go across the river and raid the settlement on the other side. Without waiting for daylight, we crossed the river in the night. It was quite a sight—a line of policemen in uniform stepping on stones to walk across the shallow river in the dark, with me leading the way. We lost our footing and got wet, but we did not turn back.

In the settlement, we started a house-to-house search, and discovered the entire loot from that evening in one hut. We arrested the criminals, seized the loot and returned just as dawn was breaking. We called the aggrieved parties, including the two girls. They gave whoops of joy upon seeing their belongings. One girl was crying, 'My father had given me this ring, thank you! I never thought I would see it again.' Her sister was ecstatic to see her brand-new steam iron. Exhausted as we were, it was heartening to see their excitement at being reunited with their belongings.

The news of the recovery spread like wildfire. That year, we conducted a drill every fortnight to control crime. We would go across the Garga and raid the *basti* (settlement) on the other side. It was a little dangerous, sometimes we would be surrounded by hostile villagers, but I refused to budge from my firm stance.

I wanted to stamp my authority to intimidate criminals and have a firm upper hand. My strategy was to convey an aggressive message right from the beginning to keep them under control. I also developed a network of informants. One of my telephone operators was a sly, clever guy. I asked him, 'Can you go and live in that village and keep us informed about their comings and goings?' He agreed. He disguised himself as a local and started living in the basti. He passed on a lot of valuable information, telling us when to raid and recover stolen articles as well as apprehend the criminals.

The first year I was in Bokaro, there were forty-seven dacoities; the next year, just six. My old boss, L.V. Singh, who was now the IG of the Ranchi zone, came to Bokaro to inspect my office. 'How can it be? You must have under-reported the dacoity cases,' he said, perplexed.

I showed him the case records of the dacoities we had detected in the past year. 'This is the reason the numbers have come down,' I explained. The IG was still a little incredulous. I allowed myself a quiet smile.

A year after I arrived as SP Bokaro, Prime Minister Indira Gandhi was due to visit Dhanbad. She was expected to arrive on 1 May 1984 by helicopter at a makeshift helipad near the meeting ground. I was asked to assist the Dhanbad SP in the bandobast (arrangements). Huge crowds had gathered near the helipad to welcome the PM and we were on our toes, keeping a hawk's-eye on the surging crowd. At one point, it did seem that we would have a situation on our hands when the barricade threatened to give way under the press of eager bodies straining to get a look at Mrs Gandhi. But my team and I were quick to react, and a disaster was averted. Later, I received a very encouraging note from the zonal IG, L.V. Singh.

This is to put on record my appreciation of your services rendered at Dhanbad helipad during the Prime Minister's visit to Dhanbad on 1st May, 84. Your successful performance has further reinforced my belief in your ability to face [a] difficult situation. The situation was complicated because of the infirm barricade of the helipad as they did not adhere to

regulations in creating [the] barricade, which did give way
when people started moving towards [the] helipad in great
number[s]. There was murmur and suggestion that a lady
officer may not be able to handle the mob. I could not have
agreed to this and you held your ground with determination
and firmness to my satisfaction. I thank you for the same
and hope that in [the] years to come you may cherish these
qualities and develop them by your sincerity and devotion
to duty.

I was grateful to him for his vote of confidence in my abilities,
but it now surprises me how openly and easily people could
question an officer's abilities simply based on gender. Even
today many such biases remain within the police force and in
many workplaces, but they are not discussed so brazenly. This is
gender discrimination and there is no other way of describing it.
It was my good fortune that my seniors reposed faith in me and
did not allow this inherent bias in our society to guide them in
entrusting important tasks to me.

* * *

While our early successes are always memorable, there are some
cases that haunt every officer. For me, it was the murder of a
young doctor.

Late one night, I received a call from Bokaro General
Hospital that a young man had been brought dead with stab
injuries. He turned out to be the son of a very important
minister in Bihar, Jaipal Singh Yadav. I scrambled into my
uniform and rushed to the PO, which was his home in Chas,
a town adjoining Bokaro Steel City. The deceased was a doctor

with a private practice. It was 2 a.m. when I arrived at his house. Other officers also arrived one by one as the information got relayed on the wireless.

As I entered the house, I saw a stream of blood. While I was skirting the blood to make my way in, a young woman emerged and fell at my feet, clasping my knees. She started crying desperately, 'Save my husband, please save my husband!'

Those were some of the hardest moments of being a police officer. I knew her husband was no more, but I could not tell her anything yet. Also, I needed to start the investigations right away if there was any hope of catching the perpetrators. My team was looking at me for instructions and the victim's wife was holding me and beseeching me to save a dead man. These emotions were terrible to bear, more so when I looked at their two little children, just about four and six years old.

We started piecing together the night's incidents. The couple was asleep when they were awakened by the sound of movement in the house. The doctor got up and found four or five intruders in the living room. They were all youngsters, very shabbily dressed, according to the wife. 'They didn't look local,' she said.

The doctor tried to resist them and they stabbed him in the chest with a small knife. They were several small stab wounds, not really meant to kill, but they must have punctured a critical blood vessel. Even as the wife shouted for help, the neighbours came and took him to hospital, where he bled to death.

The construction of the house was still underway; the first floor had stairs leading up to the roof, where a door had been left open. We concluded that the criminals had entered through the roof. We learnt that the doctor had made payments to the construction workers that night and wondered whether the murderers had assumed the victim had more money in the house. One team went looking for the construction workers, but found that all of them were still around, they had not fled. We sent teams everywhere, we hired local men who were familiar with the hinterland to act as sources. We looked at every angle— robbery, enmity, political equations—but every lead brought us to a dead end.

Only one clue held some promise. There used to be wandering criminal tribes and gangs who were notorious for such crimes. They would put up temporary tents, do some local bartering, commit some petty thefts, pack up and move away. We were told that one such tribe, the Gulgulias, had been seen in the vicinity recently. We went in search of them in every direction, but we could not trace them.

The morning after the doctor died, his father arrived from Patna. I was convinced that because Jaipal Singh Yadav was such a powerful minister and his son had been killed under my watch, I would definitely be transferred. I was surprised that he did not express any anger or annoyance that we had not solved the case yet. He was stoic throughout the day. He asked me to make every effort to apprehend his son's killers. He then took his daughter-in-law and grandchildren with him and left for Patna. I realized that not every person is vindictive, not every politician throws his weight around. As soon as they understand that you are genuinely working hard on their case, they tend to trust you and not put undue pressure on you.

For days on end, I could not forget the young wife clinging to my knees. I made it a point to visit her whenever I went to Patna, just to give her the consolation that we were still trying our best. Later, someone told me that the minister had established a small school, and she was helping him run it.

Not having been able to bring her husband's killers to justice still torments me.

* * *

While I had established a certain amount of authority in the constabulary, the senior men would often try to challenge me, especially the OICs. It took time, but slowly most of the officers also started cooperating with me, because I would take them along and treat them with respect. Some sub-inspectors were direct recruits of the 1976 batch, as old as me. They were smart, young officers, and I would give them the freedom to do their work. They felt very enthused to go on a raid or a night round and were ready for anything. SIs R.R. Singh and B.K. Sinha remained in touch with me throughout my career. Even after I retired from the service, I continue to get calls from them to consult me on their personal or professional matters, to wish me on festivals or just ask after me.

The deputy superintendents of police (DySPs) were less enthusiastic. They invariably seemed to have an excuse to avoid every task I assigned them. Women in positions of authority were very few in those days and these were seasoned policemen, so they thought they knew everything. To gain their acceptance and cooperation, I had to prove to them that I knew things better. Soon they fell in line because they understood that I knew my work.

Sometimes you have to adopt ingenious methods to bring the officers in line. The OIC of Balidih police station thought he was very smart, but I felt he was more macho than smart. On one of my night rounds, when I went to his thana, I saw there was nobody there. I picked up his cap and brought it home. In the morning, he looked for his cap high and low, and asked everybody. He later discovered that I had gone to his police station in the night. So, he came to my house, very sheepish and apologetic. He collected his cap from my driver and left. From then on, he knew who the boss was.

* * *

In Bokaro, theft of plant material was very common. Items like diamond-tipped instruments or extremely expensive conductors used to be smuggled out of the plant and sent by train to Calcutta to be sold. The money earned then led to gambling, drinking and fights.

I decided to nip things in the bud. Whenever any crime was reported from inside the plant, I would take quick and firm action. The plant had vast stores and it was not possible to see the wall at the other end if you were standing at one end. No outsider could possibly know what was inside and in what quantity. One day, a theft of a large number of conductors worth lakhs of rupees was reported. This could not have happened without the knowledge of the three storekeepers in charge. We raided their flats, but they were not at home. Their wives feigned ignorance, therefore I decided to search thoroughly and discovered a huge haul of conductors on the terrace of one of the homes. We raided the homes of the other two storekeepers and recovered more stolen conductors.

I took a bold decision that day. I picked up the wives for hiding stolen material, put them in our jeep and brought them to the plant, to send a message to the absconding men.

Word spread rapidly that the SP had arrested women. The husbands came out of hiding in no time and surrendered. It became the talk of the town. There was now a fear among the criminals that this SP would stop at nothing. Incidents of theft actually started declining in the plant. Or perhaps the managers started under-reporting the thefts because all this was plant property and not their own. My hunch is that they must have told themselves, this SP is here only for a few years, so let us not report the thefts and get everyone into trouble. Although I do not know how they managed their annual audits, the number of cases of theft reported from the plant came down.

Another problem at the plant was rampant pilferage. I was told that good quality coke and steel would be taken out as scrap. Only coke of a particular size could be designated as waste, but coke of much higher grade would be pilfered by contractors in connivance with plant employees and sold off in Calcutta.

One day, I got information that good-quality coke was being taken out. I immediately seized all the trucks carrying the purported scrap coke. I sent a sample for testing to the laboratory of the Central Fuel Research Institute (which later became the Central Institute of Mining and Fuel Research) in Dhanbad. It was found to contain coke of a higher grade than what was acceptable as waste. I registered an FIR and started my investigations.

The case became the talk of the town. There were rumours that I was going to arrest the MD and GMs of the plant, although I had given no statement to that effect. There was a big scare, as people recalled an incident when one of the previous SPs had arrested a plant GM—an expert on the blast furnace—without sufficient evidence and was transferred overnight for this uncalled-for action.

Zonal IG L.V. Singh started breathing down my neck, asking me what I was doing and why. I could not understand the politics that the top police officers were playing, or why they were not giving me proper directions yet finding fault with everything.

The IG called me to Ranchi with all the records. He was very perturbed, but not at all forthcoming about what he wanted me to do. Not that I would have agreed to do anything unlawful, but I simply could not understand his intentions or on whose behalf he was speaking.

DIG Srivastava, a very practical officer, advised me that I should do my investigation by the book, and not try to arrest any bigshot unless I had evidence of connivance against them. 'Try not to draw too much attention. If you need to record the statement of the MD or the GM, fix an appointment and go to their office, instead of calling them to the thana and sensationalizing the matter further,' he said.

I think it was a piece of very sound advice. I chargesheeted the contractors and plant employees involved in loading and theft of the coke. My investigations revealed that the MD or the GMs had no hand in this matter. I felt the timely guidance helped me get out of a very tricky situation, which could have snowballed into a major issue.

* * *

At home, I had to shed the skin of a ruthless police officer and become a mother. My children needed a lot of attention during this time. I always felt I was depriving them of a mother's time. Anshuman was a few months old, learning to sit and crawl around the house. Tushar was attending Mrs Girgila's school in the colony, which was a very well-known nursery school. But he was growing up and had to be admitted into a proper school soon.

Rakesh and I were always very concerned about our children's education. In Bokaro, St Xavier's School was considered the best, and I was really keen for Tushar to get admission there. The competition was tough. People used to say that the entrance exam was like an 'IAS exam for children'. The queue to pick up admission forms was about 2 kilometres long!

Around this time, a very disturbing incident occurred, which angered me as an officer and upset me as a mother. I received an anonymous letter threatening to kidnap my son. I showed the letter to DIG Srivastava, and both of us felt that an inspector against whom I had taken action might be behind this threat. But we could not prove anything.

'Why don't you drop your son to school yourself in the mornings? Don't let him go alone with the driver,' the DIG advised. So, I started taking Tushar to school myself.

I also enrolled Tushar with Mrs Dora Bose, who used to coach children to get into St Xavier's. Poor child, there was so much pressure on him to prepare for the entrance exam. I had put myself under a lot of pressure too about his admission. So, it was a huge relief when he was accepted there in class 2.

We lived very close to St Xavier's School and the students had to go past my house to get there. In the mornings, when I came out in my uniform and got into the jeep, I would notice a bunch of girls watching me curiously from the fence. It felt good to see them. Even now I sometimes meet girls from Bokaro who have joined the civil services, and they always say they remember me. They tell me about the time when I went to their school for prize distribution or they saw me in uniform driving a jeep, and how they were very inspired.

One day, there was a complaint of eve-teasing outside St Xavier's School. Boys from other schools would gather outside the gate and harass the girls as they walked by. When I heard this, I deputed two constables at the school gate and asked them to catch the boys.

The next morning, they picked up four boys and brought them to my home. I took down their addresses and sent my driver and bodyguard to go bring their fathers. When the fathers arrived, they were livid to learn what their sons had done.

One of them said, 'The minute your police vehicle stopped in front of my house, *mera toh izzat chala gaya* (my reputation was ruined). I have been such a straightforward person all my life.'

Another father said, 'We send him for tuition in the morning and this is what he is doing!'

Yet another started thrashing his son.

The men were grateful that I had brought their boys to my home instead of sending them to the police station. Yes, I could have booked them for eve-teasing but what good would that have done? It may have ruined their lives and actually pushed them into crime. Here it was a mother's instinct that kicked in—it would be better to call the parents to my home and let them deal with this wayward behaviour.

I think sometimes these little things do bring about a more positive approach to policing. I felt glad that the boys got the scolding of their lives from their parents, and it also set an example for the other boys in the locality to behave themselves. The SP was watching them!

One day I was called to St Xavier's School as Tushar's teacher wanted to meet me. She said, 'You should not discuss your cases with your son, he comes to school and narrates them to his friends. Yesterday you made some arrest, and he was talking about it.'

I was stumped. Of course I was not discussing my cases with my six-year-old son! In fact, I was quite particular about my children not getting affected by the trappings of power. I made sure that the orderlies did not stay in the house, even the orderly on telephone duty would live outside. I had also decided not to have guards in front of my house. Normally guard rooms are located in front of an officer's house, but I had relocated them to the back of the house. I had put up barbed wire fencing so that the children could not go there, and the men did not come to the house. It was all to protect the boys from the extra attention that comes with being a senior officer's child in a district. I also wanted to ensure that the children never had access to the firearms kept by the guards.

So, I kept wondering how Tushar had come to know about the previous day's arrest, which had been dramatic no doubt, but I had not mentioned a word to him.

There had been a massive strike at Bokaro Steel Plant over bonuses, started by a union leader called Samresh Singh. When an FIR was filed against him, I got information on the wireless that he was fleeing Bokaro in a green Ambassador. This was early in the morning and I had just dropped Tushar to school.

Suddenly I spotted a green Ambassador on the road and asked my driver to chase it. I saw the car was going in the direction of Dhanbad. As we neared Chas rural police station, I informed the OIC on the wireless to come out on the road and stop that vehicle. Suddenly Samresh Singh found the entire road ahead of him blocked by cops, and a police jeep behind him. He screeched to a halt.

When I got off my jeep to arrest him, his eyes bulged in disbelief. He had not expected the SP to be out on the road at 7 a.m.! It was actually quite amusing to see the shock on his face. That evening, I had narrated the incident to my DIG over the telephone from my residential office, which is when Tushar must have overheard me. I resolved to be extra careful about what was spoken in the house.

Samresh Singh became a political prisoner, but the strike continued because he was able to monitor the agitation from behind bars. So, it was decided that we would move him from Bokaro to Bhagalpur jail. It had to be done quietly and quickly, so that his supporters could not come to the jail and create a ruckus.

Yet I felt bad for him. He was not a criminal, he was only a union leader playing his brand of politics. I telephoned his wife and told her that we were transferring him to another location. 'I cannot tell you where, but if you want to send something for him, we are ready to take it.' The wife was very grateful that I had called her. These little things make a difference, especially as I had come to think of the people of Bokaro as my people.

Which is why I still cannot forgive myself for not being there when they needed me the most.

12

An Aching Absence

October is a month of heavy bandobast. Durga Puja brings with it pandals, fairs, crowds and revelry. Diwali brings with it fireworks and more revelry. Then comes Chhath Puja, the most sacred festival of Bihar, where the rising and setting sun is worshipped with immense *shraddha* (devotion).

It is only after Chhath Puja that the police get a bit of a break from deployment duties. That year, I had decided I would take the boys on a holiday to visit my youngest sister, Mini, and her family in Bombay after Chhath Puja. My leave application was granted, and we left. We had a lovely time together, and the children enjoyed playing with their two little cousins.

Two days before we were due to return, we were out shopping. All of a sudden, we saw shopkeepers hurriedly pulling down their shutters. The date was 31 October 1984. Prime Minister Indira Gandhi had been shot dead by her bodyguards—Satwant Singh and Beant Singh—in retaliation for Operation Blue Star.

Around 1983, the Golden Temple in Amritsar had become the nerve centre of the Khalistani separatist movement, with

Sikh separatist leader Jarnail Singh Bhindranwale taking up residence inside the temple complex. There were reports of the presence of a large number of militants and huge stockpiles of arms and ammunition within its confines.

Operation Blue Star was a military operation carried out on the orders of the PM between 1 and 8 June 1984, to flush out Bhindranwale and other armed militants from the Golden Temple. Sikhs across India, as well as the world over, were horrified and incensed by this attack on their holiest shrine. Four months later, her Sikh bodyguards pumped thirty-three bullets into Mrs Gandhi at her residence in New Delhi.

Upon learning of the assassination, we rushed back home. This was before the age of 24 x 7 private news channels and social media. Sitting in Bombay, I had no idea of the fires burning across India in the wake of Mrs Gandhi's death. The following evening, I received some vague reports of disturbances in Bokaro and yearned to get back to my post. But there was no flight available and the best I could do was take the train on the morning of 2 November, as planned.

When we boarded the train, I still did not know the severity or extent of the riots that had broken out. While passing through Madhya Pradesh, I began to get a sense of what had begun unfolding throughout the country. Railway stations were completely ransacked, shops destroyed and fires burning. I realized it had been foolhardy of me to have left Bombay on an overnight train with two small children. There was no milk or food available. After every station, the train's catering staff would come back with more stories of devastation and, occasionally, a packet of biscuits.

We arrived in Dhanbad to an empty, desolate station. It was reassuring to see my bodyguard Havildar Dhruvraj Singh waiting for me with my driver and jeep. But beside it stood an open army jeep.

'Why is the army here, Dhruvraj Singh?' I asked, perplexed.

'*Bahut hungama hua hai,* Madam Sir; *bahut log maare gaye hain* (There was a lot of chaos, Madam Sir; a lot of people have been killed),' he said grimly. This was the first time I was hearing about the deaths and devastation in my city. Without wasting a minute, I got into the army jeep and we sped towards Bokaro. Unnerved by all this hurly-burly, little Anshuman started bawling.

On the way, with a crying child in my arms and another clinging to my side, I received a briefing about the riots that had broken out in Bokaro on the morning of 1 November. I was told about mobs attacking Sikh residents, resulting in many deaths, as well as widespread looting, arson and destruction.

I was beyond shocked. I had left a happy city that had just celebrated Chhath Puja together, and here I was returning to a ghost town. I could not believe what had become of Bokaro in a few short days, with blood on the streets, fear in the air and a curfew in effect.

I dropped off the children at home, got into my uniform and left without a moment's delay. I don't remember when I came back home after that.

I met DIG Srivastava, who had been holding the fort in my absence. He looked exhausted and overwhelmed by the tragedy that had struck Bokaro. He briefed me about the incidents that began around 9 a.m. on 1 November 1984.

'*Do din se hum log aur kuch nahin kiye hain* (We have not done anything for the last two days), we have just been rescuing people. Please take charge,' he said, the horror of the last two days writ large on his genial face.

I learnt that when DIG Srivastava had heard Sikhs were being attacked in Bokaro, he had immediately left home with his own firearm. He saw some Sikhs had taken shelter in a local gurdwara, and a mob was preparing to attack. Standing in front of the gurdwara, he fired a few rounds and the mob dispersed immediately.

He started getting distress calls from all over Bokaro and decided that the Sikhs should be rescued and brought to a safe place. His first concern was finding a secure building for the Sikh families. He rang up Father McNamara, the principal of St Xavier's School. The school was closed for holidays, so he requested the principal to allow the police to open a relief camp on the campus.

A *shok* sabha (condolence meeting) had been held at a Ram mandir in town the morning after Mrs Gandhi's killing. Tempers had flared, and immediately after the sabha disassembled, the attacks on the Sikhs had started. Angry mobs, armed with guns, swords, rods, petrol and kerosene, targeted Sikh homes.

Chas, a town across the bridge from Bokaro, had a prosperous Sikh population of businessmen, transporters, contractors and owners of large shops who had come to Bokaro when the steel plant and ancillary industries were being set up. On that day, Sikh families, both in Bokaro and Chas, were brutally attacked.

I started piecing together the chain of events to understand how the situation had spiralled out of control. The DySP (town) who was in charge of the district in my absence had already faced a commission of inquiry (CoI) in his previous posting for opening fire in a law-and-order situation. So, this time, he went by the book. When he saw a mob approaching from Chas via the bridge, he sent his jeep to get red flags and a loudspeaker to announce that the assembly was unlawful. He contacted the OIC of Bokaro city police station, the main police station, in sector 3 and asked everybody to reach the spot immediately.

As a result, when distress calls from Sikh families started pouring into Bokaro city police station, there was no force present to respond because everybody had rushed out to Chas instead, including the OIC. The mismanagement and lack of proper leadership was apparent.

There was so much anger that day—suddenly neighbour had turned against neighbour, forgetting decades of friendship and amity. Some officers told me we still did not know how many had been killed or where their bodies were lying. There was also talk that leaders of the Congress Party had instigated the mobs.

Dashmesh Nagar under Marafari police station was badly hit. Welders, khalasis and workers lived there in an unauthorized colony that had come up when the plant was being built. Mobs attacked these hutments and a number of Sikhs were killed. There were also isolated attacks wherever a Sikh person or family was known to reside.

There were many killings in sector 9 in Bokaro. The attack was systematic and targeted; it lasted only a few hours but caused immense damage to life and property.

Zonal IG L.V. Singh had arrived from Ranchi to take stock of the situation. He was very upset that I had not been present to handle it. I tried to explain to him that I had been away on sanctioned leave. 'I came as soon as I could, Sir. There was no flight; this was the earliest train available to me,' I explained miserably.

But this was not the time for explanations. It was the time to take charge. I consulted all my officers—the youngsters were rudderless and were looking for a leader to guide them on how to handle the aftermath of the carnage.

I went and met the families, huddled many to a room inside St Xavier's School. When they saw me they rushed to me, demanding why I had left them. Many of them just clung to me, crying, 'Where were you? Why did you leave us? Because you were not here, see what has happened to us.'

Their anguish hit me like a ton of bricks. Was it true? Was all this the result of my absence? Would I have been able to stop this madness had I been there? How many lives were lost simply because I was not there? My conscience begged for answers, but my mind was numb. Guilt washed over me in waves, rooting me to the spot.

Maybe if I had been there, I would have ordered advance deployment as soon as news of the PM's assassination broke. Had police presence been more palpable on the streets, perhaps the mobs might have been deterred from going on a rampage.

Right after Operation Blue Star in June, several Sikh army men had resigned and left the Ramgarh cantonment in the neighbouring district of Hazaribagh. They had marched in a procession and there was speculation that they would enter Bokaro because of our sizeable Sikh population. I had ordered heavy deployment and blocked the roads so that we were prepared for any incident. Fortunately, the procession did not come to Bokaro.

However, the Sikh community in Bokaro had been agitated ever since Operation Blue Star. In the gurdwaras, they spoke about *ghallu ghara* (holocaust or massacre in Punjabi) and took out protest marches. Whenever the Sikhs congregated for a meeting, we would always make proper deployment, talk to them and make sure that nothing spun out of control. I would personally liaise with the leaders and elders of the Sikh community to ensure nothing untoward happened.

But when the Sikhs became targets, there was nobody to handle the enraged mobs. There were a few killings in neighbouring Dhanbad as well, but the situation was immediately controlled because the SP was present. Nowhere else in Bihar did riots break out on such a scale.

As I stood at St Xavier's mulling over my absence, I was jolted out of my reverie by an elderly Sikh lady. She simply embraced me and kept saying, '*Aap aa gaye hain*, Madam, *aap aa gaye hain* (You have come).' There was so much relief in her voice. Many more women crowded around me. They all wanted to tell me the horrors they had faced: about the husbands and sons who were missing; about the children who could not sleep at night because they were terrified; about burnt homes; and about looted possessions.

I realized that although I may not have been there on that critical day, there was still a lot that I could do for them now that I was. I got into action mode. Every Sikh family had been brought to St Xavier's School for protection. I gathered all the OICs and announced, 'All OICs will now sit here. Each of you bring one writer and start registering cases that have happened in your areas. Let every dead body, every missing person be accounted for.'

We eventually recorded more than 100 FIRs. We found that sixty-nine people had been killed in the Bokaro–Chas area. By evening, we started getting names of the accused who had led the mobs and perpetrated the violence and killings. I requested the district commissioner not to lift the curfew.

'Tonight, we will pick up everybody who has been named; let us extend the curfew by a couple of days,' I said.

We worked the entire night and arrested many of the accused. We started locating missing persons who were either dead or alive. Raids were conducted for the recovery of looted material. When word spread that the SP was back, people started throwing out things they had looted, probably because they believed I would not spare anybody.

One of the places that was attacked was Mrs Girgila's home and school, where Tushar had studied earlier. Because the Sikhs are industrious and prosperous people, some of the attacks were also prompted by jealousy. The miscreants had looted everything in her house but had, thankfully, spared her life. The morning after we started our raids, her fridge, almirah and other items were found abandoned beside the Garga river. It was a little baffling to see how the recovery of even a few of her belongings gave Mrs Girgila so much relief in the midst of all that she had lost and suffered. I suppose in moments of great distress, we cling to any vestige of familiarity.

People told me that some policemen had joined in with the looting of shops, they also gave me a few names. In that tense atmosphere, it was not possible to start cases against policemen. I called my men and told them, in no uncertain terms, that I was aware of the complaints of looting against our people. '*Agar kisi ne koi cheez uthaya hai, toh aap abhi usey wapas kar dijiye* (If anyone has picked up anything then you return it now),' I ordered. Otherwise, I assured them, I would personally go and raid their homes. Of course, I had no time to go and mount raids, I said it merely to instil fear in them. 'If I find a single item of loot, I will register an FIR and arrest you.' The next morning piles of tyres and motor parts were thrown out on the streets.

* * *

The story of one family was particularly traumatic. There were five children and they had lost both their parents. The father, Ajit Singh, was a very successful transporter-cum-contractor living with his family in Cooperative Colony. When the mob came to their home, the children hid in the bathroom and, through a crack in the door, saw both their parents being dragged out. Four of the children were in the house, the youngest among them barely two or three years old. The eldest sibling was an eighteen-year-old girl studying in Chandigarh. She came to Bokaro the day after the attacks with her chacha (uncle) and *chachi* (aunt).

Taking the two older girls into confidence, I went to their house to understand how the incident had unfolded. The younger sister, who was about fifteen to sixteen years old, was able to give us the names of the attackers. We had already picked them up—notorious local goondas who would align themselves with whichever political party was in power.

There was blood everywhere, and the whole house had been ransacked. The almirah had been broken into, there was nothing left in it. In the locker of the almirah I found a small key, which looked like it belonged to a bank locker. But the girls did not know in which bank their parents had a locker. I thought to myself that since Ajit Singh was a rich contractor, if we could somehow find his locker, maybe the children could have access to some money. They had nothing left anymore.

I took the elder girl in my jeep. 'Let us drive around and try to locate your father's locker,' I told her. We went to a couple of banks, with no success.

At our third stop, the manager of Punjab National Bank said, 'Yes, this key belongs to one of our lockers.'

'Can we open it?' I asked.

'No. The locker is in the name of Mr Ajit Singh and his wife; how can we allow it to be opened by anybody else?' the manager replied.

I took him aside and told him about the tragedy that had befallen this family. 'Look, there are five children and they have nothing. You know their father was a rich businessman. We want to open the locker. How can you help us? Just look at the condition of the children,' I implored the manager.

He was in a dilemma, but he wanted to help. 'If you give me in writing that the locker has to be opened under these extraordinary circumstances—and that if any question is raised subsequently, you will take full responsibility—only then can I allow you to open it,' he said.

Looking at the plight of the children, I did not think twice. I assured him that I would take personal responsibility and immediately gave him the surety he wanted in writing. We went down to the vault in the basement and opened the locker. There were passbooks of various bank accounts, licences of five trucks, Rs 40,000 cash and several pieces of jewellery. I was so relieved for the sake of the children, and I could see a flicker of hope reflected on the face of this eighteen-year-old girl. Now she could at least take care of her siblings.

Armed with the licences, I made police teams and sent them out to trace the trucks. The moment the news of Ajit Singh's death had spread, the drivers, khalasis and subcontractors had all run away with his trucks. With our prompt action we managed to retrieve all the vehicles and hand them over to the family.

Ajit Singh's eldest daughter was a very sensible girl. When we were collecting the jewellery from the locker, she said, 'My parents had these made for my wedding.' Later, I came to know that she never married, and dedicated her entire life to bringing up her siblings, with help from her uncle and aunt.

That day, I had taken an on-the-spot decision to take full responsibility for opening the locker for the sake of five orphaned children. I have always believed that if your intentions are good, even bending the rules is acceptable. I feel, in fact, in certain situations, officers should not hesitate; they should have the courage to take responsibility for an action that may not be strictly going by the rules. Especially if the purpose is to help somebody. Often, we police officers find ourselves in a quandary such as the one I had faced. We have to be willing to take a personal risk to help people in distress.

There was another case of a Sikh gentleman whose cries still haunt me. He lived in Sector 9 with his wife and two young sons.

'We were trapped, there was a huge mob outside our flat. They started throwing petrol-soaked flaming objects inside and kept calling out to us: "Come out, come out of your home, we will not harm you." I did not trust this bloodthirsty mob. There was smoke everywhere and we were choking.

'Suddenly my wife stood up and said, "If we stay in the house we will die." Taking each of our sons by the hand, she opened the front door and walked out into the crowd. That was the last time I saw my family. I have been searching for them ever since that moment. They are not in the relief camp, they have not come home nor have I found their bodies. Can you help me, Madam?'

I accompanied him to his flat. Everything was charred, and whatever had escaped the flames had been either destroyed or stolen. We looked all over the flat and all around it. We could not find any clue as to the whereabouts of the missing wife and sons. The gentleman kept saying that he feared they had been burnt to death.

The road outside the building appeared to have been freshly swept and we noticed a heap of ashes on one side. Both of us crouched on the ground and started sifting through the ashes. Suddenly he let out a cry. In the ashes lay his wife's gold *jhumka* (earring) which she had been wearing that day. We started looking for more clues and found tufts of human hair. 'These are my boys! These are my boys!' he said in exultation.

I could not process his reaction. Here was a man holding his dead children's hair as the only proof of their demise and he was tearfully ecstatic. I realized not knowing what had happened to them had been driving him to the brink of madness. He now looked relieved, having found some answers. Then the finality of this discovery hit him and he crumpled to the ground. I did not know what to say or do in that moment. I did not have the words to console this broken man. I just stood beside him in silence as he wept over his dead wife's earring and his children's remains.

Another time, a woman in the camp was telling me about her family and sobbing uncontrollably. 'They came into our house and threw all the men from the terrace. I watched all of them die, my husband, my children . . . everybody.' Listening to her trauma, I too started crying, standing in the middle of the relief camp. I could empathize with her. Others gathered around and started consoling us. I realized that even in the midst of their own misery, the people were so large-hearted that they were comforting me.

Even as each individual story broke my heart, and I tried to do whatever I could to comfort them, I simultaneously took charge of the other activities. CM Chandrashekhar Singh came to Bokaro, and we had to do heavy bandobast for his visit. He conducted a peace march in the Chas area.

When he met me, he said, 'For the first time I have members of the public telling me, "You should not grant leave to our SP without asking us. She would have saved us if she had been here."'

The CM was a level-headed, respected leader. His presence and words helped assuage the people's feelings. The arrest of the accused also pacified exacerbated tempers immediately.

I was barely home for days and nights on end, and my two boys were miserable and confused. They were alone with the help; Rakesh was not able to come to Bokaro from Munger either. He was very concerned and was constantly telephoning me, but I could not even take his calls. Tushar, who was always a very mild-mannered boy, smashed the telephone in frustration one day because I was never home. Anshuman was not able to understand anything and was getting cranky missing his mother.

A week after our return from Bombay, I realized that it would take many days for things to normalize in Bokaro. So, I sent the children to my parents in Patna with my bodyguard and the maid. Now when I think back, I cannot believe I allowed them to travel by train all the way to Patna without either Rakesh or myself. I shudder to think of it even now. But at the time, I just could not understand what else to do. It was yet another on-the-spot decision I was forced to make, this time in my personal life.

I am eternally grateful that both those snap decisions worked out well.

* * *

After about ten days, Father McNamara requested me to shift the relief camp out of St Xavier's School so that classes could resume and life could return to normal. The way Father

McNamara and his team welcomed the members of another community into the Christian-run school was very inspiring, and the Sikh community of Bokaro remained ever grateful to the Father. But we knew it was time to move out and let the children begin classes.

The Sikh families were still scared. The riots had widowed many women, leaving them alone with little children. They did not want to go back to their homes, they did not trust their neighbours anymore.

We needed a place to move them. I turned my attention to our newly constructed barracks in the police lines, which were lying vacant. These were two sets of double-storeyed barracks that could house 200 people. But they were uninhabitable as yet because there was neither electricity nor water.

During the riots, the Hindustan Steel Construction Limited (HSCL) colony in Marafari had suffered many deaths as well. The head of HSCL, Mr Subbiah, was regularly in touch with me about the relief and rehabilitation of the Sikh families. I had very cordial relations with him and his wife as we lived in the same sector. When I discussed the problem with Mr Subbiah, he said, 'We have pipes, we will get you water.'

I immediately seized the opportunity. For two years the barracks had stood empty. Who knew when the Bihar government would have money to give us water and power? If HSCL was offering a water connection, best to just take it, I told myself.

Within a day, Mr Subbiah and his team of engineers had laid out pipes and made provisions for water in the barracks. They also brought power lines and gave us electricity. So, we were able to move all the people from the relief camp to the police barracks in sector 12.

While we were able to at least put a roof over their heads, we did not have the provisions to feed them. But more help was at hand. Here I witnessed the true meaning of *seva* (service) as practised by the Sikh community. Members of the community from Dhanbad and other neighbouring areas came to set up langar (community kitchen) so no one would go hungry, bringing food, clothes, utensils and blankets with them. They wanted to hand over the relief material to me personally for distribution, to make sure there was no misappropriation or theft. Gradually, we encouraged the families to rehabilitate themselves and leave the barracks.

Rehabilitating the victims' families, especially the widows, became one of my top priorities in the following weeks and months. Bokaro Steel Plant announced that they would give compassionate appointments to dependents of all plant employees who had been killed in the riots. HSCL also offered the same. Many of the widows were not confident about taking up a job and their families wanted to take them back to the safety of their homes in Punjab. But I felt that a job was a necessity for them as it would give them an independent status in their family, besides securing their financial future and their children's. This was more important than going back to their hometowns. So, I spent time counselling and convincing them to accept the jobs being offered and helped them fill out the necessary forms.

In those days, the SP had the authority to appoint five persons to the police. Among the five I selected, one man, who had lost his wife to the mob, said, 'Please give the job to my brother-in-law. He and his wife will be looking after my children.' Taking a compassionate view of the family's needs, I bent the rules and appointed his wife's brother as a driver, who turned out to be a very hard-working man.

But there was still a large number of women whose husbands were neither in the employment of Bokaro Steel Plant nor HSCL. They had been private workers, welders or contractors. I tried very hard to convince the government to do something for them. Later, after I had left Bokaro, I learnt that the government had taken a decision to appoint all these women to the posts of constables.

I was not present when my city needed me most. It's a truth I have lived and grappled with for decades now. I did everything in my power to help the people as soon as I returned, but will that ever be enough? This thought still haunts me.

But this incident taught me one important life lesson—it is not just during the darkest hour when people need the police, they need us every day, and it is our duty to stand with them every single day.

13

The Aftermath

General elections were announced immediately after the demise of Mrs Gandhi, to be held in the last week of December 1984. Her older son Rajiv was scheduled to come to Bokaro for campaigning, and I was given charge of handling the helipad of Dhanbad. I had to leave home at 4 a.m. in the bitter cold to reach the helipad in time for his arrival. I decided to take my older son, Tushar, along.

When I was a little girl, my father had taken me along when he went to attend a session of the All India Congress Committee (AICC) in Patna. Pandit Jawaharlal Nehru had come to address that session and I had been fascinated by the experience. Even though I was a girl—and back in those days, girls were not taken to attend such occasions—my father had made an exception. I still remember that day fondly, how Pandit Nehru came riding a bullock cart, how the crowds swelled just to catch a glimpse of him, how the audience hung on to his every word. I had observed all this sitting in a corner of the dais.

Eager to share the experience with my son, I bundled Tushar in heavy woollens and took him in my jeep. If the grandfather had made a grand entry in a bullock cart, the grandson swooped down in a helicopter. The sun was just rising, and when Rajiv Gandhi got out of the helicopter, the morning rays fell on his face, lighting it up with a golden hue. Together with a red tika on his forehead and a red and white *angavastram* (stole) around his shoulders, Indira Gandhi's elder son looked like the crown prince that everyone believed him to be. '*Yeh kitne* handsome *hain* (He is so handsome),' Tushar exclaimed, rubbing the sleep from his eyes and staring in awe as Rajiv Gandhi started walking towards the stage.

During his campaign, I witnessed how the popular vote was completely with this young man who had just lost his mother and had been thrust into the spotlight. All the women would shout '*Hamaar aashirvad, bachwa ke vote daib* (Our blessings, son, our vote is for you).' Everybody was all for him, and it was obvious that he was going to sweep the general election, which he did.

The Congress Party won a landslide majority, securing 404 of the 514 seats in the Lok Sabha, and Rajiv Gandhi became the prime minister of India on 31 December 1984, exactly two months after his mother had been gunned down by her bodyguards.

In 1985, assembly polls were announced in Bihar. Elections in Bihar tended to be extremely unruly, with rampant booth capturing, proxy voting, bombs and deaths, and even the outbreak of riots. Dhanbad was considered an especially notorious district because of the warring coal mafia.

Just before the assembly elections, I was having a discussion with DIG Srivastava when one of the candidates came to him with folded hands, cutting a humble figure. 'Please protect me. My life is in danger,' he implored us.

'We will deploy enough manpower to protect the candidates and ensure their safety,' the DIG reassured him. 'Nothing will happen to the candidates.'

The candidate was O.P. Lala, who was contesting for the first time on a Congress ticket from Dhanbad. He feared that the coal mafia would assassinate him, indicating the infamous Singh brothers of Dhanbad—on whom the film *Gangs of Wasseypur* is said to be based.

That year, the Bokaro elections had been countermanded because one of the candidates had died of natural causes. Since our elections could not be held, the DIG directed me to go to Dhanbad for deployment on election day along with all the men from Bokaro police. Large-scale violence was expected, and we were asked to be very alert. I left home at 6 a.m. and met the DIG on the way to Dhanbad.

'I am carrying my personal firearm,' he confided. I was quite taken aback, wondering what lay in store for us that day.

We were on patrol duty. Our strategy in those days was to stop all vehicular movement. Political parties would bring their goondas in their vehicles for booth capturing, bogus voting, intimidation and other illegal activities. I started aggressively patrolling the roads, checking every vehicle.

After some time, I heard people taunting me with a bizarre allegation. 'We know why Madam is here. They are from the same community.'

It turned out that O.P. Lala and I belonged to the same community, a fact that I had been completely unaware of. Hearing this ridiculous charge, I started checking even more strictly, not sparing any party's vehicles.

About thirty minutes before voting stopped at 5 p.m., a man came running to me, 'Madam Sir, see, all these people have collected here to cast false votes because this polling station is in a secluded spot.' So, I decided to stand 200 yards from the polling station until voting finished. Seeing an officer in uniform, the crowd slowly melted away.

Mr Lala won with a thumping majority. That year, Dhanbad saw peaceful voting for the first time. Ashish Ranjan Sinha, who was SP Dhanbad at the time, and all of us had really worked hard that day, and we received appreciation all around.

By this time, my first IG, Rajeshwar Lal, had joined politics and had become a member of the legislative council of Bihar. For the assembly elections of 1985, he came to Bokaro to campaign for one of the candidates, and we had an interesting meeting.

'I must tell you, people really admire you here; they think very highly of you; you have done very well,' he said, all smiles. I felt he took some credit for my success and said he was very proud of me.

I don't think he remembered how he had treated me when I had first joined the force. The lady officer whom he had found difficult to post had made the posting she was given her very own. I let bygones be bygones.

Bokaro voted in the assembly by-elections in the summer of 1985. I was in charge of the entire election bandobast. We did meticulous planning, carried out preventive arrests and properly deployed manpower for patrolling and checking crime. We also made lists of people with private gun licences and asked them to deposit their firearms for the duration of voting. All these steps ensured that the elections in Bokaro went off peacefully as well.

* * *

On another front, however, things were far from peaceful. The Justice Ranganath Misra Commission of Inquiry was set up in April 1985 by Prime Minister Rajiv Gandhi, which was, as stated in the Commission's report:

> . . . to inquire into the allegations in regard to the incidents of organised violence which took place in Delhi and the disturbances following the assassination of the late Prime Minister Smt. Indira Gandhi.

In September 1985, the scope of the inquiry was expanded to look into 'the disturbances which took place in the Bokaro Tehsil, in Chas Tehsil and at Kanpur. . .' Delhi had borne the worst brunt of the riot, with 2146 deaths as per official records, followed by Kanpur, with 135 deaths and the Bokaro–Chas area with sixty-nine deaths. Thus, these two places also came under the purview of the Commission.

Facing a CoI entails thorough preparation and detailed documentation to establish the chain of events from case diaries and station diaries—which call came when? Who responded? What was the incident? What action was taken? My experience of preparing meticulous paperwork during the inquiry into the Bhagalpur blindings proved invaluable in guiding my team.

With the CoI hanging over our heads, officers started turning against one another. 'This officer did not listen to me; that subordinate did not follow my orders; or that senior officer took the wrong call.' Allegations started flying thick and fast among my men.

Although I knew I would not be in the dock because I was on sanctioned leave during the incident, as SP, I wanted to present a united front before the Commission. I assembled my men and addressed them, making it clear that this was not the time to find fault within our own ranks. Everybody was in this together; everybody's neck was on the line. I pointed out that I was going to be with them every step of the way as they faced the CoI, but that they would have to work together. 'You cannot abandon ship when there is a crisis, *sabko saath chalna hai* (we all have to stick together).'

Zonal IG L.V. Singh guided me through this process, and we tabulated all the FIRs we had registered after the attacks. Each case was accounted for, and we made a very meticulous presentation of all documents. The sub-divisional officer (SDO) and others in the district administration were apprehensive about whether the police would stand by them, but I made sure that everyone worked together.

Before the CoI came to Bokaro, I displayed all the cases on the notice board: the number of deaths, the cases of looting, destruction or violence and all the FIRs we had registered. To ensure as much transparency as possible, I asked the public to come and see the board and told them to write to the CoI if they had any grievances.

The Commission completed its inquiry and submitted its report in 1987. The report stated:

The police at Bokaro were not as ineffective as at Kanpur or Delhi. Many of the affidavits indicate that the police came and helped. The Administration actually sought the help of Central Industrial Security Force which was put into use and the situation in Bokaro was contained within 7–8 hours. The Commission takes notice of the fact that most of the incidents are subject-matter of FIRs which more or less have complete particulars. In almost every case an investigation has followed and a large number of cases have ended up in charge-sheet. As noted in another part of the Report, some of these cases are already under trial.

Bokaro police was not found guilty and the report provided closure to one of the toughest periods in my career.

* * *

What gave me even more solace than my men being exonerated by the CoI was the warmth I received from the Sikh community of Bokaro. When I finished my posting and was being transferred out, they invited me to a Sikh *sangat* (gathering) to honour me. They gave me a plaque in gratitude for what I had done for them. This community had lost so much because I was not present, yet they did not lay blame on me or feel any rancour towards me.

One day, a group of Sikh widows came to my house to meet me. 'We feel so empowered because of you, Madam,' they said. I had counselled many of them to take up the jobs being offered to them on compassionate grounds. They presented me with a beautiful silver chain for which they had all pooled in money and bought for me. It was straight from their hearts, something I could not refuse.

There were many such instances, and, as I wrapped up my stay, so many people came to say thank you. In Chas, there was Chas Sweet House, a sweet shop run by the Chatterjee family. When I came back from Bombay on 3 November 1984, I was told the OIC of Chas police station had locked up its owner, Rohini Kumar Chatterjee. He was over eighty years old. People from Chas came to me and said, '*Bahut galat hua hai* (What has happened is not right), Madam, this old man has been put in the lock-up. They are accusing him of instigating the attacks only because he is a Congress sympathizer.'

I knew the OIC was capable of high-handedness when unchecked. I had to be vigilant with him all the time. I directed him to release Mr Chatterjee immediately.

Months later, when the Bokaro Chamber of Commerce held a farewell for me at Bokaro Club, an old gentleman walked up to me, held my hand and started crying softly. He put something in my palm and walked away. At night, when I opened the packet, I found a small ring. I suddenly remembered who that elderly gentleman was—Rohini Kumar Chatterjee! I was so touched. He never said a word, just gave me that ring and left. I have preserved it till date.

I felt I had built a relationship with the town, including with the plant management. I had nurtured a collaborative relationship with the senior officials that paid us rich dividends in terms of improving law and order, besides controlling crime. When I was leaving, the MD organized a very warm farewell for me. Several schools and colleges invited me for farewells as well, as I had a close relationship with all of them. The nuns of St Xavier's School invited me to have a meal with them in their living quarters, which is very rare. The nuns of Holy Family Hospital called me to their school and gave me a box full of coconut macaroons, which they had baked themselves. I treasure these memories as much as my children, and I enjoyed the macaroons.

My farewell became quite a spectacle, with people coming, sector by sector, to meet me before I left. I got busy vacating the house for the next SP and saying goodbye to all my friends.

My closest friends in Bokaro were a doctor couple who lived next door. Drs Dinesh and Asha Srivastava were a few years older than me, with two small boys as well. They were an invaluable support system for me, especially because I was alone with a small child and a baby. They would take charge of my children whenever I needed help. Tushar and Anshuman would play in their home, and if they fell ill while I was not around, the Srivastavas would take over. I truly valued their friendship, especially because they did not see me just as a senior police officer, they were genuinely fond of me as a person. I spent a lot of time with them.

I think it is very important for police officers to have a support system. We must develop good relationships with neighbours and friends, especially because there is no family in remote postings. As an IPS officer, it does us no good to walk around with our noses up in the air, we have to reach out to people. Not only because they can help us out, but to forge genuine bonds of friendship.

* * *

I had one piece of unfinished business—the departmental proceedings against those six constables who had troubled my predecessor. The week before I left Bokaro, I finally passed an order on their file. It had been hanging over their heads the entire time I was there, and, as a result, during my tenure they did not trouble me at all. They had cleaned up their act and become very disciplined. In fact, I never once saw them in anything but their uniform ever since that first police sabha, when I had thrown them out.

So, I decided not to dismiss them, which is what they had been fearing all along. But to send across a strong message to them and the other men, I cancelled several of their increments. It was a harsh punishment but not severe. They were eternally grateful to have retained their jobs.

Krishna Chowdhury of the 1979 batch succeeded me as SP, Bokaro. He was the son of DG A.K. Chowdhury, whom I would work with in Patna a few years later. In between, DIG Y.N. Srivastava had left, and Santosh Kumar had come as my DIG. A fine officer, I got along very well with both him and his wife.

I had carried out extensive recruitments in my tenure. It was said that this was the first time in Bokaro that recruitments had been done without a single rupee changing hands. Apparently, for a constable's post, a candidate was expected to shell out as much as Rs 40,000 in those days. I ensured that no police personnel took a bribe. When I learnt that a government doctor was demanding money to conduct their medical check-ups, I telephoned and warned him that I would register a case against him.

On the day I was leaving, the new recruits came to my house with a small gift to express their gratitude, saying that they had not needed to spend a single paisa on their recruitment. I wished them all the best and proceeded to the police lines for the farewell parade.

After the parade, I found a large procession had gathered at the police lines to accompany me to the railway station. I was quite shocked but did not object to anything, because now that the new SP had taken charge, the arrangements had been made under his orders.

Many people stood on the roadside and waved to me as we proceeded through the town. A shamiana had been erected at the station. When I arrived, it appeared that half the city was already there, including people from the steel plant, my neighbours, Father McNamara and even those six constables, who were now shouting 'SP, zindabad!'

I waved one last goodbye to Bokaro and its people and stepped into the train. Rakesh was already there with the boys. It finally hit me that I had lived in Bokaro for three years and must have done well for them to give me such an overwhelming send-off. As soon as the train started moving, I could not hold back my tears. All the pent-up emotions that I had bottled up during the series of goodbyes and farewells came rushing out.

Although Bokaro was considered a rather comfortable posting compared to busy and big districts like Patna, Ranchi or Munger, I felt this posting had allowed me to experience everything—a massive strike, two elections, the aftermath of devastating riots, and a CoI. I felt I had played a positive role and was leaving Bokaro richer in experience and relationships.

14

'Yes, Yes, We Will Go!'

It was 26 January 1986, a few months before my emotional and memorable farewell.

We had just finished attending the Republic Day parade. It was one of those rare days when Rakesh, the boys and I were all together, enjoying a holiday at home in the winter sun. Suddenly, we received a call from the Bihar home secretary, B.K. Singh. There was already speculation about my next posting. Some people were convinced my next stop would be SP, Jamshedpur.

Rakesh took the call, his face inscrutable. I wondered what the home secretary wanted to discuss on Republic Day. 'Yes, yes, Sir. We will go, we have no problem,' Rakesh said, and hung up.

My heart skipped a beat. 'What happened? Where is it that we are going?' I asked anxiously. It was not like Rakesh to take a major decision without consulting with me, that too about a posting.

'It's the academy, they want us both,' he said, beaming.

I felt a rush of excitement at the thought of the NPA in Hyderabad. My next thought was that we had not even applied! My mind was full of questions although I was incredibly happy at this surprising turn of events, especially because it meant a joint posting.

We had been married for eight years. As we were batchmates, often we could not be posted to the same place. While our careers had taken us to some exciting and challenging postings, our family life had been rather disrupted. As ASP, I had been in Patna, and Rakesh in Ranchi. Then Rakesh went off to Nalanda as SP. We were together in Patna again for some time when he came as SP city and later as SP rural, while I was in the CID. But soon we were living apart again—I went as SP, Bokaro, and Rakesh got posted as superintendent, Railway police (SRP) in Dhanbad. I do not know whether he was disappointed, he did not say anything. He has always been very encouraging about my job and felt I must go to Bokaro. Still, he was concerned about my health since I was still recovering from jaundice after Anshuman's birth.

'You have been so ill, it is better that I stay nearby, in Dhanbad,' he said simply.

But within a year, Rakesh got posted to Munger, nearly 300 kilometres from Bokaro. Munger was a very heavy charge, and the constituency of the then CM, Chandrashekhar Singh. It was also politically sensitive, being the home of twelve MLAs of the Bihar assembly. I was happy for him, but I was also sad that he was going away. He was my emotional support; I knew I would miss him very much, not just for family matters, but also because we were peers. He was the one with whom I would discuss my work. The police is a very hierarchical service which makes it quite a lonely job for officers, especially in senior positions.

Those days, there was no STD connection. If you wanted to talk to someone in another town, you had to book a trunk call. More often than not, the call would not even go through.

Munger was rather remote, and Rakesh was frequently touring. As a result, it was quite difficult to speak to him.

Talking to each other was always an awkward exercise. The range DIG's office had a radio telephone. Rakesh would send a message to the operator in my DIG's office to call me. The message would be relayed to me and I would have to go over to the DIG's office to speak to my husband. It was not a private connection, operators across the entire wireless network of the state could listen in. It was embarrassing to even ask something as simple as, 'How are you?'

My parents-in-law had shifted to Munger with Rakesh. The SP's accommodation there was a lovely, colonial-era bungalow in a huge compound on the banks of the Ganga. The river here is massive—mighty and beautiful in all its grandeur. My father-in-law had a foreboding when he moved to Munger. 'My time has come, for I am now beside Ma Ganga,' he would say.

Little did we know he would get his wish.

I used to visit Rakesh sometimes with the boys. There was no direct train. We would come to Dhanbad from Bokaro by road and take a train in the middle of the night, arriving at a small station called Kiul at dawn. It was hard to disembark with two little children, and Rakesh would come to Kiul to help us get down from the compartment. We would then drive for about 50 kilometres, arriving in Munger completely exhausted. That entire day would be spent in recovering from the arduous journey. It felt like a punishment visit. But there was no other way. Rakesh could never come to Bokaro given his heavy workload in Munger.

In March 1985, while I was in Bokaro, my father-in-law fell extremely sick. He was moved to Jamshedpur for treatment at the Tata Main Hospital as a former Tata employee. When his condition worsened, I went to Jamshedpur. I wanted to do my bit and take care of Rakesh's father. After he passed away, we returned to Munger to perform the *shradh* (funeral rites) ceremony.

Soon enough, I got a call from my DIG, asking me to return to Bokaro as I had been away for too long. The assembly by-elections had been announced, so I left immediately.

Just after my return, Rakesh fell sick with jaundice. I fretted about his health but could not leave Bokaro to tend to him. On Rakesh's request, luckily, the government posted him to the 4th Battalion of Bihar Military Police (BMP) headquartered in Bokaro. We got a little respite.

So it was no wonder that when the Bihar home secretary offered both of us a posting at the NPA as assistant directors, Rakesh immediately said yes. At the time Rakesh lost his father, one of his sisters was still unmarried, and he had taken on the responsibility of finding her a good matrimonial alliance and arranging her wedding. Merely a week before the home secretary's call, we had organized her wedding.

We felt God was telling us that we had fulfilled our commitments here, and our services were now needed elsewhere.

The home secretary told Rakesh that PM Rajiv Gandhi and Union home minister Arun Nehru were keen on revamping police training in India, which was why we were being hand-picked for the job. The PM had visited the NPA and had not been happy with whatever he had seen.

As soon as we gave our consent, our release orders followed quickly. Before proceeding to Hyderabad, we were asked to meet Julio Ribeiro in Delhi, the celebrated IPS officer who was then special secretary to the government of India in the ministry of home affairs. Neither of us had met him before and we were quite perplexed as to why he had asked to meet us.

But first, we went back to Patna. It was very calming to stay with my parents for a few days. We also met with many of our friends and colleagues in Bihar police.

S.B. Sahay had just taken over as DG, Bihar police. When we called on him, he said, 'Mr Ribeiro has given me a task. My first job as DG is to convince you to go to the NPA.' We assured him that we did not need any convincing.

Many officers were surprised at our decision to go on central deputation, that too on a training assignment. One person even insisted it was the 'wrong time' for us to leave Bihar.

'You are Kayasthas,' he said, referring to the caste both Rakesh and I belonged to. 'At this moment, there is a Kayastha DG heading Bihar police, the DIG (admin.) is a Kayastha, even the IG, CID, is a Kayastha. This is the *best* time for you to stay in Bihar, the golden period for Kayasthas.'

We found this line of thought quite ridiculous. But it was true that the culture of officers going on deputation was not common in Bihar. We were one of the first few Biharis to go out of the state, which is why we faced so many questions. Even at the academy, people would ask us if we had left our home cadre because we had gotten into trouble in Bihar!

* * *

We arrived in Delhi just as the heat of summer was kicking in with soaring temperatures. Mr Ribeiro invited us to his house as it was a holiday and sent his car to pick us up. On the way, we got chatting with the driver, who was all praises for his sahib. '*Woh toh bhagwan jaise hain*,' he said, as he explained to us that his staff looked upon Mr Ribeiro as a god because he took such good care of them.

When we arrived at his house, we were taken aback by the humility and simplicity of the couple. Mrs Ribeiro went to the kitchen to make coffee for us, and Mr Ribeiro carried the tray himself. There were no orderlies, no retinue. I was impressed, and this was the beginning of a lifelong association with Mr Ribeiro.

He gave us the backstory to our sudden posting. After PM Rajiv Gandhi had expressed his disappointment at the present condition of the NPA, a decision had been taken to revamp police training. A fine IPS officer of the Madhya Pradesh cadre, A.A. Ali, had been appointed the director of the academy with a clear mandate to improve its working. He requested the home ministry to post officers with proven abilities in the field to the academy, and to draw them from different states so that the IPS probationers would be exposed to the police ethos from across India.

He had also pointed out that since more women were qualifying for the IPS now, a lady officer should be posted at the academy. They had asked Kiran Bedi, but she declined the offer. The home ministry then looked through the list of women IPS officers and arrived at my name. They discovered I had a good record and was married to an IPS officer, which made them doubly happy.

Mr Ribeiro said many facilities and incentives were being provided to attract good officers to the NPA. 'Your pay will be enhanced by 30 per cent and we will make sure you are sent abroad for advanced training,' he said, giving us a pep talk, because back then no one opted to go into police training. It was not a priority posting, compared to getting the charge of a district or range.

That is how Rakesh and I found ourselves back at the Sardar Vallabhbhai Patel National Police Academy in Hyderabad ten

years later; this time as members of the faculty in the summer
of 1986.

* * *

The four of us took the train and reached Secunderabad on
a May afternoon. I remember it being an extremely hot day.
A vehicle that looked like a minivan was sent for us. We piled
into it and set off for the long journey to Shivaramapalli, where
the academy is located. I was excited to see NPA again, and to
show off the beautiful campus to our children.

But the going was far from smooth. The vehicle was an
ancient jalopy that would judder to a halt every few minutes,
compelling the driver to get down and pour water to cool the
engine. We trundled along, mile after mile, stewing and sweating,
the children crying from the sweltering heat and exhaustion.

From being SP in a state to being received this way was a
bit of a shock. We finally swept through the academy gates and
heaved a sigh of relief to see the familiar, serene surroundings.
After settling in at the senior course mess, we wanted to first
wash away the day's exhaustion, but there was no water in the
taps. We were told the water was released only twice a day; we
would have to wait until the next day to take a bath!

We were given two rooms in the mess, which were neither
welcoming nor comfortable. The children were cranky after the
long train journey and the interminable car ride. We decided to
put them in the two beds in one of the rooms while we opted to
sleep on the floor.

As night fell, we felt our enthusiasm ebbing. Nobody
had come to ask after us, and we had been just left alone. We
switched off the lights and tried to sleep, hoping that all would

be well in the morning. But in the dark, the cockroaches came out. Could it get any worse?

The following day, remembering the big breakfast that used to be the highlight of my mornings as a probationer, I got up hoping the children would at least get a good meal now. But there was no hot breakfast. The food was prepared at the IPS officers' mess and came to the senior course mess in steel tiffin carriers—the omelettes soggy from condensation, the toast leathery. None of us felt like eating, and even the sight of the food was sickening.

When we had arrived at the NPA as probationers, we had felt so welcome and were treated like officers. This felt like a real comedown from those days, ten years later. That night, I could not sleep. I sat up and nudged Rakesh. He was awake as well.

'Rakesh, I hope you took the right decision. Have we made a huge mistake coming here?' I asked.

His silence in the dark, still night spoke volumes.

15

The Best Years

'Have we made a huge mistake by coming here?'

When I look back now, I can truthfully say that those were the best years of my career. For me, it was exhilarating to be involved in shaping the future leadership of the Indian police. The IPS leadership is the thin khaki line between order and chaos. Every trainee leads thousands of personnel, who in turn interact with lakhs of citizens in every part of the country, providing succour and security. While my official personality had flowered in Danapur and Bokaro, the five years at NPA brought me standing and respect within the IPS. I learnt mentoring and counselling skills of a high order, besides honing my own professional skills. I also got a chance to interact with senior officers of all the services and eminent persons from all over India. I learnt from their experiences, which helped me better understand the different challenges facing our country.

Both Rakesh and I have always felt very strongly about the importance of training, which is often forgotten amid the trappings of power and glamour of postings. We were there to share our experiences in the field, to help train young IPS officers. But we were also there to learn and grow ourselves.

I still remember the words of PM Rajiv Gandhi at the POP of 1987:

'Passing out' does not mean an end to training. Training is a continuous process and it must go on throughout your career. Continuous training must include learning from your own experience and learning from the experience of others, interacting with your colleagues, not just horizontally but equally with your seniors and, perhaps, even more important, with your juniors and your subordinates . . . Training is, also, being re-trained at periodical intervals. It is keeping trained, keeping fit, keeping in touch, and a part of any of your duties must be the training and uplifting of your subordinates.

In September 2020, Prime Minister Narendra Modi raised some pertinent points about the correlation of training and good governance during the POP of the batch of 2018, which I found very promising for the future of the IPS:

We should never underestimate the importance of training. Very often, in government services, training is looked upon as punishment. The impression is that if someone has been given training duties, he must be a useless officer. This belittling of training is at the root of all ills plaguing good governance. We must come out of this mentality.

Between 1985 and 1991 we trained six batches—over 500 IPS probationers. My colleagues and I helped them grow and come into their own. In the process, we built everlasting bonds with

some of the brightest young minds of India. To date, we remain
close to many of them.

Within a week of arriving, we discovered that Mr Ali was
a gentleman and an able administrator. His first job, he said,
was to get assistant directors (ADs) from various states. R.K.
Johri from West Bengal, K.R. Nandan from Andhra Pradesh
and J. Mahapatra from Gujarat joined as ADs along with us. A
year later, S. Ramakrishnan came from West Bengal and P.P.S.
Sidhu from Uttar Pradesh. Two deputy directors (DD) were
already there—V.K. Deuskar from Madhya Pradesh and A.V.
Subba Rao from Kerala. For the first time, the academy had a
full strength of senior faculty.

The director shared his vision with us—turning the
academy into a centre of national excellence. He showed us
a video to apprise us of the present conditions, which left us
horrified. I still cannot shake off the revulsion I felt as I watched
the footage of a cook chopping onions right on the floor of the
IPS officers' mess!

The kitchen was in shambles, the food looked far from
appetizing, not least because of all the flies buzzing everywhere.
The classrooms looked rundown, with hardly any modern
teaching aids. But the outdoors had become lush and green by
then, with beautiful lawns and a huge number of trees. A closer
look, however, revealed the accumulation of garbage behind
many of the buildings.

We were taken to the tennis courts, which were piled
high with stacks of discarded items that had come from the
Mt Abu campus in 1974. Broken tables and chairs, chamber
pots, mats . . . they made the tennis courts an eyesore. In the
government, an item can be discarded only after a process of
'condemnation' but no one at the academy had found the

time to form a board and condemn these items in eleven long years.

'Our academy represents the entire country's police service to trainee officers, visitors and international guests. We cannot run such a shabby campus. Shouldn't we feel proud of our alma mater and be happy to serve here?' the director asked us all.

His words were very encouraging for me; I was ready to do my best for this institution that had given me everything—a new life in the police service, respect, job satisfaction and devotion to dedicated hard work.

* * *

I was asked to teach the crime records and crime prevention paper as well as one half of the investigation paper. Rakesh was to teach the other half, dealing with special crime investigation.

Along with teaching, the faculty members were put in charge of various clubs and activities on campus. An officers' club was started and I was put in charge of it. I established this club from scratch—from buying the furniture and crockery to organizing the weekly programmes. As soon as the swimming pool became operational, the club was integrated with the pool. Mr Ali wanted to use the club to teach the probationers the social graces expected of them.

He, in fact, put much thought into teaching social etiquette. He decided that in the evenings, probationers should 'call on' faculty members. Whenever officers join a posting, they are expected to call on their senior officers—once in their office in full uniform, and later at their home, after taking an appointment. The director also laid out dos and don'ts for us for receiving the probationers at home: how we should conduct ourselves; what we should talk to them about. He was a stickler for details, and I admired him for it.

We were expected to start teaching immediately—but the problem was, although I knew how to investigate a case, I didn't know how to *teach* it. We were trained to be IPS officers, to handle policemen or command a force. We didn't know how to be lecturers!

It took me five hours to prepare my first forty-minute lecture. With new-found respect for all my teachers, I understood what a difficult job it was. To get all your facts together and hold the attention of a roomful of young, extremely intelligent officers, fresh from taking one of the toughest exams in the country. They had all kinds of queries and I had to be well-prepared to answer them.

I was quite intimidated to enter the classroom on the first day, but I could not show it. However, I soon discovered that I could establish a rapport with the students easily. I was the first among the ADs to remember the names of all the 100 or so probationers within a week. Knowing their names helped control the boisterous ones. When you called them out by name, the boys were forced to be alert. Otherwise, there was a tendency to either sit at the back and doze off or be disruptive.

Being particular about the quality of teaching, and aware that his ADs were not trained teachers, the director started a system of confidential feedback from the probationers. It sure kept us on our toes! He would share this feedback with us individually and it was a matter of great satisfaction when I saw I had received extremely positive feedback.

* * *

Phenomenal changes were taking place at the academy. From facilities to activities, construction to publications, we embarked on a thorough revamp. Each AD was assigned several duties. I was made in charge of the NPA publications and magazines and the ladies' welfare society on campus, apart from the officers' club, while Rakesh was made AD (admin.).

But all this required funding. It was decided that Rakesh would go to Delhi and pursue the matter with the ministry of home affairs. This yielded excellent results. The effect of the enhanced funding was soon evident. Broken furniture and crockery were replaced; civil construction work picked up; the classrooms and rooms of the probationers were repaired; the cleanliness and maintenance of the campus became easier; library books and facilities were enhanced; office machinery as well as classroom, sports, training and hospital equipment was procured; training literature was printed; vehicles were condemned and replaced . . . the long march to a world-class institution had begun.

Several guesthouses and cottages were set up with the help of state governments—Orissa Bhawan, Bihar Bhawan, Meghalaya Cottage, CISF Cottage, among others. At Orissa Bhawan, which was located in site A, where the NPA staff lived, I started the ladies' welfare society with the wives of all the subordinate ranks as members. Drawing upon all my social welfare experience since childhood, I got the women trained in embroidery and tailoring. Soon, the uniforms of the entire NPA staff began to be made by members of our welfare society, besides embroidery and handicrafts items, which were displayed at a stall during the annual POP. This increased the family earnings of the staff and helped integrate the officers and junior ranks on campus.

One of my biggest contributions, I feel, was revamping the *NPA Magazine*, which received a makeover after thirty-seven years. I changed the layout and started printing it on offset machines, which improved its look and feel. Throughout my childhood, I had been inadvertently exposed to the production, design and publication process of *Nayi Dhara*, the Hindi publication my father used to run, so I knew how to make a layout, proofread pages and other nuances of publishing.

The new *NPA Magazine* received appreciation from all quarters, and, for the first time, all copies were sold out.

The director had long wanted to start an NPA newsletter as well. In 1987, I was visiting Reshma in California when I chanced upon a campus newsletter at the renowned Stanford University. The elegantly designed, four-page pamphlet caught my eye and I picked one up. When I showed it to Mr Ali, he said, 'I want this. Exactly. The layout is beautiful!'

The *NPA Newsletter* started coming out on a quarterly basis, with news about the academy and other related topics. It was very well-received. I felt so glad I had chanced upon the Stanford newsletter and had brought it back with me for inspiration!

Not only the director, his wife, too, was involved in making the NPA a happy and vibrant campus. Under Mrs Ali's guidance, we started a range of activities for the officers and staff. Festivals, cultural programmes, cooking contests, elocution and children's fancy-dress competitions—we were organizing something or the other every week. All these experiences helped me later when I took charge of battalions in the paramilitary forces.

* * *

Mr Ali would often tell us, 'If things have to go wrong, they *will* go wrong, you have to be prepared for it.'

In 1987, the POP was organized for the 1985 batch. Whereas earlier the POP used to be held in November, it was now brought forward to August. Our parade ground was soft, easy to march on with boots. But now, since the POP would be held in monsoon, the ground was concretized. What if it rained on the day of the parade was the worry. So the director insisted we make alternate arrangements. We made the probationers practise the parade inside an auditorium as well.

It did not rain on our parade that year, but I learnt an important lesson: a good administrator prepares for the worst while hoping for the best.

As I was watched the video of the POP of the 2018 batch held on 4 September 2020, amidst the coronavirus pandemic, I was reminded of Mr Ali's words. The chief guest, Prime Minister Narendra Modi, could not even come to the parade. He addressed the officers via video link. I can well imagine how much the present director, Atul Karwal, would have made them practise for this—marching in masks, maintaining social distancing on the parade ground and then in the auditorium, setting up the audio and video for live streaming—it must have all been so new, requiring meticulous planning and execution!

Coming back to 1987, Rajiv Gandhi's visit was the acid test for all of us, more so because the last time he had been there, the NPA had left him disgusted. He seemed quite pleased with what we had done to the campus, and we all heaved a sigh of relief.

The ladies' welfare society put up a handicrafts stall for the first time, requesting Sonia Gandhi to inaugurate it. All the members of our society were very enthused by her kind appreciation of our efforts.

The year 1988 was a landmark in the life of the NPA—
its fortieth year. In recognition of its distinguished service in
the onerous task of nation building, the NPA received the
President's Colours on 15 September 1988. It was a moment
of pride, fulfilment and satisfaction to see our alma mater thus
honoured. The Presentation of Colours is a ceremony that
marks an anniversary or event in the history of a regiment. In
the commonwealth countries, the Presidential Colours award is
presented to a military educational institute or training institute
as well.

The 1987 batch practised hard for this parade. Keeping the
significance of the occasion in mind, AD-OD Mr Ramakrishnan
himself was the parade commander. The ensign officer, the
policeman who receives the flag, was Sanjay Chander, a very
smart and impressive probationer.

Another big event during this time was the introduction of
official reunions. After officers leave the NPA, they rarely get a
chance to meet one another during the rest of their careers. Mr
Ali felt there was a need for officers to meet and share their stories
of service from different corners of India, and we got permission
from the government of India to hold a reunion. The first
reunion was for the batch of 1956, who came to celebrate the
thirtieth year of their passing out. It was wonderful to witness
their bonhomie and to watch such senior officers become like
young probationers as soon as they met their batchmates.

The tradition of reunions continues at the NPA. Rakesh
and I have gone back for our batch's twenty-fifth, thirtieth and
thirty-fifth year anniversaries, and have thoroughly enjoyed
meeting our colleagues. Everybody is asked to say something
about their experiences, and you come away with many insights
and learnings from each occasion.

The NPA reunions became so successful that the other services also adopted it. Now the IAS, income tax, customs and other services all hold reunions. Aided by social media, officers have started having informal get-togethers as well.

* * *

We had an active social life at the NPA, with so many ADs of the same age group being posted together. While we adults sat together and chatted over a meal, we were happy to let the children play about as the campus was very safe.

But there was one big bother in our lives—water scarcity. Hyderabad was reeling under a drought. Sometimes it seemed that our concern for water was overtaking every other domestic issue. Unlike in our district postings, we did not have the frills here—no drivers, bodyguards or orderlies. Water would be supplied to us in tankers, we had to collect the water in buckets and store it in large drums in our bathrooms and kitchens. Sometimes it felt unreal that where once we had been SPs in charge of a whole district, our lives now revolved around hauling buckets of water!

Since Rakesh was AD (admin.), the director asked him if he could do something about the water problem. Rakesh moved heaven and earth, quite literally! He first requested the Remote Sensing Agency of the Indian Space Research Organisation (ISRO) in Hyderabad to provide a satellite map of the campus, which was then given to the Geological Survey of India (GSI) to identify potential spots with underground water. The Central Ground Water Board (CGWB) eventually identified two locations which turned out to be perennial sources of water. Over twelve months later, when water finally gushed out from borewells dug at these two locations, it became a day of great jubilation on campus.

I could not believe my eyes when our taps sprang to life. 'Will we always get running water from now on?' I asked my husband incredulously. Our sons refused to come out of the shower.

The director complimented Rakesh, 'You are a *bhishti*. Bhishtis give water to injured and dying soldiers on the battlefield. In Persian, it means a person who goes straight to heaven.' That was vintage Mr Ali—his thanks conveyed vividly.

To date, people remember Rakesh at the NPA as their bhishti.

As soon as we had water, our Olympic-sized swimming pool became operational and the officers' club was shifted to the pool compound. Swimming lessons were started for probationers. I too finally learnt to swim and soon became quite a decent swimmer.

* * *

The first batch we taught was that of 1985. I found the probationers to be rather subdued, reeling under the strict regimen. After we arrived, the atmosphere livened up almost overnight, possibly because we were all young ADs and our enthusiasm was contagious. We could establish a rapport with the probationers. Rakesh and I had been at the academy just nine years ago and we were the youngest faculty members there.

Our duties as faculty included counselling the probationers. The batch was divided into groups and assigned to the various faculty members. We had to counsel and mentor them as well as accompany them on all their excursions, like the Bharat Darshan, village visit and parliamentary training.

In every batch, I noticed there were some probationers who struggled to adjust to the NPA way of life. Many of them were very young, away from home for the first time. We had to be sensitive to each of their predicaments. Some found it extremely hard to complete the rigorous outdoor training, while the regimented life made some of them rebellious. But it was important for them to accept this discipline. In the field there is no escaping the hierarchy; you *have* to listen to your boss and carry out commands unquestioningly and with implicit obedience.

Often, I would notice that some officers who came from very humble backgrounds would feel like fish out of water in the elite IPS atmosphere. A sense of insecurity would creep in, a feeling of inferiority compared to those who had come from a reputed college in a big city. We had to watch out for these youngsters caught between cultures and counsel them individually if required.

And, of course, every batch had its share of inflated egos—young officers who walked with a swagger because of the privilege of their birth, treating everyone else as lesser beings just because they knew how to knot a tie or speak English fluently. The UPSC selected meritorious candidates from varied backgrounds. Some had never visited a village in their life, and some came straight from villages.

The outdoor staff—the ustaads and AD-OD—would sometimes be very harsh with the probationers, and we would have to intervene.

In the batch of 1986, there was one officer who was very diffident. Bhupender Singh would say during his individual counselling sessions with me, 'Ma'am, I am an idealist at heart, I don't think this regimented life is for me.' He said he was planning to resign.

I would spend a little extra time with him, be like an elder sister. I tried to make him see that if he persevered, things would get easier. Like many others before him, he too would adjust to the demands of the training. I think I was able to instil a degree of confidence in him; he did not resign. Perhaps what convinced him was my telling him that idealists are needed in the police much more than anywhere else.

I never met him after he left the academy and often wondered whether he continued in service. In 2019, I received a call, and recognized his voice immediately. He told me that he had just taken over as the DG of Rajasthan police. He said he always remembered me as the mentor who had persuaded him to stay on in service at a time when he had lost his way. It felt very fulfilling to know that I was able to contribute to someone's life so positively, and that even thirty-five years later he thought of me.

Another officer about whom I always worried hailed from Bihar. He was a humble young man, the studious kind with thick glasses and a quiet manner. He was so frail that I often wondered how he would cope with the hard life here, with its overemphasis on the outdoors. My worry was not misplaced.

The officer could not handle the exercises. AD-OD Mr Ramakrishnan—who was so strict that even the director would call him a 'martinet'—kept pushing him to do better, but he failed the first outdoor test. The boy was so shaken that he seriously contemplated quitting.

While it was true that all of us had to be pushed beyond our endurance those early months by our ustaads, I thought I should have a word with the AD-OD. I told Mr Ramakrishnan that this officer was unable to cope with the physical demands of outdoor training and suggested giving him some time to adjust.

Mr Ramakrishnan was not convinced—he was always on the lookout for probationers shamming to get out of exercises—but seeing the young man's sincerity, he relented. Today, Arun Kumar Sinha has become one of the most successful officers in his cadre, holding an extremely senior and sensitive position. It warms my heart to see how well he has shaped up, holding such a top post yet remaining humble in his approach to the service.

Sometimes we had to convince officers to continue in service even as our hearts were clouded by doubts over the fairness of our counsel. I can still remember the unease with which I talked probationer Satya Sundar Tripathi into going to Nagaland.

In the 1989 batch, for the first time, two IPS officers—S.S. Tripathi and Ved Prakash—had been allotted Nagaland cadre. There was always a fear that Naga rebel groups would not accept the All India Services. After the cadre allotment, Tripathi handed me his resignation letter to be forwarded to the authorities concerned. I kept the letter in my drawer and persuaded him to go to Nagaland, all the while fearing for his safety. After he completed his training and left for Nagaland, I tore up the letter.

I was horrified to learn that while Tripathi survived, Ved was killed in an ambush. Today Tripathi is a high-ranking officer with the United Nations. When I went to the NPA for their batch reunion recently—as the faculty for the batch is also invited now—it was heartening to hear him say that it was my persuasion that helped him stay on in service.

I was wracked by similar doubts when another probationer, Lal Tendu Mohanti, was allotted the Jammu and Kashmir cadre. He came from a very well-connected family in Odisha. Every night his father would telephone him, asking him to resign and return home immediately. He was in a dilemma, torn between his father and his desire to stay on in the IPS.

My job was to counsel him and make him stay. But those were such turbulent times in Kashmir—who knew what fate awaited him? I motivated him to continue in service. Although I lost touch with him after he went to his cadre, the anxiety for his safety never left me. Many years later, I met him in Delhi and was delighted to see how well he was doing.

As a result of these experiences, I was happy when the rules of cadre allotment were later changed. Now, cadres are allotted before the commencement of training, rather than midway. The old way would often leave officers who were allotted a sensitive cadre feeling trapped in service.

***

While you often tend to remember those who struggled and overcame their problems more fondly, a few probationers are also etched in my memory because they impressed us from Day 1.

In the NPA, the most coveted honours are the best all-round probationer and best outdoor probationer. The best all-round probationer receives the prime minister's baton and home ministry's revolver at the passing out parade. The tradition of presenting the probationer who ranks first in each batch with a baton started after Prime Minister Jawaharlal Nehru came as guest of honour and gave away his own baton to the best all-round probationer. This baton is kept in the academy and ceremonially presented to the first rank-holder every year, along with a new revolver. The best outdoor probationer receives a ceremonial IPS sword of honour.

The first POP we oversaw as ADs was of the 1985 batch. Anup Kumar Singh was adjudged the best all-round probationer. He went on to become the DG of the National Security Guard (NSG). Be it his demeanour, conduct or personality, I consider him a cut above the rest. In 1986, V.S.K. Kaumudi became the best all-round probationer; in 1987, it was Nand Kumar Sarvade; in 1988, Atul Karwal; in 1989, Sanjay Kundu. Each of them has done very well.

The reason I mention these five is because over the years, I have come to realize that sometimes officers who impress at the academy do not necessarily turn out to be good in the field. Some get into bad ways, some abuse their authority while others are poor performers. But these five best all-round probationers excelled in the police service and beyond, and, as their mentors, we feel that the faith we reposed in them was justified.

Conversely, I also realized that the bad eggs continued to be bad, if not worse, after they left the academy. This impression was shared by other faculty members as well.

Indiscipline, rude behaviour, shirking work, lying, misbehaving with colleagues—we saw all this and more. We could discipline, reprimand and punish but could not improve them. Once they were out of the academy, they were free to revert to their old habits.

Having handled one too many troublemaker, I became sure of one thing—the weeding out of bad officers must happen at the academy itself. Too many undeserving officers continue in service for a minimum of thirty-two to thirty-five years because the states refuse to act even after the NPA writes against them. They bring a bad name to the police and harass the public, manipulating the system and vitiating the atmosphere within the service.

* * *

All the ADs had been promised mid-career courses for skill development, including training abroad. I, too, believe you must make every effort to upgrade your skills throughout your career. It is wrong to think that once you have joined the service after completing your training, there is nothing more to learn. Some people wish to avoid training opportunities because they do not want to lose out on a coveted posting; others look upon courses as a chore or an excuse to travel. But I feel that, even if you come away with *one* learning from a course, it is worth your time and effort.

Early on, I went for a week-long course conducted by the Indian Institute of Management (IIM), Bangalore, on human-resource management. It helped me hone my communication skills. My key takeaways were how to focus on the main points while speaking to an audience and how to hold a discussion in class.

In 1988, I returned to IIM Bangalore for a course for women executives under IIM Bangalore's Kalyani Gandhi as course director. The participants came from different walks of life: the government, police, NGOs, banks and the railways, among others. Other than the lectures, it was a pleasure to interact with an eclectic mix of high-achieving women.

A senior executive with the State Bank of India raised an issue that is uppermost on the minds of us working women—time management. I shared that playing host to a stream of visitors at the NPA and being compelled to take them shopping in the evenings was cutting into my time with the children, and stressing me out.

'You have to learn to say no. You cannot please everybody. You must be enjoying the shopping expeditions a bit yourself too, but if you lack the time, you have to learn to say no to others and to yourself,' Ms Gandhi explained.

Such a simple thing, really, but sometimes you need to be reminded of the simple things.

Upon my return, I requested Mr Ali to allow me to organize an in-service course for women officers as I felt there was a need for women in the government to share and understand their experiences. As always, he was most enthusiastic. Along with Kalyani Gandhi, I designed a programme for women in bureaucracy. It was highly successful, and we did another one the following year.

For the first one, we invited women executives not just from the IPS but from the other All-India services as well, like the railways, customs and income tax.

Here, too, there were useful discussions and the interactions outside the classroom proved to be just as enriching. Many of them had gone to their cadres as the first women IPS officers, just I had. Each had faced similar challenges—be it gaining acceptance among the men, inspiring the confidence of seniors, or getting a field posting. As we shared our stories, I realized how each of us thought that this was happening *only* to us. There was a lot of bonding, sharing and understanding of women's problems, which helped me mentor the lady probationers under my care better, preparing them for what lay ahead.

Meeran Chadha Borwankar from the Maharashtra cadre shared how she never smiled in the police station during those early days because she was always so tense. There were only men! Finally, some colleagues pointed this out to her, saying, 'It is okay to smile at your subordinates, not all men are bad.'

Kanchan Chaudhary Bhattacharya, who later became the DG of Uttarakhand police, spoke about the sense of isolation she had felt at the beginning of her career. This experience was captured by her sister, Kavita Chaudhary, in the popular

Doordarshan serial *Udaan,* which she wrote, directed and acted in. I then shared how when I travelled by train and my co-passengers came to know I was an IPS officer, people would often ask me if I had acted in the serial. They would see a resemblance between me and the '*Udaan* lady'! We all had a good laugh over it.

Kiran Bedi was invited as well. Although she came to address the participants, she did not join the course.

One of the jobs of the NPA faculty was to counsel probationers. Many of us found this role rather difficult, having never done anything like this before. Mr Ali organized courses for us so that we could learn to counsel. A team of experts came from IIM Calcutta, including Dr Gouranga Chattopadhyay, who had explained to me the impact of my own strict upbringing in my nana-nani's house.

Dr Chattopadhyay taught us the basics of counselling. 'When a person starts sharing, you have to first put yourself in their shoes. Be on the same wavelength and understand where they are coming from. Once you have built a rapport and gained their trust, they will be more receptive to your suggestions,' he taught us.

In 1987, Rakesh went to England for a course on the management of training at the Royal Institute of Public Administration (RIPA). The institute was in the heart of London. I took leave to accompany him, leaving the children in the care of my parents in Patna.

After the course ended, we took a bus tour across Europe. It was an exhilarating experience, the honeymoon that we had never had. I found England beautiful, as also France, Germany and Switzerland. When will India become like this—no poverty, no hunger, no uncared person—I wondered. It made me even more determined to give my best upon my return.

From Europe, I went to America. Reshma had been settled there with her husband Anil since 1977, but we never had the money to go all the way to the US from India. So, when I finally arrived in San Francisco, she was eager to show me everything, including the hallowed Stanford University campus. I also flew to the East Coast, where my brother Samir was studying at the University of Pennsylvania, or UPenn.

I was impressed to see that the sky was the limit in America when it came to higher education. You could study Greek literature along with music, physics with a language, biology with philosophy. It took India another three decades to come around to this system of education, viz., the New Education Policy 2020.

I would particularly notice the girls on campus. They were studying at such premier institutions and accomplishing so much. There was no segregation between the sexes and both boys and girls were studying through the night in the library. I felt I had missed out on something valuable by not studying in a place like America.

In August 1989, I was selected for the ten-week course on the management of training at the RIPA. Although I was a little intimidated about going abroad alone and apprehensive about staying away from the children for such a long time, I was happy that I was going to London, a city I had become somewhat familiar with. I stayed as a paying guest with the same landlady Rakesh had stayed with. Mrs Asha Kohli was a Pakistani lady married to a man from Jammu. We developed a very warm bond, sharing our food and free time with each other. It was easy to realize that the religious divisions and national enmities we feel in India often melt away when we go abroad—our common history and geography bringing us together.

There were thirty-two participants from developing countries across Africa, the West Indies and South–Southeast Asia in my course, including seventeen women. The biggest learnings outside the classroom came from my interactions with these women. It was fascinating to see that if I was worrying about my children, a lady from Sudan or Kenya was equally anxious about hers. We were all talking about almost the same issues that confronted us in our personal and professional lives. I felt part of an international sisterhood.

I found the course to be well-designed and apt for my line of work at the NPA. We learnt about interpersonal skills, communication and how to design a course based on a job-requirement analysis. This was particularly helpful.

Upon my return, the director asked me to take over as course director for the batch of 1989, as well as oversee the junior management course, which was an in-service training course.

This role taught me how to mentor and take charge of an entire batch. It instilled in me a greater sense of responsibility towards shaping the young officers as future leaders in the service. I also learnt how to multitask. Constantly juggling myriad duties, I matured in a way I had never envisaged before coming to the NPA.

* * *

If mentoring bright young officers was a fulfilling experience, losing them in the line of duty was just as devastating.

I remember our probationer, Ashok Kamte, the sword of honour recipient from 1989, for his unending enthusiasm for everything outdoors. Kamte was martyred in the 26/11 terrorist attacks in Mumbai along with Hemant Karkare, the chief of the Mumbai anti-terrorist squad.

When I saw Kamte's funeral on TV, I was at the CISF headquarters. I broke down, the smiling face of this talented and brave officer flashing before my eyes.

The death of our fellow officers always deals a hard blow, but while we were at the academy, the losses hit us harder. Perhaps it was because we were in the cradle of IPS officers, maybe it was the reminder of the danger in our line of work or our collective grief but every death enveloped the academy in a pall of gloom.

As editor of the *NPA Magazine*, I would write the obituaries with a heavy heart. The first obituary I wrote was for Arun Kumar Arora, the best all-round probationer of the 1984 batch. In July 1986, Mr Arora was an ASP under training when he was fatally injured in an explosion in Jodhpur during an investigation. One more name was added to the martyr's memorial at the NPA.

This memorial is sacrosanct in the IPS. On 21 October, which is Police Commemoration Day, there is a parade and we all pay our respects to IPS officers martyred in the line of duty.

Another incident that hit us hard while at NPA was the loss of two young officers in Patiala. A.S. Brar of the 1979 batch was SSP Patiala and K.R.S. Gill of the 1982 batch an ASP under his training. They had led several operations against the terrorists in Punjab. On the morning of 14 December 1987, they were jogging together when they were attacked by terrorists and killed on the spot.

There was a horrified silence on campus when we received the news. 'Who is going to be next?' the silence seemed to scream.

The most difficult loss for me, personally, and for others at the academy was the death of probationer Vandana Malik of the 1987 batch. She had been allotted the Manipur–Tripura cadre, where she was undergoing her district practical training at Lamshang police station in Imphal. On 8 April 1989, Vandana was returning to her police station after overseeing bandobast duty for a public examination when her vehicle was attacked by insurgents and she was killed.

I was extremely fond of Vandana. A bright officer, she had done well in both indoor and outdoor training, besides participating in various extracurricular activities. As part of my counselling duties, I had gone to Imphal to check on her. I stayed with her and we spoke about many things. She was looking forward to going home, albeit with a heavy heart, as she had lost her mother to a heart attack a few months ago.

The day we received the news of her death, I had gone out of the campus. I returned to find the probationers of the 1988 batch all gathered in hushed silence at the IPS mess, totally shaken. I still remember officers Sundari Nanda and Rashmi Shukla standing outside, shocked and tearful. Everybody was numb: we did not know how to react.

The following day, Mr Ali and I travelled to her hometown, Faridabad, for her funeral. She seemed to be lying so peacefully, like she would wake up at any moment. In full uniform, she was cremated with full police honours. To see her go broke my resolve and I cried bitterly.

When I returned to campus, I received a letter from Vandana. She must have posted it a day before she died. In the letter she spoke about missing her mother. It was one of the hardest and cruellest moments that I faced in the academy. There had been five girls in her batch, and my heart ached for them. I realized they must be devastated to lose one of their own, so I decided to write to each of them to console them and share their grief.

When probationers join the academy, they are asked to fill up a form. Under the question, 'Why do you want to join the IPS?' Vandana had written, '. . . the challenge offered to a lady police officer, the expectation of an eventful life.'

This vibrant, young girl paid with her life to live up to the challenge. Writing Vandana's obituary was heart-breaking. I poured out my anguish on the printed page:

> For martyrs we say it with flowers but how do you say it, when the flower itself is a martyr. On 8th April 1989, Vandana Malik gave the greatest gift to the country and to her service—her unfinished life. We cherish her memory with reversed arms and with good-bye unspoken.

Over the years, we lost more officers who we had trained. As already recounted, Ved Prakash, a very brave officer of the 1988 batch, was killed by Naga rebels in Mokokchung in August 1994. He never baulked at the dangerous posting.

Ravi Kant Singh of the 1987 batch was killed by the United Liberation Front of Asom (ULFA) when he was handling insurgents as SP, Tinsukia, in Assam in 1996. I still remember what a sensible and down-to-earth boy he had been. G. Pardesi Naidu of the 1987 batch was SP, Mahbubnagar, in Hyderabad when he was killed by Naxalites in a landmine blast in 1993.

Losing our probationers was very traumatic for Rakesh and me.

We also had to grapple with losing our friends and batchmates during this period. I was utterly shocked and dejected to learn of the death of Sital Dass, a very bold officer from Punjab. He was posted as SSP, Patiala, in August 1988 when he went to disarm an ASI who had gone rogue. When

Dass asked him to hand over his revolver, the ASI shot him at point-blank range.

Our batchmate, Daulat Singh Negi of Himachal Pradesh, was posted to the Assam–Meghalaya cadre. He had been in the Indian army and fought in the 1971 war. I was not close to him when we were probationers, but when he came to the NPA for an in-service course, we got along very well. He wanted me to help him buy Hyderabad's famous pearls for his wife. In July 1990, soon after he returned to his post as SP, Dibrugarh, he was ambushed and killed, reportedly by ULFA activists.

Every death felt like a personal loss—it wrenched us, shattered us, left us numb.

* * *

Yet another goodbye awaited, this time on a high and happy note. We all looked up to Mr Ali. He was a good boss, deeply committed to improving the academy. But that did not stop us ADs from cracking a joke or two. He was so exacting that we would joke that Mr Ali gives the order now and expects the work to be finished yesterday.

I feel the reason the academy blossomed under his leadership was that he knew exactly what needed to be done, having been an AD when the academy was at Mt Abu. He knew the academy inside out. Very often, senior officers come to the NPA as director towards the end of their careers, attracted by the prestige associated with this position, despite having had nothing to do with training all their lives. The academy has seen all kinds of directors: some who worked hard to take things forward, others who just whiled away their time.

Mr Ali's term as director came to an end in March 1990. Every rank was sorry to see him leave. He had inherited a campus on the decline and in four short years he had turned it around. His farewell was a grand affair, befitting his invaluable contributions to the academy, the Indian police and to the lives of each one of us.

Nearly thirty years later, the academy is again under a director who had previously served as an AD there. I feel the appointment of Atul Karwal, my probationer from the 1988 batch, was a good decision. A very capable officer of the Gujarat cadre, Atul had asked to be posted to the academy as an AD midway through his career because he believed in the importance of training. As his teacher, I feel happy to know that our beloved academy is in the care of this very able trainer.

Being posted at the NPA fairly early in my career was an unusual experience, which came as a surprise and changed my career trajectory. Stepping outside Bihar, I became part of a national discourse on policing, interacting with top civil servants, experts on law-and-police procedure as well as national-level policymakers. Shaping the future leaders of the IPS and building a personal bond with many of them was another matter of great satisfaction. All these experiences expanded my horizons far beyond a district or a range that I would have handled back in my home cadre.

The NPA truly gave me my best years of service.

16

My Girls

While attending an event at the Lal Bahadur Shastri National Academy of Administration in Mussoorie and interacting with probationers, Julio Ribeiro had once been asked, 'Sir, if you had another life, what would you like to be?'

Mr Ribeiro thought for a while and then said with a smile, 'I would like to be the wife of an IPS officer.'

It is often said in the police that IPS officers' wives have the best life. They enjoy all the perks of the service without suffering the tension of the job.

I remember thinking, 'I am an IPS officer's wife too, but this is not true for me at all!'

I was happy to be an officer myself, tensions notwithstanding. Especially at the NPA, where I felt that I was fulfilling an important role as a woman mentor of women probationers.

Throughout my initial years in the service, I had been wary of being treated differently because I was a woman. Therefore, it was quite a pleasant surprise when I was picked to serve at the academy *because* I was a woman.

I had not been trained by a woman myself, and would have appreciated a woman mentor in this all-male environment. So, I made it a point to help the lady probationers settle down and be there for them when they needed a sympathetic senior to talk to.

Suman Bala Sahoo of the batch of 1987 recounts her memories of the NPA, capturing beautifully why it is important to have women mentors if we want to raise a balanced force:

I was just 23, living away from home for the very first time. Eight girls joined in our batch, but some left for other services, five of us remained. The IPS was still a very male-dominated field. It was very comforting to have Manjari Ma'am with us. She used to take care of us like an elder sister, she had such a motherly touch.

Ma'am would guide us about the expectations from us as IPS officers, especially how to conduct ourselves as an officer and how to wear our uniform. She instilled in us the concept that when we are in uniform, we are an officer first. So, no make-up, no big bindi.

She also advised us on very delicate matters, like our time of the month. She spoke from experience, assuring us that soon our bodies would become accustomed to the outdoor activities. Except swimming, we did everything throughout the month.

She counselled us if we struggled to cope with the outdoor training, even speaking to our AD-OD, Mr Ramakrishnan, on our behalf. All our faculty members loved us like their own children, even though the age gap was not much.

Ma'am would also worry about our marriage! It was a sweet, affectionate relationship. Only a lady senior officer can have such an equation with a junior officer. Having Manjari Ma'am with us at the beginning of our IPS journey was indeed fortunate for us. We forged a relationship that continues even today, 33 years since I first met her.

* * *

Often, the girls would be unhappy with the police uniform. 'Why should we wear the men's uniform, ma'am? Why can't we have something more comfortable, more suitable for us?'

It is true that the uniform *is* designed for a man. No concessions are made for women's bodies, let alone their preferences. The rules are clear—we have to tuck the shirt in, with exactly four buttons above the belt. The cross belt across the torso is also not designed for a woman's comfort.

Yet I feel there should not be any difference in uniform. Because, to me, the uniform is the big equalizer. 'The moment we start wearing a different uniform, others will perceive us differently,' I would tell the girls. When you are breaking into a male bastion, you must first blend in, before standing out. I hope that one day there will be so many women IPS officers that they will stop being an aberration.

Even in training, there are no concessions for women. We have to undergo exactly the same training as the men. We may score less in certain activities, but we could not fall out or leave an activity incomplete by making excuses.

When Kiran Bedi had qualified for the IPS in 1972, it is said that she had been given the option of picking any other service. But she chose to stay with the IPS and never asked for any concession in uniform rules or training regimen. She started a healthy tradition, which is why all of us have done the same training.

Therefore, today any lady IPS officer can look her male peers in the eye and say, 'You and I have done the same training, I am no less than anybody else.' This is important if we want to be on par and not segregated into a separate category within the IPS.

Another concern that frequently cropped up among the girls was swimming with their squad. Just like in my time, often there was just one girl in each squad. Some of them would flatly refuse to wear a swimming costume and get into the pool with the men.

One girl said she had a mark on her back and tried to persuade me to exempt her from swimming. I gave her a patient hearing before pointing out the realities of our service. 'In a flood situation, you will *have* to jump into the water with the men. If a criminal is escaping, you have to wade through a flooded field. You cannot stay away from your duty citing inhibitions. It is better to get over these mental blocks right away.'

I would tell them about my own experiences. I still remember how awkward it was practising unarmed combat with my squad mates. But you have to come to terms with a man touching you and lifting you over his shoulders. In a real-life combat situation, no one will cut you any slack because you are a woman.

Though I always say that we are officers, not 'women officers', I did not believe in losing my femininity just because I was an IPS officer either. Outside duty hours, I was always in a sari. I had long hair and loved to dress up. I did not feel the need to give any of it up. I have had many lady officers tell me that when they got selected for the IPS, they had feared that they would have to cut their hair and give up their saris in order to 'fit in'. But as soon as they met me, they knew otherwise.

Srilakshmi Prasad, my probationer of the 1986 batch, has quite the story to tell:

We were just two girls in our batch, but we did not feel out of place even in that crowd of men because we saw there was a lady IPS officer in the academy. It was comforting to know she was there. We saw a role model in her, we had never interacted with a woman IPS officer before.

We met our faculty during the orientation courses. Madam was in uniform—no bindi, no nail polish, hair in a tight bun; very fit and trim. She was rather stern-looking, we figured she was a no-nonsense officer. We enjoyed her class, we liked how she approached the subject.

Later that evening, we attended a social gathering organized by the academy. Here, I spotted a lady in a vibrant sari with a long plait, decked up in lipstick, nail polish, bindi . . . I thought maybe she is the twin of the lady officer who took our class in the morning.

I was confused for quite a while, I kept looking at her. I think I even asked the other girl in my batch, 'Do you think they are twin sisters?' When I learnt that this was the same lady, my jaw fell open.

Till then, our idea of a woman IPS officer was Kiran Bedi Ma'am. We thought if we must fit into this service, if we have to wear the uniform and do law and order work, we must be manly. We must cut our hair, be rough and tough, act like a man, speak like a man, dress like a man even when in civvies.

I come from a conservative family in South India, by nature and temperament, I am a traditional woman. When I was selected for the IPS, people told me now you must chop off your long hair and dress like a man. I love to wear saris; I was worried that I would be giving all that up once I became a police officer.

When I saw Manjari Madam, I knew that we need not be like that at all. We need not try to look like a man or behave like a man. We need not hide our femininity, rather we should bring our feminine touch to the service.

I would observe everything about Madam—how a woman officer fits into the uniform, fits into the service, what is her interaction with the men like, how is she different, how is she similar . . . I learnt all this from her. Learning how to orient my gender to this male-dominated service was especially important to me at the time, 35 years back.

She not only set an example with her behaviour and personality, she would also guide us, giving us tips and worldly wisdom. She would narrate her experiences in the service so that we would not receive a rude shock when we went out to the field ourselves. She remains a life-long inspiration and friend to me.

Among all the girls I taught, I particularly remember Meera Verma of the 1985 batch. The only lady in her batch, she was possibly the toughest girl I have come across, with a life story that was as hard-hitting as inspirational. I got to know her closely when I accompanied their group on the Bharat Darshan tour. As she was the lone girl, she had to share the room with me.

Meera grew up in a remote village in Rajasthan, too poor to go to school. 'I had no time for school, I had to draw water from the well and help out in the house. Then, a convent school opened nearby, and the nuns went around the village asking to enrol the girls. My father refused flatly,' she told me.

But the nuns were a committed lot. They begged and cajoled and finally convinced her father to send her to their school.

'I started studying for the first time. To my own surprise, and everybody else's, I did very well,' she smiled as she recalled the memory.

When her *mama* (maternal uncle) came to the village from Jaipur, he was astounded to see that a girl in the family was going to school. 'It is to my mamaji's credit that he saw some potential in me. He brought me to Jaipur and put me through school and college.'

Her education opened up a whole new world; she started preparing for the UPSC examinations and made it to the IPS. It warmed my heart to learn that her one mission in life was to educate all her brothers and sisters.

I used to think that mine was quite a story of how circumstances propelled me to the IPS. But here was a girl who *literally* had nothing, yet she made it to the prestigious service through sheer grit. I admired her courage and spirit. I was also impressed with how tough she was physically. I realized that, even though I was her teacher, I was learning so much about life from her.

Many years later, I visited her in Gujarat, which was her cadre. She had married a police officer and I was glad to see that she continued to display courage and grit as an officer.

* * *

Sometimes the ustaads would expect impossible feats from the probationers. One day, I was aghast when AD-OD Mr

Ramakrishnan said he would not allow one of the girls to participate in the POP. It had never happened at the academy that a lady officer had been barred from the parade because she had not done well in her outdoor training.

I pleaded with Mr Ramakrishnan to not take such a harsh step; it would impact her confidence adversely. She was very sincere in her training, her poor performance outdoors was not for the lack of effort. Although the AD-OD was sceptical, he agreed to allow her to participate in the parade. I am happy to report that this lady officer has gone on to become an able officer and has done well in her cadre.

Sometimes, in the academy we get so caught up with physical training that we do not realize how well an officer might do in the field despite being unable to climb a rope or complete a jump!

With the presence of a handful of women amid so many male officers and staff, we had to always keep an eye out for the safety and security of the girls. Stray incidents of misbehaviour did happen and the faculty members as well as Mr Ali brooked no nonsense in this matter. One day, a lady doing a foundation course at NPA had complained about one of the drill instructors. As soon as the allegation was proved, Mr Ali showed no hesitation in repatriating him back to his organization.

Sometimes, I would be faced with a tricky situation, where one had to walk the fine line between the letter and the spirit of the rules. One day, early in the morning, a lady probationer arrived on my doorstep, extremely distressed and tearful. The previous night, one of her male colleagues had gotten drunk and had physically misbehaved with her in the mess.

She said her other colleagues were pressurizing her to not make a complaint, saying that this behaviour was an aberration. 'What should I do, ma'am?' she asked me.

I listened to her, sympathizing with her predicament. Finally, I asked her what she wanted to do. She said she was unable to come to a decision. Seeing how she was in two minds, I advised her that we should report it to the director. I believe strict disciplinary action should be taken in such matters.

But later, as she pondered her colleague's behaviour, she realized that it was not premeditated, neither was he a habitual offender. When she informed me that she wanted to close the matter, I respected her decision.

* * *

While several probationers, both men and women, have done us enormously proud, there are a few girls whom I recall with particular fondness both for the good work they have done and the close bond we have nurtured for thirty years.

Both the girls in the 1986 batch, Srilakshmi Prasad and Dyuti Rani Doley Barman, shone in service. Srilakshmi was a principled, practical officer who believed in quietly getting the job done. She retired as DG, Tamil Nadu Human Rights Commission, in 2020. Dyuti Rani was the first lady IPS officer of the J & K cadre. She later made a name for herself as director, North Eastern Police Academy (NEPA), and director, NPA.

From the 1987 batch, R. Sreelekha was the first woman IPS officer in Kerala and Suman Bala Sahoo in West Bengal, while their batchmate A.R. Anuradha went to the Andhra Pradesh cadre. Sreelekha is a trailblazer who held many important posts in the police and public-sector organizations yet managed to write several books.

Being the first woman in her cadre, Suman was unable to get a field posting under the Left Front government of West

Bengal. Undeterred, she did extremely well in whatever post she was assigned. I am hoping to see her as the head of one of the police organizations one day.

I remember Rashmi Shukla of the 1988 batch. She was clearly not built for the physical rigours of IPS training, but how she overcame the challenges impressed everyone in the field. It was heartening to see a frail girl like her transform into a 'tough' cop, going on to become the commissioner of police, Pune. Her batchmate S. Sundari Nanda did us proud, becoming Puducherry's first woman DGP, while B. Sandhya charted an impressive career in Kerala. She later completed a PhD in criminal justice and has published several books.

From the 1989 batch, I was happy to follow the career achievements of B. Radhika, who was the first woman in the Odisha cadre. Regarded as a tough, honest and sincere officer, she is now with the Sashastra Seema Bal (SSB) in New Delhi. Her batchmate Nina Singh, the first woman in the Rajasthan cadre, who went to Harvard University for a master's, is known for the innovative steps she introduced in Rajasthan police. She also made a name for herself in the CBI. I was extremely proud to learn that Nina has co-authored two research papers on police reforms and evidence-based policing with Nobel laureates in economics, Abhijit Vinayak Banerjee and Esther Duflo.

From 1990, Renuka Mishra, Savita Hande, Seema Agarwal, Tanuja Srivastava and Tilotama Varma were the standout girls. Renuka did a great service to the police by making the recruitment of constables transparent and fair in her cadre, Uttar Pradesh, ending nepotism and corruption. The standard operating procedure (SOP) she developed is now being followed all over the country, garnering her widespread admiration for helping end a highly corrupt practice. Savita has travelled the world, undertaking all kinds of challenging work for the United Nations. She is currently in Afghanistan.

I was moved to read about Seema Agarwal, who, during her posting in the Tamil Nadu Crime Records Bureau, helped reunite missing persons with their families.

Tanuja's work on women's issues and the sensitization of police personnel in Uttar Pradesh has been widely appreciated. Tilotama joined the Wildlife Crime Control Bureau (WCCB), where she is doing a great job protecting the faunal treasures of the country.

Just like me, Renuka and Tilotama joined the NPA as ADs along with their IPS husbands, where they acquitted themselves creditably.

Another remarkable girl in the 1990 batch was Anuradha Shankar, the daughter of a Bihar IPS officer, who came to train at the academy as the mother of two small children. Being a very frail girl, she found the outdoor training extremely tough, while staying away from her children left her feeling guilty and distressed. Yet she managed to complete her training and went to the Madhya Pradesh cadre, where she did very well.

Each one of them was the first or among the first few women in their cadres, facing all the challenges that come with having to pave your own way, sometimes in an unwelcome and hostile atmosphere. Through their determination and hard work, they opened up each state for all the women IPS officers who followed. I am proud of each one of them.

In September 2020, Kiran Shruthi D.V. of Tamil Nadu was adjudged the best all-round probationer from among 131 officers, twenty-eight of them women, in the batch of 2018. When PM Mr Modi addressed the probationers via video link, and asked her, 'Why did you leave engineering and opt for the IPS?' she said, 'I've always had the ambition to go for civil services, Sir. My family held great regard for the uniformed services. My name is Kiran Shruthi because of Kiran Bedi ma'am.'

From Kiran Bedi being asked to pick another service since there was no precedent of a woman joining the IPS to Kiran Shruthi D.V. being adjudged the best all-round probationer in a mixed batch, we have come a long way indeed.

17

Back to a New Bihar

There had been a regime change in Bihar in 1990, with the Janata Dal forming the government after years of Congress rule. Lalu Prasad Yadav had assumed office in March 1990, and he was creating waves.

While at the NPA, we would read about the happenings back home with great interest. One of the biggest pieces of news was when Lalu Prasad famously had BJP leader L.K. Advani arrested on 23 October 1990, halting his rath yatra (chariot procession). According to the newspapers, the CM had appealed to Mr Advani to suspend his yatra, but since he did not pay heed, he was arrested in Samastipur.

From our colleagues in Bihar, we would hear stories of a complete overhaul of the state administration under Lalu Prasad: that he was a man of the masses or that he had a very different style of functioning. We heard he was making sweeping changes in the state and did not brook any kind of opposition. All kinds of stories—some positive, others alarming—were emerging from Bihar.

In April 1991, our tenure at the NPA ended. Rakesh and I were excited and a little apprehensive about going back. We thought March–April would be a good time to relocate, because the children could start the new school term. Their education continued to be our overriding concern, especially now that Tushar was growing up. Our sons had been attending Little Flower High School, one of the best in Hyderabad. Tushar was turning out to be a good student while Anshuman was the mischievous one.

Having grown up in one town right up to college, I always worried about the effect of our various transfers on the boys. They have had to change schools seven times thanks to our careers. Apart from friends and favourite teachers, they had to often leave behind what they had learnt or learn an entirely new language.

So, when our five years at the NPA gave them a stable home and school life, we were greatly relieved. While the workload kept us busy, we were home every evening to spend time with them. The academy was a great place for kids to grow up. In a district, children may develop a sense of entitlement or superiority as their parent is the only SP or DIG in that place. They get marked out for special treatment, however much you try to shield them from your job. But at the NPA, shorn of all the perks and trappings of a district posting, the boys were growing up with children their own age from other IPS families. It was a big leveller, and I feel it grounded them.

Our posting orders arrived even before we returned to the state, leaving our colleagues at the academy just as surprised and impressed as us. Was this how Bihar was functioning now?

After a spate of very warm farewells from our probationers, colleagues and the NPA staff, we left for Patna.

Upon our return, I was posted in the special branch as SP(G), and Rakesh in the CID as SP(C). Both of us would be in Patna, which made us happy. In fact, we would be working in the same building.

The first floor of my parents' house was lying vacant, and we decided to set up home there. This made my parents doubly happy as they would now have their grandchildren near them all the time. As a working mother, I also felt a great deal of comfort knowing that my children were growing up with their nana-nani, just as I had.

We were hoping to enrol Tushar in Patna's prestigious St Michael's School, but all-boys' schools in Patna had switched from English to Hindi medium while we were away. Our sons had already had to learn Telugu in Hyderabad, and this would mean another change. But our friends and relatives assured us that this would not be so hard, and Tushar was admitted in St Michael's School in class 7. Anshuman started going to a local English-medium school called Rosebud in class 3.

* * *

I found my work quite interesting. The special branch (SB) acts as the eyes and ears of the government. It collects intelligence of every kind—criminal, law and order, political, agricultural, social, et cetera, from across a state—collates it and keeps the government informed on a daily basis. Supplying advance and real-time information is a big part of the job.

The DG of Bihar police was A.K. Choudhary and my boss in the special branch was DG Krishan Prakashji.

As I settled back into the groove of Bihar police, I saw Bihar with an outsider's eye. I felt our state had not moved forward.

Having worked in an academy where things were happening all the time—we could get things done, were encouraged to take initiative *and* there was a decent budget—I found Bihar to be lagging behind. Things were slow here, and getting anything done was a long, laborious and cumbersome process. I felt people were more interested in cabinet meetings, where transfers of officers were decided, than in getting their work done.

At the same time, a lot was going on because of the new CM, who wanted to make things happen. I was keen to meet Lalu Prasad as I had never seen him. One day, there was caste-related violence in Arrah in the Bhojpur district. My boss, Krishan Prakashji, took me along when he went to brief the CM. As soon as I walked in, the CM looked me up and down. I think he was a little curious to see a lady police officer. I also figured he must have heard about my work in Bokaro, because he told the DG, 'The situation in Arrah is bad, why don't you send her there? Let her go and take charge.'

Mr Prakashji was as taken aback as I was, but he covered it up well. He explained to the CM that I had just returned to the state after five years and joined the SB. Thankfully, the CM saw his point of view; I managed to escape being sent off to Bhojpur even before I had settled down in Patna!

I oversaw intelligence collection in sections like labour, constabulary, atrocities against Harijans, agrarian services and Naxalite activities. It was not a very tough assignment. After about eight months, in December 1991, I was posted as SP(A) in the special branch. It was an important post with an interface between the districts and senior officers, who, in turn, would brief the CM.

I had to keep both my boss and the DG of Bihar police abreast of important developments, especially because whenever any major incident occurred, Lalu Prasad would directly ask him what steps had been taken. The DGs depended heavily on me to get them the right information at the right time.

In those days Bihar was besieged by caste tensions, often leading to riots and carnages. The problem was between the rich landlords, who mostly belonged to the Bhumihar community, and the poorer villagers and labourers, who were mostly Yadavs and Dalits. Naxalism was also becoming a thorn in our side. The Maoist Communist Centre of India (MCC) which later became the CPI (Maoist) was making its presence felt.

The SB was faced with a peculiar problem. The CM was a leader of the masses, with a vast network of loyalists spread across the length and breadth of the state. Very often, after an incident went down in a remote village, he was the first to get the information. It was extremely embarrassing for us when he called up the DG to say, 'Do you know that this has happened?'

It became a challenge for us—getting our officers in the field to report the matter first. It was almost like a race: who would get the information first, us or the CM?

We were constrained by due process. For example, if a crime was committed in the night, the OIC of that police station would receive the information, reach the PO and verify the situation. Then, when the wireless sets were switched on at 8 a.m., he would send a report. If it was a big incident, he would inform his SP, who would go to the village to inspect and relay the information to us on the hotline. So, there was always a time lag. But any person who had access to a phone could just dial a number and give all the details to the CM or his party men or the press before we could do so. It was a huge challenge, which kept me on my toes throughout my time in the SB.

Bihar of the 1990s was a place of brisk politicking. I had to remain alert and keep briefing the CM about whether anybody was holding meetings against him or hatching a political plot, or if any dissident group was gaining ground. I worked very closely with my immediate boss, DIG Ashish Ranjan Sinha, developing a good rapport with him. I would rely on his insights into the crosscurrents of Bihar politics to understand the caste dynamics. He was extremely hardworking and had good political contacts on the ground.

As SP(A), my work also entailed looking after the establishment and personnel management. I completely re-organized the Naxalite Cell for better manpower utilization. My Bokaro DIG, Y.N. Srivastava—who had been SP(A) in the past—had advised me to occasionally sit in the special branch reserve lines, which SPs rarely did.

I heeded Mr Srivastava's advice and started going to the reserve lines once a week. This streamlined our operations; everybody seemed relieved that I had put a system in place. From the men in the field, there was a demand for an officers' club in the reserve lines for them to use when they came to Patna. I got the club sanctioned, and subsequent SPs got it built. It came as a big relief to SB officers.

* * *

Two significant things happened in our family in 1991. My brother Samir got married in July. He had continued to study in the US, following up his engineering degree with a master's and then a PhD. It was interesting to see that our parents fretted over his marriage as much as they had worried over their daughters'.

'When will he return? When will we see him married?' was a constant refrain. Proposals kept coming in, for he was considered a very eligible bachelor. Finally, our parents found a bright girl from an accomplished family whom Samir also liked. It was a major event in the family because a wedding was taking place after so many years. I was happy to be back in Patna and got involved in helping my parents make all the arrangements. Everybody in our extended clan came to Patna and there was a carnival-like atmosphere in the house.

I had sent invitation cards to my colleagues and bosses, as well as to CM Lalu Prasad's office. But I was just an SP, and did not really expect the CM to come for my brother's wedding. But he did, causing a mini stampede at the reception! All the guests wanted to see him.

Reshma told him that she remembered him as a student leader at Patna University. 'Sir, you had come to Patna Women's College to campaign when you were contesting the students' union elections. My friends and I had all voted for you.'

Lalu Prasad beamed at this story; it was something he would repeat many times in the future, telling people that this officer's sister and her friends had voted for him in the students' union elections.

The wedding festivities came to an end and Samir left for the US with his wife, Gauri.

But our joy was tinged with sadness. My mother's elder sister, Leela, who was like a mother to me, had been diagnosed with cancer. My mausi's house was in the same compound as my parents', so we were all extremely close to her and her children—Ranjit, Ranjana and Ritu. My aunt had visited me wherever I was posted, including Hyderabad. I was thankful to be back in Patna now, able to be with my mausi in her last days. She passed away in August, leaving all of us heartbroken.

* * *

During my tenure as SP(A), a carnage took place in Bara, Gaya district, in February 1992, a major incident that shook up the entire administration. Thirty-five upper caste men of the Bhumihar community were massacred. We were told that members of the MCC had brought all thirty-five landlords to the banks of a canal and slit their throats.

The SB had to coordinate with the local police, collating all intelligence for swift action. But everybody feared taking on the MCC, including the local police officers. Eventually, we managed to gather enough intelligence for the police to conduct multiple raids over many days and round up many of the suspects.

Five years later, in 1997, the Bhumihars formed their own party—Ranveer Sena—and took their revenge for the Bara carnage, killing fifty-eight Dalits in retaliation. This became known as the Lakshmanpur Bathe carnage.

The early 1990s was when the march of technology had just begun in India. I feel one important contribution I made was initiating and overseeing the computerization of the entire records of the Naxal section. It was a mammoth task, much appreciated by everybody.

On 15 August 1992, I received the police medal for meritorious service.

Rakesh and I were due for our promotion now, having put in the requisite years of service. But we could not be promoted as three colleagues of the 1975 batch were facing vigilance and corruption charges, because of which their promotions had been held up. They took a stay from the Central Administrative Tribunal (CAT), which handles all such cases related to bureaucrats. But, unless these officers received their promotion, nobody below them could get promoted.

The post of SP(A) essentially meant waiting for a promotion as DIG, so there was some speculation about where I would be posted next. I let it be known that I would like to go to a range. I felt SB was a good posting to get back into the groove, especially since there had been a regime change while we were away. But I was ready for the field again.

As SP(A), I would have frequent interactions with Lalu Prasad during meetings or when my boss would ask me to brief the CM directly. In the summer of 1992, I received a call on the hotline. '*Main* Lalu Prasad *bol raha hoon* (This is Lalu Prasad speaking). I am posting you as DIG southern range. Please go and join at Ranchi.' He was very brief and direct. I was stunned.

Range DIG, Ranchi, was considered a very good posting. I did not disclose this piece of good news to anyone, thinking I should wait for the notification. But it never came. I later learnt that the current DIG did not want to move out of Ranchi, so he had manipulated our infamous caste-ridden system and ensured that no notification was issued.

So, I continued as SP(A) and Rakesh as SP(C). Some of our friends said that instead of waiting indefinitely for our promotion we should challenge the stay. We had put in sixteen years of service and should be DIG now. They suggested we become interveners in the case. But we did not have so much money that we could hire a lawyer. We requested our friend Chandramauli Prasad—a young and upcoming lawyer—to contest on our behalf. He argued forcefully, but the case dragged on for another five months before the stay was vacated.

A few days later, I had just come home for lunch when I received a call from the special branch control room. I still remember the date—17 November 1992. They informed me that a cabinet meeting was in progress and the CM had asked me to go to him 'immediately'.

Anxious about the sudden summons, I went straight back to the Secretariat. I entered the room where all the cabinet ministers were seated at a long table with Lalu Prasad at the head. As soon as he saw me, he pointed towards someone and said, 'You have not recruited this lady . . .'

I looked around the room and saw that some SB constables had brought a woman to meet the CM. She was standing with her head bowed, one child in her arms and another clutching her sari. I could not recognize her. The CM sounded rather upset. 'You should have appointed her,' he continued.

It dawned on me that she was the widow of an SB constable who had been offered a constable's job on compassionate grounds, which was the norm. I tried to tell the CM that we were following the due process for her recruitment, which often took time.

My boss, Krishan Prakashji, came in soon after. Lalu Prasad repeated his grievance. The DG was, as always, unflappable. He simply told me, 'Expedite the process.' I nodded.

As we prepared to take our leave, Lalu Prasad suddenly turned around and addressed me again: '*Aaj aapke liye bahut shubh din hai* (It is an auspicious day for you),' he said with a broad smile.

I wondered what more was in store for me that day.

'*Aapko hum* DIG Patna *bana rahe hain*,' he said.

I could not believe my ears. Did he say he was making me DIG, Patna? *DIG, central range, Patna*? The shock must have been apparent on my face, as all the cabinet members turned around and stared at me. I was at a complete loss for words.

'Sir, DIG Patna *toh bahut* senior position *hai* (But Sir, DIG Patna is a very senior position),' I stammered.

The present DIG Patna was M.K. Sinha, six years my senior. And here was the CM casually telling me to go and take charge!

'How can I take over from Mr Sinha, Sir? He is very senior to me,' I said, faltering. But Lalu Prasad's mind was made up. 'No, no, no . . . I am posting you, please go and take charge.'

I left the room, still shell-shocked. I returned home for that long-delayed lunch but received yet another call. This one informed me I was to take charge as DIG before 5 p.m. that very day! There could again be a stay order on promotions, therefore, I had to take charge immediately.

I wore my uniform and headed to the office of the DIG central range, Patna, still wondering how I could simply walk into his office and say, 'I have come to take charge.' Matters of discipline and seniority are sacrosanct in our service. Thankfully, there was no awkwardness. Mr Sinha had already been informed, and I was able to take charge without a fuss.

When I look back at those years in the special branch, I feel it was a very stable period, with extremely cordial relations between the special branch and the district police. Headquarters had a friendly atmosphere because both DGs—Krishan Prakashji and A.K. Choudhury—were honourable, uncomplicated people. Traditionally, there had always been tension between the SB and the district police, but that was not the case during my time in the SB. There was implicit trust and we ensured we did not breach our boundaries in a game of one-upmanship.

18

'Do You Need Some Help?'

Of all my postings, taking over as DIG, central range, Patna, was possibly my most emotional moment. For, this was where my journey in Bihar police had begun.

The DIG's office is housed within an old British-style building with imposing pillars and red bricks beside Patna's huge Gandhi Maidan. I can still remember hesitantly entering the room of L.V. Singh back in the winter of 1977 as an ASP under training—nervous, excited and full of awe. The DIG seemed to be the epitome of authority, the repository of all police wisdom.

I always say I owe a lot to L.V. Singh; he made sure I had a well-rounded training. He threw me into the thick of things straightaway, believing that I should be trained like everybody else. I held him in such high esteem that it was quite overwhelming to now find myself sitting in *his* chair.

A few weeks after I took charge, L.V. Singh came to see me in my new office. After retiring from service he had joined politics, going on to become a minister of state for defence in the previous central government. He cut an imposing figure in his crisp white dhoti-kurta. I immediately got up and asked him to sit in his old chair.

'No, you sit there, I want to see you in that chair,' he said with a wave of his hand, and sat down across from me, smiling. He said he was delighted to see my career progressing so well. His praise—which had been so hard to come by when I was an ASP—warmed my heart and renewed my resolve to do my best in this post.

As range DIG, I was responsible for the police administration of central range, which consisted of the Patna and Nalanda districts. I was reporting to IG Mr K.A. Jacob, a 'gentleman' officer in our cadre according to everyone.

While taking stock, I discovered that routine police work had been neglected for a while; officers were busy handling law and order and day-to-day problems. I resumed inspection of the offices of the SPs and launched a drive to clear the backlog of cases and departmental inquiries. All this improved the general working of the districts and boosted the morale of the force.

As DIG, I also had to supervise the training of ASPs and DySPs. This brought back such a rush of memories! Remembering everything that L.V. Singh had taught me, I took them under my wing. There was one lady ASP, and I made sure she was not handicapped in any way during her training.

* * *

Bihar of the early 1990s was rife with caste and communal tensions, Naxalite activities and notorious criminal gangs. As DIG, Patna, I was right at the centre of the maelstrom.

The demolition of the Babri Masjid happened on 6 December 1992, just three weeks after I took charge. The news was conveyed to me on the wireless as I was having lunch; widespread trouble was anticipated. I left my food half-eaten and rushed out.

The divisional commissioner of Patna district, Rahul Sarin, and I immediately headed for the old Patna city area, where communal troubles usually flared up. The SPs had swung into action, calming nerves, holding meetings, preventing gatherings and urging people of both communities to maintain peace. We started heavy patrolling. Every branch, section and every police cell went into top gear, collecting intelligence and trying their best to prevent any untoward incident.

As soon as news of the demolition spread, crowds surged into the streets, tempers rose and people started pelting each other with stones. In the Sultanganj police station area, officers had fired shots to disperse a mob and prevent large-scale violence. One person died in the firing; seeing that the police were ready to take strong action, the area became completely deserted and quiet.

Within hours, saffron flags went up in most parts of Patna city. This was a new development, and all of us were surprised by the speed with which the flags came up on buildings and roadsides. We had our work cut out for us. We increased the boots on the ground and remained in the old city area late into the night.

I had always heard that Lalu Prasad was a 'hands-on' CM, I saw his style of functioning up close that day. He came to the old city with his convoy late in the night to take stock of the situation. All of us senior officers sat with him in one of the police stations to draw up a strategy for the next few days.

Our immediate concern was the return of *kar* sevaks (devotees) from Ayodhya. 'You have to be extremely careful right from the moment they arrive at the railway stations.

Whoever is returning is likely to carry bricks from the demolished mosque. They might create mischief and provoke sentiments,' he pointed out.

It was reassuring to have the CM out on the streets, as his presence had a calming effect on people from all communities. He had a good rapport with Muslims as well as Hindus. While we were sitting with him, he kept receiving distress calls from people caught in the violence outside Bihar. He was also constantly talking to his counterparts in other states to help the stranded people. I saw how everyone reposed faith in him; he was completely in charge.

Thanks to proactive patrolling and a concerted effort by the entire district administration, there was no major incident in Patna-Nalanda in the wake of the Babri Masjid demolition.

* * *

Bihar, perennially mired in caste conflict, was witnessing a new kind of caste politics. The victory of Lalu Prasad's Janata Dal had energized the Yadav community and its affiliated so-called 'backward' castes, while reservations recommended by the Mandal Commission Report 1980 had made the OBCs (Other Backward Castes) more aware of their rights. Of course, the upper castes were not going to relinquish their position without a fight. The result was recurrent clashes, agitations, demonstrations, violence and deaths.

As DIG, Patna, I was frequently on tour, defusing situations in sensitive areas like Barh, Mokama and Bakhtiyarpur in the Patna district, as well as several areas of Nalanda, like Biharsharif town and Harnaut. I would go and hold meetings with the district police, local people and caste leaders. I also organized cooperation meetings with the neighbouring districts and range (Bhagalpur).

In 1993–94, I noticed a new trend—caste rallies. Encouraged by the politics of Lalu Prasad and his party, the OBCs began asserting their political presence. Between January 1994 and May 1994, an unprecedented number of caste rallies were held in Patna. Each drew members of a particular backward caste from all over Bihar. They would come to the state capital in a show of strength and camp at Gandhi Maidan. For us, it meant relentless bandobast duty. Those were very tense months; we were always on tenterhooks, apprehending trouble and trying to stay one step ahead in our preparations.

Even a simple parliamentary by-election in Patna was fraught with worry. Given the newfound empowerment of the Yadavs and other backward castes, commissioner Sarin and I decided to be present in the Danapur subdivision on the day of voting. Sure enough, bombs were hurled—several booths were being captured for 'bogus voting'. We had a busy day ensuring free and fair elections.

Nalanda saw caste and communal tensions as well. Commissioner Sarin and I would have to routinely rush to Nalanda to defuse situations. I got to know Mr Sarin quite well during these two-hour road journeys; I found him to be sincere, level-headed and very cooperative.

One day, there was a communal flare-up and we rushed to Nalanda to oversee deployment and patrolling in the old part of town, which abounded in narrow, congested lanes. Suddenly we were informed that the CM was on his way there.

Upon his arrival, we briefed him about the incident, in which one person had been killed. He insisted on visiting the spot. That day, I witnessed Lalu Prasad's famed mass appeal.

He decided to address the people at a *nukkad* (street corner), with several tall old buildings around. We were all horrified at the security risk. Never one to back out of a public show, the CM climbed on top of a jeep and started speaking.

He was such a crowd-puller; within minutes entire neighbourhoods emptied out as everyone gathered before him. They listened to him in pin-drop silence. He appealed to them to maintain communal harmony, to not allow things to go out of hand. 'If something happens, everyone will suffer,' he told them, his voice ringing clear in the quiet evening.

It was getting dark, and we were getting seriously concerned about the CM's security, worrying what would happen if somebody threw a bomb at him. Oblivious of the danger, Lalu Prasad continued to speak, a picture of confidence. Thankfully, nothing happened that evening, and we all returned to Patna safely.

* * *

The road connecting Patna and Nalanda used to be perennially congested, with traffic from these two cities jostling with vehicles from Ranchi, which lay further ahead. Whenever people had any grievance, they would come out of the villages and block the road at Nalanda. It was a strategy of minimum effort, maximum effect. This became one of my big headaches during this tenure.

In Bihar, most main roads have villages on either side. People are crossing these busy roads on foot all the time, dodging traffic, with scant regard for road rules. Very often, there would be an accident.

One afternoon, a person died in a hit-and-run accident, prompting the villagers to come out in big numbers to block the road in Nalanda, demanding compensation and arrest of the accused. But paying compensation for road accidents was not a prevalent practice back then. I was monitoring the situation from Patna all day. I was told the blockade would soon be lifted; the district magistrate and SP were at the spot, talking to the agitators. Around 7 p.m., I received a call from Mr Lalu Prasad: 'Night is fast approaching, things will go out of control; it is better if you go and sort things out.'

When I informed commissioner Sarin, he was kind enough to offer to come along. Within a few minutes, we left for Nalanda. We arrived somewhere near the site of the blockade in pitch darkness. There was a long line of cars. Unable to proceed further, we got off the car and started walking in the dark along with my escort and some extra force. I briefed my men that the first thing we had to do was lift the body and clear the road.

The protesters had placed the victim's body on the road to block traffic coming from Ranchi on one side and Patna on the other. I took a chance, which, in hindsight, I think was risky.

I started shouting into the darkness, 'Clear the road, clear the road! Everybody must leave immediately. Otherwise we will arrest you. *Khaali karo, khaali karo!*

The constables also started shouting, banging their lathis. The protesters were taken by surprise, not knowing what was happening. My men forcibly picked up the body and put it in a jeep. All the while I kept shouting, 'If anybody wants to talk to me, to negotiate, I am willing to have a conversation. Find five people, come outside and we will talk. But the road has to be cleared.'

The stranded drivers and passengers had been walking by the side of the road listlessly. Suddenly there was a scramble to get back into their vehicles, and soon the police started directing the flow of traffic. The angry crowd melted into the night.

The impasse that had started at 2 p.m. that day and had gone on till past 9 p.m. was defused within a few minutes. Yes, negotiations are necessary to pacify a crowd; but, at times, what is required to bring a situation under control is firm and decisive action. That day, even I did not anticipate that the prolonged blockade would fizzle out so quickly. It was dangerous for me to enter the agitated crowd in the darkness, but it was the need of the hour.

My action became the talk of the town in Patna. Later, I came to know that some of my relatives and friends had also been stuck on their way from Ranchi that day. They had never seen this side of me and were taken aback to see how boldly I had handled the situation. They went on to narrate the incident to everyone we knew!

* * *

Those days Patna police had a notorious reputation of bumping off criminals. It was an open secret, which led to a scare among the people. This worked to the advantage of many, be it the police or their political bosses, and even some sections of the population. But a sense of resentment had begun festering in the city.

I had always been opposed to any kind of extra-legal action. Having seen the aftermath of the Bhagalpur blindings from close quarters, I knew that this was a slippery slope that only took you down. I had seen how police officers had become embroiled in the gross violation of human rights in the name of speedy justice, and I did not want the same to happen under my watch. Nor did I want to become party to any wrongdoing. Left unchecked, I felt that Patna police would get into serious trouble one day.

In March 1993, a teenage boy was killed in Patna city in a daylight encounter. The police alleged he was a thief who was carrying a pistol. The people of his mohalla (area) were extremely agitated by this daylight killing and a police force had to be deployed to disperse the crowd.

Some mohalla residents came to meet me. 'Madam, although you are here, look at what is happening!' they said sadly. They wanted justice, insisting that the boy was not a hardened criminal and that the pistol had been planted on him. He was at best a petty pickpocket and they alleged that he was being made a scapegoat by the Patna police.

Perturbed by what I heard and moved by the plight of the parents, I asked for the supervision note on the case. I made several inquiries into the matter, recording my observations in writing. I also let word go out that I did not approve of this action.

Early one morning, my hotline rang. The instrument was in my bedroom, so I reached across and picked it up. Someone at the other end said the CM wanted to speak to me. I sat up, wide awake now. Within a second, Lalu Prasad was on the line. He was not happy and did not mince his words.

'The city SP tells me that you are not allowing them to work properly. If they do not take action, crime will get out of hand in Patna, as in the past. The situation was brought under control only because of the action the SP was taking, and it will be better if you don't interfere.'

I do not know what struck me in that moment, but I decided to refute the CM's argument. I replied frankly, 'Sir, I do not approve of this action, I do not think this is the right thing. This line of action must stop, otherwise a lot of people will get into trouble,' I paused for breath after saying this passionately.

There was silence at the other end, so I continued.

'The person who was killed was just fourteen years old. Sir, your child could be fourteen, I too have a son who is nearly fourteen. How would you or I feel as a parent if something like this were to happen to our child? A child can make a mistake, but does he deserve to be killed?'

Hearing my tone, my husband was shocked out of his slumber. He sat up and started asking me, 'What are you saying? Who is it?'

But I kept speaking, strongly and emotionally. 'Suppose something had happened to your son for snatching a purse, or to my son . . . how would you or I feel, Sir?'

The CM finally said, '*Nahin, yeh toh galat hai* (No, this is wrong),' and hung up.

I assume the CM must have spoken to the SP because, after that, there was never any talk on this topic, and during my tenure in Patna district, we did not have any more encounters. Incidentally, the SP who had probably complained about me was also transferred.

Although I never spoke about this conversation to anyone, it has remained with me. We are always wary of politicians as we believe they do not like plain-speak. My respect for Lalu Prasad went up as I felt he did he see the point in what I was saying. It was good for me, and it had an impact on everyone—the officers in the CID also heaved a sigh of relief that there were no more encounters. But nobody knew how and why they stopped.

Another menace in Bihar in those days was kidnappings for extortion. It was a kind of urban terror that had gripped the well-heeled and kept the police on their toes. One of the most high-profile kidnappings in Patna during my DIG days was that of Ram Kailash Saraogi, a prominent businessman in Patna. There was a big outcry across the city, especially within the business community, which was living in fear. Protests broke out, the media went into a tizzy and there was tremendous pressure on us to recover the hostage. We were very perturbed by this case; as it had come just after the encounter of the boy, the reputation of Patna police was at stake.

To the credit of the SSP and his team, Mr Saraogi was released within twenty-four hours. The Bihar chamber of commerce sent me a letter expressing gratitude,

> . . . for the good work leading to the immediate recovery of Mr Saraogi, which boosted the morale of the general public and business community.

* * *

Crime and law-and-order problems had increased manifold in the past twenty years, but the strength of the police had not kept up. There was an acute shortage of manpower in police stations all over Bihar, especially SIs.

One of the most significant developments in Bihar police in 1993 was a massive recruitment drive. Lalu Prasad decided to hold the biggest-ever recruitment in Bihar, of 1600 SIs. Despite the shortage, there was widespread criticism that such large numbers of police were being recruited. Opposition parties and the press alleged that the CM would ensure recruitment of only members of his own caste.

Reservations recommended by the Mandal Commission in 1980 had already come into effect, but Bihar's proclivity for seeing caste in everything added to the atmosphere of distrust and speculation. Lalu Prasad did not bother about this; he had a good majority in the legislature so he just went ahead with his plans.

The recruitment drive was to be held in every district of Bihar. In Patna alone, as many as five recruitment boards were being set up, to select over 500 SIs. Each board would consist of three senior members and one chairperson. To my utter surprise—horror, in fact—I found my name as chairperson for all five boards!

A recruitment board tests candidates on parameters like running, high jump and long jump, among others, and records their physical measurements before making the final selection. The greatest scope for wrongdoing is during the physical fitness test as the results can easily be fudged.

Even as the corridors of power came alive with whispers of, 'Why has Manjari Jaruhar been given *five* boards?' I protested to my seniors, pointing out how one person chairing five boards was fraught with the possibility of corruption charges. They were aghast, as the CM had personally asked for me to chair these boards.

But I insisted, and finally my boards came down to three, while IG K.A. Jacob would chair the other two. Although I felt three was still too many, I agreed. How much can you protest in such matters?

Mr Jacob was laughing when he telephoned me, 'Okay, you have had your way, but I can tell you one thing, all the work must be done by you; I will only sign on the dotted line of the documents that you place before me.' Although I shook my head in resignation, I could not say anything further, but I was even a little pleased at the trust he had reposed in me.

Preparations were being made for the recruitment drive across the state. Several of my colleagues who were DIGs in other parts of Bihar would telephone me and ask, 'Manjari, what if we get a *list*? Have you received one?'

A rumour was doing the rounds that lists of 'preferred candidates' would be sent to DIGs. Being away from Patna, they were not sure which way the winds were blowing in the state capital.

'I have not received any "list"; if that happens, you have to handle it yourself. I have made up my mind. I am going to go by the book and do whatever is correct,' I replied. Seeing the mood of the Opposition, I felt the recruitment could get challenged in court at any time and we would be held accountable for our actions.

A day before the recruitment drive started, I got a strange call from Lalu Prasad late in the night, 'I have a lot of expectations from you. Everybody's eye is on the Patna recruitments as there are five boards here. The leader of the opposition, Jagannath Mishra, is camping in Patna. He is watching very closely, waiting to raise the matter in the assembly, which is in session. Nothing should happen in the recruitment that can be challenged to cast aspersions on my government. That is why I have entrusted you with this task.'

The call took me by surprise and only strengthened my resolve to ensure free and fair recruitment. We completed the process without a hitch. The drive went on for several days, it was a massive exercise—there were as many as 65,000 applications for the 500 vacancies being handled by the five boards in Patna.

I must say, contrary to everyone's expectations that Lalu Prasad would favour his own people or that he would circulate lists, nothing of the kind happened. Later, some people did challenge the recruitment in court, and it was mired in controversy for a while, but, ultimately, 1600 SIs were recruited in one go—for the first time in Bihar—which was a big relief to the police force.

* * *

I was DIG, Patna, from November 1992 to July 1994. In between, Mr Jacob left and Mr Anil Kumar came as the IG. I found him to be a mild-mannered boss who did not interfere in the work of his juniors. I felt comfortable turning to him for advice when confronted with a vexing problem.

On my promotion, I had wanted to be in charge of a range, although I had not imagined that I would be given an important charge like central range straightaway. I was lucky to have been selected by the CM himself for the post. At the same time, it was an extremely exhausting charge. In the eighteen months or so that I was DIG, Patna, I was hardly ever at home, racing from one situation to the next, with no time to pause for breath.

I remember how one year we were celebrating Holi at home. Covered in the festive colours, I received information that some miscreants had desecrated a grave in old Patna city. Leaving my family and guests, I immediately changed into my uniform and left for the spot. Since this was one of the most communally sensitive places in Patna, anything could happen.

I started feeling that I was neglecting my children too much. They were growing up so fast! As a mother, my only solace was that we were still living on the floor above my parents' house, so the boys were well looked-after. Thankfully, Rakesh was always there to shoulder parenting responsibilities, often doubling as both parents when I was out touring, which was almost always.

During that time, another exciting opportunity came my way.

Those days, some lady police officers were being sent to Australia for mid-career training courses. I got selected for a twelve-week course on organizational behaviour at the University of Wollongong in New South Wales, Australia. Many people were shocked that I was even thinking of leaving a post like DIG, Patna. But I knew my mind, and it was made up.

When I was on the verge of leaving for Australia, there was a custodial death in Naubatpur police station. The deceased was from one of the so-called 'upper castes'. The unfortunate death heightened caste tensions in the area, with members of the upper castes staging multiple dharnas outside the Bihar assembly demanding an inquiry. Some of them were also demanding that the inquiry should be conducted by Manjari Jaruhar. But I did not want to get sucked into what I knew would be a prolonged and controversial inquiry, on the eve of my departure.

When a decision was taken by the government that the DIG, Patna, should inquire into the matter, I requested my boss, Anil Kumar, if I could be exempted as I was about to leave for three months, and this was bound to be a controversial inquiry.

Mr Kumar told me something important that day—a lesson I remember to date: 'No, Manjari, you *should* go and hold the inquiry. It is because people have faith in you that they have been asking for you. Whenever people trust you, you should honour their trust and not run away from it. Therefore, I will not advise you to excuse yourself from this case. You go and record whatever you think is right.'

I felt trapped. I could see the merit in what he was saying, but I did not wish to get embroiled in Bihar's perpetual caste politics. Then I remembered my mentor L.V. Singh's words when I was an ASP under his training.

'An IPS officer is always expected to lead . . . in the course of your career, there will be many times when you will be asked to adjudicate or to brief seniors. Being decisive is a requisite for leadership.'

So, I went to Naubatpur, completed the inquiry and submitted my report to the government. My inquiry confirmed my suspicion that the man had been killed in police custody, and I recommended that action be taken against the officers responsible.

Before I was to leave for Australia, the IG said, 'The CM has always shown so much confidence in you; I think you should go and personally inform him that you are going to Australia for this course.'

It was raining. Lalu Prasad was sitting under a canopy in the lawn at his home at 1, Anne Marg. When I walked in, he asked me to sit. I was in a sari that day. He was relaxed, he even commented that I looked taller in a sari than in a uniform. It amused me to note how observant people are about lady police officers.

The CM asked his coterie to leave and turned to me. He wanted to know what had happened. I said, 'Sir, I am going for a training course for three months. I am leaving for Australia, so I have come to meet you.'

He could not quite fathom the reason. 'Why are you going? Nobody leaves the post of DIG, Patna.'

'Sir, it is an extremely prestigious and well-designed course; I think I will greatly benefit from it.'

'*Theek hai, aapka baat maan lete hain* (All right, I accept your decision),' he said with a smile.

Then he lowered his tone and whispered conspiratorially, 'Do you need any help?'

I was at a loss. What exactly was the CM asking me? Being an astute politician, he immediately sensed my confusion. 'No, no, for officers like you who are honest and straight, we have a small fund. We know going abroad is expensive . . . we keep something aside for helping officers like you.'

I did not know how to react—I was embarrassed, amused and confused, all at once! I think I mumbled something like, 'No, no, Sir, everything is being paid for by our government and the Australian government,' and look my leave.

When I told the IG about this exchange, he was quite shocked. And then he smiled and said, 'I have never heard anything like this before! He must really value you.'

Mr Lalu Prasad did have a lot of confidence in lady officers, he treated them with respect. There were many important posts being handled by women during those days. Whenever I interacted with him, I found him to be very dignified in his behaviour.

Being at the heart of Bihar administration as DIG central range gave me a rich experience of handling one crisis after another: be it caste or communal tensions; important political developments; or criminal activities. It exposed me to good police work and gave me a quiet confidence in my own self that I could handle whatever responsibility was given to me.

* * *

Ever since I had visited UPenn and Stanford, I had been regretful about missing out on an American education. Just being on a campus where boys and girls were engaged in the pursuit of knowledge, making their dreams come true, was exhilarating, and made me wistful. Although not exactly an American Ivy

League experience, the course in Australia would finally give me a taste of campus life in a 'western' country.

I landed in Sydney in July 1994. Coming from a teeming city like Patna, the absence of people in Sydney was striking. Wollongong is a small university beach town in the state of New South Wales (NSW), about 90 kilometres from Sydney. It was a scenic place, although sparsely populated. Located in the Illawara region of NSW, the University of Wollongong (UOW) is said to be one of the most picturesque university campuses in Australia.

I was assigned a beautiful studio apartment. Fully furnished, it was as comfortable as it was functional. One day, I was in the well-stocked university library, marvelling at their fully computerized requisition system, when a boy walked up to me. 'Ma'am, are you DIG, Patna?'

'How do you know me?' I asked, instantly intrigued. He said he had seen me when I had visited Patna University for some law-and-order duty. He and his friends were fascinated that a DIG was doing a course in the same university as them. It amused me to see how excited they were to discover that a police officer they had held in awe in their college days was now a student along with them.

Little did he know how excited I was, too, to become a student again, and in a university that was so different from my own colleges. Just to leave behind the daily hurly-burly of policing and engaging in an academic pursuit was invigorating.

* * *

I learnt various new concepts in class. One was total quality management (TQM). This concept was developed on the principle of *kaizen*, a Japanese term meaning 'change for the better' or 'continuous improvement'.

The teaching methodology was vastly different from colleges back home. The professors would discuss various concepts and we were expected to do extensive reading on our own. But there was no written work, no tutorials or papers to be submitted and no exams at the end of the course either. I was only expected to listen and learn.

The course on 'management of change' was of particular interest to me. I found it fascinating to learn how, as the head of an organization, you could effect change: the steps you should take, the conversations you should have and the kind of communication that should go out to all members of the organization.

This topic seemed especially relevant for a service like ours, which is hierarchical and rule-bound. I learnt that when you want to introduce change, it is always good to take everybody into confidence and explain to them why the change is required. This makes the process participatory. But if you impose it, your team may not accept it because lack of information makes people suspicious. They will make the process of change difficult.

At the same time, I also learnt that not all change can be brought about through consensus. Sometimes a leader has to insist on change even if people resist it.

I used both the approaches later in my career. Whenever a change was required, I would always consult my seniors and subordinates to get their views and build a consensus. This helped me make any organizational change faster. But I did not shy away from taking a hard decision even if it required me to impose a change. To add to what I learnt at UOW, I feel that when you are enforcing change, you have to rely on your own experiences as a leader. Sometimes I did have to follow this method, especially in senior positions.

Another interesting module was on stress management. The professor spoke about the various kinds of stresses and also taught some exercises to help us de-stress.

She explained to us how stress had never been measured until then—especially what causes it and how much. She had made a chart during her research, where she had calculated that the maximum stress to an individual is caused by the death of their child.

This was something I had felt while dealing with various kinds of cases as well. The greatest agony I had witnessed was the loss of a child. I particularly remembered the case of a small boy when I was SP, Bokaro. A boy of about five or six had been run over by a vehicle. He was trying to cross the road and go to the other side to play. The mother had probably just taken her eyes off him for a moment and he was hit by a car. I had rushed to the spot after receiving the information. It was gut-wrenching to watch the mother cry over her dead child. I cried with her too.

I feel lucky that I was picked to attend mid-career courses in London and Australia, apart from various short modules in India. The exposure to new cultures, classroom lectures, mixed groups of participants and even the experience of living alone in another city added significantly to my professionalism and personal growth.

19

The Paramilitary Challenge

When Bokaro bade me a touching farewell, I should have known that bonds forged with warmth and goodwill do not change. For I was back in Bokaro eight years after I left the Steel City as SP. My later charge was vastly different. I was now DIG CISF, Bokaro Steel Plant, a position I had taken up in October 1994 upon my return from Australia.

The CISF had started out as an armed force of the government of India, responsible for the security of public-sector undertakings like steel plants and power plants, mines, oil fields, refineries and ports all over India. Later, the force was inducted into airports, metro railways and critical private establishments as well.

When I was first approached by the CISF, I was not sure whether I wanted to be a DIG in charge of the steel plant in a district where I had been SP earlier. My change of heart happened by coincidence. One of my DySP probationers who had been with me in Bokaro, visited me while I was DIG, Patna. He mentioned that Bokaro now had a Delhi Public School following the CBSE pattern. I knew Bokaro had excellent coaching facilities for engineering aspirants as well.

Tushar was now in class 10 and would be choosing a career path soon, while Anshuman was still attending a mohalla school in Patna, which was far from ideal. Perennially worried about my job impacting my children adversely, I felt their education should take precedence at that juncture.

Just as I was mulling this over, I was selected for the three-month course in Australia, which left me in a dilemma. After much hesitation, I rang up the DG, CISF, S.C. Mehta, and he immediately said, 'No, no, you must go. IPS officers rarely get an opportunity to attend a course like this. It's only for twelve weeks; the DIG's post in Bokaro will be kept vacant for you.'

And so I went.

* * *

After my return from Australia, I left for Bokaro with Anshuman. Rakesh stayed back in Patna with Tushar, who was preparing for his class 10 board examinations. I was upset about not being around during his first big examination, but my husband assured me that Tushar would be fine.

As soon as we arrived in Bokaro, my old friends, the Srivastavas, came over to the CISF mess where we were staying. It was a happy but hasty reunion. They promptly took charge of Anshuman, and I left to take charge as DIG, CISF. I called on K.A.P. Singh, the managing director of Bokaro Steel Plant. I found him to be pragmatic and professional, and I felt we would get along well. Anshuman was admitted to Delhi Public School in class 6 after a test and an interview. This came as a big relief to me.

Just as when I took over as SP, Bokaro, my predecessor in the CISF, too, had been transferred under a cloud. There were serious charges against him. A commandant had been suspended and a CBI case registered. The men had been involved in the smuggling of plant goods, a practice rampant among the villagers as well. Disputes over sharing the looted property led to a violent clash between the CISF and the villagers, leading the CISF men to torch several trucks and go on a rampage.

When the plant administration appealed to the DIG and the commandant, they were found to be involved in the smuggling racket themselves. All this had dragged the reputation of the CISF through the mud.

So, I hit the ground running, starting with matters of indiscipline. Wherever I was posted, the first message I gave out was that discipline was one thing I would not compromise on. At the same time, I made every effort to ensure that their lives were a little easier outside duty hours.

In a déjà-vu-like situation, I found the CISF men posted at the plant had become carefree and wayward, behaving like a workers' union rather than a disciplined force. Many would report for work in civilian clothes. I issued the same order I had as SP—that nobody would enter the plant except in uniform. To set an example, in the four years I was there, I never once visited the plant in civvies. I was always in uniform.

The men had also gotten into the habit of hitching a ride on the two-wheelers of plant employees. Because a constable was travelling with an employee, the CISF would not check them at the gates. This enabled them to successfully steal plant material. It was a nexus that needed to be broken. I ordered that no one in the CISF would take a lift from an employee. When the men protested about there not being enough buses, we ensured that adequate transport was available at shift changes.

Since Bokaro steel plant was a profit-making establishment—one of the *navratna*s or nine gems of Indian PSUs—they looked after the force well. My office, provided by the plant, was big, clean and comfortable, located on a compact campus with adequate barracks. Despite this, a large number of CISF personnel were living inside the plant, which led to various malpractices. We shifted all of them to the barracks on the CISF campus, leaving only a small contingent inside for emergency duties. We started weekly parades on the CISF campus and a monthly police sabha, where I would address the men and listen to their grievances. It was important that they understood that the DIG was as concerned about welfare as discipline. Gradually, my message began to percolate, bringing in a sense of responsibility amongst my men.

As with the district police, there existed a confrontational relationship between the CISF and the plant, perhaps because smuggling, pilfering, theft and under-reporting involved everyone, from the paramilitary and police to the employees and locals. The plant management, who were totally dependent on the CISF for the protection of plant property and their own safety in the face of union trouble, felt helpless because the very force assigned to protect them had turned suspect.

I began to work closely with the plant management, hoping to repair some of the damage caused by all that had transpired before I arrived. Since I had to protect the plant, it was also in my interest to understand the problems its management was facing.

The MD started inviting me to their monthly meetings, which helped me understand plant operations much better.

It was also a good forum to place issues that the force was facing before the MD. The cordial, reciprocal relationship was reflected in Mr Singh's letter to me, which mentioned that the plant performance had been 'good'.

'This, to a great extent, has been possible with the active involvement and support of CISF . . . CISF could drive home synergy in all areas of their operations which eventually brought about a better image for the Company.'

It was common knowledge that the system of entry of trucks into the plant was riddled with corruption. If a truck was kept waiting outside, the transporter suffered heavy losses, so he was willing to pay a bribe to gain quick entry. When I realized the plant had vast resources that could help us improve operations, I requested the MD to computerize the system of issuing passes on a first-come, first-served basis. By stopping the corrupt practice of manually issuing passes, we provided relief to the transporters.

Another novel method that had a salutary effect on plant employees was the introduction of 'simultaneous drive'. I had learnt this tactic in the police, where there was surprise checking on a designated night across the district on the movement of all persons and vehicles to control crime. I would take the plant management into confidence and conduct this massive exercise. Every person's pass on a particular shift would be scrutinized, which amounted to checking 15,000 to 20,000 people. We detected several people trying to enter the plant with fake, expired or no IDs at all. We also checked all the vehicles within the plant. All this helped control crime to a great extent, and instilled discipline among the employees.

* * *

Just three months before Tushar's boards, Rakesh was posted to the police training college in Hazaribagh. Because of our experience at the National Police Academy, Rakesh was asked to oversee the training of the 1600 SIs who had been recruited while I was DIG, Patna. This was a massive challenge, since there was no police training school in the country that could train 1600 people together. So, some were sent to Punjab and Haryana for their basic training. For Rakesh it was all about standardization, coordination and supervision on a scale never done before in Bihar.

So, Tushar was now all alone in Patna, studying for his board exams with neither parent by his side. I felt it was truly unfair on the poor boy, but we had no choice. I give credit to my son that he kept calm. Fortunately, Rakesh was able to take leave and be with him during the days of his exams later on.

After his boards, Tushar got admission to Delhi Public School in Bokaro and started his engineering coaching. A studious boy, he did well in his class and became a squad captain, which was a big thing for him since he was new to the school. Anshuman, the mischievous one, would often be compared to his older brother by the teachers. So, I had to manage the emotions and studies of both my sons. It was not an easy period, as I felt that everybody was targeting me, implying that I was not taking enough care of my children. Those were difficult years, but then, who said bringing up adolescents would be easy?

By then the SIs had finished their training, and I learnt that the plant was looking for an IAS or IPS officer to take charge as GM (town services), Steel Authority of India Limited. I convinced Rakesh to take up the offer. He came on deputation in March 1996. After a gap, the four of us were together once again in Bokaro.

* * *

Soon after taking charge, while I was on tour one day, the IG, Ajay Prasad, informed me that fourteen CISF personnel, all hailing from Punjab, had been caught red-handed by our crime intelligence wing (CIW). The plant had a high boundary wall, topped with concertina wire, but there were many gaps. Some CISF men had entered the plant through these gaps, while others were waiting on the other side to collect the items their colleagues were stealing and throwing out.

The IG asked me to return to Bokaro immediately and handle the situation. I suspended all fourteen upon my return. I have never shied away from being ruthless when it comes to matters of criminal misconduct and indiscipline. I then tasked six inspectors with conducting departmental proceedings against them on a day-to-day basis. The fourteen were segregated in different barracks because the CISF in Bokaro had a history of revolt, which had resulted in a clash with the army and the death of a commandant a few years ago.

The proceedings were conducted in a record time of twenty-one days, and I dismissed all fourteen accused. I also wanted to drive home the message that you could *not* steal from a plant you were supposed to protect and hope to get away with it. In the following months, everybody in the CISF would ask me how I had managed to take such strong action, and even the DG was happy with how we had dealt with the situation.

On the eve of Independence Day in 1995, a massive theft was reported from the telecommunications stores of the plant. As I rushed there, I felt a sense of déjà vu. Memories of searching the homes of plant storekeepers and arresting their wives or racing my jeep to nab lorries pilfering coke flashed before my eyes.

I had called in our dog squad to assist in the investigations. The dog went and sat on a large manhole cover. I knew the premises had a network of underground tunnels for extraction of waste and supply of water as the plant needed large quantities of water for cooling the steel and other works. I remembered hearing that criminals sometimes crawled through these tunnels, removed the manhole covers, stole plant property and escaped through the same route. After we had ramped up checking at the gates, the criminals must have decided to go 'underground'. Literally.

In the half-light of dusk, I told Jagbir Singh, the deputy commandant in charge of the CIW, to open the manhole. It was pitch-black inside. We checked for toxic fumes and then lowered two members of the CIW team into the manhole. The tunnel was dry that day; it was possibly a stormwater drain. They started walking in the direction of the boundary wall, the beam from their powerful torches cutting the darkness like a knife. A little further down, they noticed something stacked against the tunnel walls.

Shocked and thrilled, they started shouting excitedly that they had found huge piles of telecommunication equipment. The theft must have been going on over a period of time, for this was not one day's loot. It took the team over ninety minutes to retrieve all the material from the tunnel. As soon as the loot was spotted in such a spectacular manner, everyone got enthused to retrieve everything.

The plant MD, K.A.P. Singh, hurried to the spot with his GMs. Although horrified at the volume of stolen items, they were impressed at how quickly we had discovered the hideout. I asked my office accountant to come with ₹10,000 from our reward funds; the MD and I straightaway distributed cash rewards to all the men who had worked on this case. Such gestures have a positive impact on the men, as they feel their efforts are being recognized.

This became a sensational case and people talked about it for days, everyone praising the alacrity with which the CISF had acted. The MD also sent me a letter of thanks. For me, it was a matter of great satisfaction, as I had inherited a force mired in controversy and accused of widespread thievery, but here we were, being lauded for our dogged recovery of stolen property.

* * *

Although our family life was peaceful in Bokaro, the shortage of IPS officers in the CISF meant that I was constantly on the move, with additional charge of coal and steel plants in Dhanbad, Rourkela and Durgapur. This, apart from travelling to attend recruitment and promotion boards. I held the additional charge of DIG, eastern sector, for a while as well.

Not just other plants, my responsibilities included overseeing CISF units posted at four mines connected with Bokaro steel plant, too—Kiriburu and Meghahatuburu near Jamshedpur, Bhavnathpur in the Palamu district of Bihar (now in Jharkhand) and the Koteshwar mines in Madhya Pradesh. These units had abysmal infrastructure. I tried to get some able officers posted here so they could function independently, and provided them with funds to improve the basic facilities.

The area around the Kiriburu and Meghahatuburu mines was particularly scenic, but you could see how mining activity was degrading the environment. Later, when I was posted in Jharkhand, I saw how this beautiful place had turned into the killing fields of the Naxalites.

Although this heavy charge required frequent, tedious journeys, I feel overseeing different PSUs expanded my understanding of the industrial contours of the core sectors of the Indian economy.

Bharat Coking Coal Limited (BCCL) in Dhanbad, with its large CISF presence of 5000 men, was always a problem charge, this being the land of the coal mafia. Huge quantities of coal would be stolen by the mafia, sometimes in connivance with the CISF personnel. I put my heart and soul into curbing crime, taking harsh action against whoever was caught. This forged a good relationship between the CISF and the BCCL.

Another interesting development was the induction of the CISF at Central Coalfields Limited (CCL) in Kargali, now in Jharkhand. It was a massive induction done over several months, where I spent a lot of time creating adequate infrastructure for the force, constantly liaising with the management.

In the course of handling these responsibilities, I realized that illegal coal mining was an extremely lucrative activity, and the gains outweighed the risks. Hence its continuance, despite our sincere efforts.

* * *

After Tushar completed school, we started looking at engineering colleges. Somebody told us about Manipal Institute of Technology, which was doing extremely well. I discovered that my NPA probationer, Savita Hande, was posted in the Udupi district of Karnataka. I telephoned her and asked whether she could find out about the admission process.

This network of genuinely caring friends and colleagues covering the length and breadth of India is one of the greatest gifts of our NPA posting.

Savita said she was going to Manipal for a case and would find out everything. She got back to me within a day, saying that there were only five seats left in electrical and electronics engineering. If we were interested, we should apply immediately. Thanks to her prompt action, Tushar got admitted to Manipal, and we were all very relieved.

It is only when I went to see him off at his new campus did the reality sink in. Our little boy had grown up and flown the nest, and we would only see him on holidays now. The extremely long journey that Tushar and I had to undertake to reach his college—Bokaro–Calcutta–Chennai–Bangalore–Mangalore–Manipal—made me even more miserable. It seemed as if we were banishing our son into exile!

Before I left Manipal, both Tushar and I broke down. I could not help but remember how my own father had changed his mind about sending me off to Lady Irwin College in Delhi. I had been so angry with him then; I wonder if the heart-wrenching experience of letting my own son go made me see my father's emotions in a new light.

When the boys were growing up, my mother had often suggested putting them in a boarding school, since both Rakesh and I had such busy work lives and would constantly worry about them. But I had resisted, as I had wanted my children near me—ever fearful that when they would come home for the holidays, I might be called away for some urgent police work. Incidentally, this is exactly what happened when Tushar came home for the first holiday break. I barely saw him and had to rush off to Delhi for a meeting, only returning a few hours before he went back to college. I would always say duty comes first, but who can quell the surge of emotions in a mother's heart?

* * *

In the paramilitary, only 14 per cent of the force is allowed family accommodation. With 2400 men posted in Bokaro, this meant the plant was providing family housing for nearly 350 men. These were spread across the township alongside plant employees, often leading to fights and arguments among neighbours. The plant had recently built a new sector in the same Russian pattern seen all over Bokaro. The MD offered us nearly 1000 flats here and I seized the opportunity. Much to the reluctance of my men—who kept saying the sector was isolated and would increase their travel time—I insisted that everyone must shift. Drawing upon my learnings from the management of change course in Australia, I explained the benefits of having everyone on one campus to my men.

In the new block, I tried to provide them and their families with several facilities—a canteen, a nursery school and a family welfare centre, where all the uniforms of the force started being stitched. These services also provided an additional income for the families of the subordinate ranks.

Because we were doing so well, ours became a showcase unit within the CISF. Whenever a new DG took charge in Delhi, he would come to Bokaro for an inspection. The DGs took note of my work and sent me commendation letters. I also received the DG's commendation disc and certificate in 1997 for controlling crime in Bokaro.

The paramilitary forces have a significant amount in their welfare funds. A few months before I joined, an ITI (industrial training institute) had been opened by the CISF, but not much progress had been made. I decided to arrange for the funds to recruit teachers for the ITI, buy equipment and organize a hostel, assisted by my deputy commandant, V.P. Prabhu. Although the work spilled outside my duty hours, I never saw welfare activities as a burden. In fact, I enjoyed doing things for my men, and headquarters supported me.

By this time, I was working with the top management of the plant which consisted of highly qualified professionals, many of them eminent experts in their field. Although they were several years senior to me, when any incident occurred in the plant, I felt they valued my advice to bring the situation under control.

Their faith in my judgement in a crisis shored up my confidence in my own abilities. I valued this later, when I was suddenly thrust into a bigger role.

* * *

Four years had passed by in Bokaro. My plan was to complete the deputation and return to Bihar police in a year's time when suddenly, in the summer of 1998, I received a call from my personal assistant: 'Ma'am, you have been posted to Delhi as DIG (admin.).'

It was a bolt from the blue! The matter became clearer after some time. R.K. Sharma, the DG, CISF, had learnt of widespread corruption in the recruitment process in Rajasthan, and had ordered the DIG to be repatriated back to Bengal right from the parade ground. Even the DIG (admin.) in Delhi had been transferred out of headquarters. This is how I came to be posted as DIG (admin.) in his place overnight.

But I was upset, because Anshuman was in class 10. Again, I would not be there for my child during an important examination. Rakesh stepped in, always the voice of prudence and common sense. 'Don't worry, I will be in Bokaro with Anshuman. Maybe after his boards, we can all move to Delhi. Let us see how things progress, but right now you should go to Delhi.'

My husband's words reassured me. Without Rakesh's calming influence, I would always be too agitated about the family suffering because of my postings.

Rakesh always encouraged me, whether we were posted together or apart. After the initial years of unexciting postings, when my career finally started taking off, he was delighted for me despite our jobs pulling us in different directions.

His unwavering support was balm for my stressed soul. Just knowing that he was there made it possible for me to take many decisions for my career and family, which would have been difficult otherwise.

Whenever I would get concerned about a posting disrupting our family life, he would calmly say, 'Go and take charge, we will figure out the rest.' At the same time, when he had a heavy charge, I would step up and take care of the extended family, sometimes single-handedly. A good partnership, I feel, is critical when both spouses have active jobs, as we did.

So, I flew to Delhi and I reported to the DG. Still, I was not at peace. 'Sir, my son is in class 10, I cannot get posted here!' I remember Mr Sharma's reply quite vividly.

'*Jungle mein mor nacha, kisne dekha*? (Who notices a peacock dancing in the jungle?)' What he meant was, even if you are doing good work but you are in the middle of a jungle, there will be nobody to appreciate you.

He explained why he had brought me to the HQ: 'I have seen your work, I inspected your unit, I feel you should work in the headquarters. The force needs you here and this will be a good experience for you.'

Without protesting further, I accepted his praise with grace and took charge. But I committed this line to memory. Later, when I was required to convince good officers from the field to come to headquarters, I would use these exact words.

20

Change Makers

Although initially distressed at the almost overnight transfer from Bokaro to Delhi, it became a turning point in my career. If all that had happened to me as a young bride had propelled me towards a life in the IPS, my years in the field had prepared me well for the next phase.

From the summer of 1998 to my retirement in October 2010, I had the good fortune of working in the paramilitary in various capacities, except for three years when I went back to my cadre. After about a year and a half as DIG (admin.), I was promoted as IG in October 1999. Since no IG's post was vacant in the CISF, I was moved to the CRPF, and took over as director of the Internal Security Academy (ISA) of the CRPF in Mount Abu, Rajasthan. Within six months, it was time to return to Delhi, this time as IG, northern sector, CRPF.

In 2004 I was back in the CISF, first as IG, eastern sector in Patna, then as IG (personnel) in the headquarters in Delhi, then as additional director-general (ADG) and finally as special director-general, the post from which I retired.

When I moved to Delhi, the focus of my work suddenly shifted from the field to the desk. As a young ASP, how I had resented being stuck behind the desk in the CID! But now, at this stage of my life and career, I welcomed it. If anything, I was excited and even energized by this 'pen-pushing' role. For now, my work would have a direct and positive impact across the entire force.

As DIG (admin.) in the CISF, I tried to draw upon my field experiences to make my office more responsive to field units. I worked closely with the DG, coordinating with the ministry of home affairs (MHA). I made sure that whatever was required by the units in terms of budget, vehicles, uniforms and provisions, was made available to them on time. The management and proper utilization of non-government funds was another area that I looked into, trying to ensure the welfare of the force.

My endeavour was to build teams to renovate accommodation, clean up officers' messes and staff canteens, start a cafeteria, provide clean drinking water, procure better utensils and organize gas-based cooking facilities. Wherever we found the office staff were in cramped conditions—in the CISF headquarters I even found some constables sitting in corridors—we managed to make space by discarding items and creating proper offices and cubicles.

Almost all the government offices that I have encountered have displayed a frustrating propensity to hoard items, thereby occupying precious space while the personnel were relegated to makeshift arrangements. Entire rooms, often entire buildings or even barracks would be piled high with discarded furniture, equipment and miscellaneous items because nobody had taken the onus of holding a board and condemning them, which is the only way things can be disposed of in the government. It was a tedious job, so no one would do it.

Such nitty-gritties would often be overlooked by the senior officers, but I felt that good housekeeping was as important as ensuring discipline and training. Possibly because I am a woman, these improvements were foremost on my agenda, not an afterthought. And they paid me rich dividends in the form of staff satisfaction and team loyalty.

* * *

Ever since my SP days in Bokaro, I had enjoyed a certain respect and acceptance within the Bihar police. But I had to yet again earn the loyalty of my team when I was sent to head the CRPF training academy at Mt Abu.

After taking over as director, ISA, I realized that most senior staff members were sceptical about a woman IPS officer being equipped to handle the tough training of a paramilitary force. This is a uniquely 'female' experience in the workforce. While a man is accepted just by virtue of his designation, even if he is not liked or respected, a woman is accepted only after she has consistently proved her mettle.

But I did not want to disrupt the status quo right away as the passing-out parade of the thirtieth batch of trainees was nearly upon us and for which L.K. Advani, the Union home minister, had already been invited. I realized headquarters, too, was anxious about a woman officer being in charge of such a high-profile visit.

Even my presence at the POP practice was received with surprise. Noticing that the marching of the colour party was not brisk enough, I asked the AD-OD how many steps they were taking per minute. From my NPA years, I knew it had to be 120 to 125 steps per minute. The AD-OD appeared taken aback, but he took note of my suggestions and tried to improve the pace of the parade. Later, he admitted to me that he had never thought a woman officer would know so much about parade!

During his address, Mr Advani expressed his surprise as well. 'I have never seen a woman officer heading a police training academy before. I did not know that a woman IPS officer was training the paramilitary forces,' he said appreciatively.

His words were quite encouraging for me; I was probably the first woman to head the training of a paramilitary force in India.

Over the next few weeks, as soon as the staff understood that I was interested in improving the facilities of the academy, they became extremely supportive of me. DIG D.N.S. Bisht and joint assistant director B.P. Singh were my constant allies. While Mr Bisht ensured total cooperation from the teaching staff to implement new methodologies of instruction, Mr Singh, who was in charge of the quartermaster stores, was instrumental in overseeing the slew of changes we managed to carry out within a short time. I must mention with particular appreciation his innovative suggestion to relocate the quarter guard to a more suitable spot and getting it done with alacrity. We resumed the morning reveille and the evening retreat bugle calls as well; all this went a long way in restoring the sanctity of this being a training institution.

None of the improvements, however, could hide the fact that Mt Abu was a wholly unsuitable location for a training academy. Before I joined the ISA, M.B. Kaushal, the special secretary in the MHA, had asked me to look into the prospect of shifting the academy to a more central location in the country.

The good weather and rugged terrain were well-suited for jungle-warfare training, but truth be told, that was all the advantage Mt Abu afforded. It was such a remote location that the probationers were denied any opportunity to interact with senior officers, academicians, or experts in the field. Hardly anyone was willing to come to such an isolated location. The remoteness also meant that no service was available locally. If anything went out of order, we had to send somebody all the way to Udaipur or Ahmedabad to procure a replacement.

The academy had been handed over twenty-one pieces of land and buildings of varying sizes. We needed a much larger and cohesive campus for training such big batches. With all this in mind, I went to Delhi to meet the DG, M.N. Sabharwal, carrying with me a big map of the terrain where all twenty-one locations were plotted to show him just how inadequate the facilities were.

But Mr Sabharwal was not prepared to listen. Visibly unhappy, he folded up the map abruptly and said, 'Please go back and work in Mt Abu.'

Perhaps he thought I was trying to push for a move to Delhi because my family was there. This was far from the truth.

I had never imagined that we would be able to move the academy during my tenure. As probationers, we had heard from the NPA director, S.M. Diaz, how it had taken several years to convince the Rajasthan government to allow the shift to Hyderabad from Mt Abu. I had merely thought that the process of relocation could begin.

Thankfully, the CRPF training academy has now been shifted to Kaderpur near Gurgaon, while the Mt Abu campus continues to hold a few in-service courses to keep the premises operational.

Personally, life at Mt Abu was a bit isolating. Rakesh had just moved to Delhi and joined the Bureau of Police Research and Development (BPR&D), and Anshuman had gotten admission to St Columbus School in class 11, while Tushar was in Manipal. Everyone would tell me what a beautiful view my house had of the famous Nakki Lake. But a view does not keep you company. Having always been surrounded by family, living alone was still alien to me.

I decided to turn this to an advantage as well, paying a visit to the officers and meeting their families in the evenings. It was a shock to discover that many of the women were living with their husbands for the first time. What a tough life these women had signed up for! I also saw the concern the men had for their families: they tried to be good fathers, sons and husbands despite the constraints of their job. It convinced me to do whatever little could be done to make their lives a little comfortable while they were there. These informal interactions strengthened our teamwork as well, and helped me forge lifelong relationships once again.

One of the most enthusiastic staff members was V.T. Matthew, the deputy commandant (outdoor), a young officer from Kerala who was always willing to learn. Years later, when I was in Jharkhand, I was extremely pained to know that he was killed in an ambush in Chhattisgarh. I had gotten to know his wife, Sally, in Mt Abu and telephoned her to share her grief. She was very touched that I had called, and it broke my heart to hear her crying into the phone saying he was so young, had so much to accomplish but had gone too soon.

In my thirty-four years of service, dealing with the loss of colleagues never got any easier.

Although living and working in a remote place like Mt Abu was a challenge, I feel the experience of working in its training academy helped me better understand the CRPF, which was so different from the CISF. The in-service courses brought to the campus CRPF officers from across India. Interacting with them deepened my understanding of the nature and needs of the force. At the same time, I too was able to contribute to improving the campus by drawing upon my NPA learnings.

* * *

The move from the CISF to the CRPF was an eye-opener. For CRPF battalions, it is a life perennially on the move. No wonder the standing inside joke was that 'CRPF' actually stands for '*chalte raho pyare* (keep moving, dear) force'!

In this respect, life in the CRPF is much tougher than in the CISF. While it is true the CISF is often deployed in very remote areas, like mines and oilfields, and may have long duty hours, it is a static force that is looked after very well by the PSU it serves. But those in the CRPF never know where they would be sent next and under what conditions. They are completely dependent on the state governments for accommodation and facilities but rarely do the men grumble about their harsh circumstances or refuse to do a duty. I empathized with this life of constant uncertainty and resolved to do whatever I could to ensure the operational efficiency of the force.

After six months at Mt Abu, I took over as IG, northern sector, CRPF—a proverbial 'hot seat' where one had to handle a large number of battalions and oversee critical deployments at the Parliament, the PMO and with Delhi police. The northern sector consisted of two ranges—Delhi and Rajasthan. Delhi was a heavy charge in itself, including not only my own battalions but also the battalions of other IGs deployed in the capital. That apart, the CRPF was called upon to assist Delhi police whenever there was a threat perception, like the aftermath of the terrorist attack on the Red Fort in December 2000 or the annual Republic Day parade on 26 January.

The primary responsibility of the CRPF is internal security. As IG, I was directly responsible for keeping the battalions in full operational readiness so that they could move within the shortest possible time when deployment orders were issued. We had to ensure all their equipment and infrastructure was available and their camping grounds had decent facilities; furthermore, the personnel were constantly undergoing training to keep them physically fit.

Since my battalions were deployed in Jammu and Kashmir and the North-east, I was expected to go and inspect those units as well. In Srinagar, one saw how life is lived under the constant threat of attack. There was palpable fear in the air, and for the first time, even I was a little apprehensive about what might happen. In 2000–01, the force had not yet been geared to handle every terrorist situation. And this was almost like guerrilla warfare, where even a child would be given Rs 50 by a terrorist outfit to lob a grenade at a duty post.

We had to exercise extreme caution in every activity. I had to travel in a convoy to visit my battalions, with a road-opening party (ROP) driving ahead of me to make sure the road was secured. Most often we would be advised not to return by the same route. I saw first-hand the harsh conditions the force was living under. I remember a small contingent guarding a bridge. They were living in such a ramshackle accommodation that it left me speechless. I sanctioned funds so that they could build a proper duty post, get water tankers and improve their cooking facilities.

I also made frequent trips to Ajmer, famous across the world for the dargah of Moinuddin Chishti. The CRPF had two group centres (GC) here. While I was happy to provide all the help that Additional DIG K.D. Pachauri needed as he efficiently managed and improved all the facilities at GC-1, it was the regularization of GC-2 that gave me huge satisfaction.

GC-2 had originally been sanctioned for Silchar in Assam, but the CRPF could not acquire land in the North-east. So, it was allotted some old barracks and land in Ajmer—it's said this was a cantonment from the time of the great warrior Prithviraj Chauhan. Since it was waiting to move to Silchar, nothing was being sanctioned for GC-2, much to the frustration of Additional DIG M.M. Sharma, who was in charge of this group centre.

A mature and practical officer, when Mr Sharma realized that I was interested in working for the force and our DG, Trinath Mishra, was a decision-maker, he pushed hard to regularize GC-2. Having two GCs in one city was unprecedented in the CRPF in those times, but we managed to move a proposal for its regularization, and got it approved. It reiterated my belief that if you have welfare in mind, people will work with you to bring about change that is beneficial and long-lasting.

I would often travel to Ajmer by the Shatabdi Express. The paramilitary forces lay great emphasis on ceremony and protocol. On one of my visits, when the train stopped for a few minutes in Jaipur, I spotted white-liveried men striding down the aisle, carrying trays of tea and snacks. To my mortification, they came and halted before me. Every single person in the chair car turned to look at me. Realizing that all the arrangements were for me, I hastily picked up a coconut water, so that they could leave and put an end to my embarrassment! I made sure that this practice was stopped in future for everyone.

My co-passengers started asking me, 'Is your husband in the army?' When they heard I was an IG in the CRPF, they were shell-shocked. 'Are *you* the IG, or the IG's wife?' one person asked again. For the rest of the journey, no one could stop talking about this 'marvellous' feat or prevent themselves from peering at me with ill-disguised curiosity.

I found myself feeling like a fish in a glass bowl yet again.

* * *

With increasing participation of women in politics, agitations and public life, the police forces began to feel handicapped in handling situations where women were present. To address this need gap, in 1986, under directions from PM Mr Rajiv Gandhi, the first *mahila* (woman) battalion in CRPF—the 88 (M) Bn— was created, headquartered in Delhi. When I joined the CRPF, a second mahila battalion had been raised in 1995—the 135 (M) Bn—headquartered at Gandhinagar. At present, there are a total of six mahila battalions.

The 88 (M) Bn, which was deployed in J&K at the time, was under my charge. It was headquartered at the Jharoda Kalan group centre, on the outskirts of Delhi, where the women were living on the same campus as the men. This had become the root of myriad problems. Their barracks were separated with barbed-wire fencing. Yet, the men would sometimes misbehave with them and they would retaliate, leading to unpleasant incidents.

I wanted to shift the 88 (M) Bn out of Jharoda Kalan to help the women live peacefully and with greater freedom.

The government had allotted us land in Pappan Kalan, in the Dwarka area of Delhi.

Trinath Mishra was then DG, CRPF. I had previously worked with him in the CISF, and we had a good working equation. He brought with him a wealth of experience of having worked with various forces, and gave me the freedom to do my work. When I discussed my proposal to shift the 88 (M) Bn, Dr Mishra saw merit in the idea and asked me to go ahead.

I have always believed in helping and mentoring the women personnel in any force, but this time we ran into a peculiar problem. As we started getting the barracks ready, the women said they did not wish to move! Some of them had developed vested interests in Jharoda Kalan—they had hired accommodation outside the GC to keep their families, and husbands of some of them had taken up jobs nearby. This group became very resentful of the relocation.

I requested P.P.S. Sidhu, the IG (personnel) with whom I had a good rapport from my NPA stint, to post an experienced officer as commandant of the 88 (M) Bn. He was kind enough to post P.P. Singh, who oversaw the contentious relocation.

Halfway into the process, we heard that the women were approaching politicians to get the DG to revoke the move. Anticipating pressure from above, I asked commandant P.P. Singh to immediately shift the quarter guard and put up the signboard of the 88 (M) Bn in Pappan Kalan. The DG suggested we organize an all-faith prayer meeting at the new venue on the date when the battalion would start functioning there.

The date was announced and everything was planned. Just a day before the function, I was hurriedly summoned to the DG's office. He, too, had been under pressure to not move the mahila battalion, but he had not said anything to me yet.

That morning, he said that Home Minister L.K. Advani had telephoned him as several women personnel had met him with a request to stop the transfer. The home minister had telephoned the DG to inquire why the women were being shifted out when it would cause them so much hardship.

'Are you sure we should do it? Perhaps you should think about it,' the DG said.

Convinced that my reasoning was sound, I replied, 'Sir, we have already shifted; the signboard has also been erected.'

The DG made a spot decision, 'If that is the case, then go ahead, you don't have to call it off.' Thereafter, everything went ahead as per schedule and we completed the move. It was a spacious and well-laid-out campus.

Over the years, I have met many women from the CRPF, and they have all congratulated me for achieving the 'near-impossible'. They are ever grateful to have their own campus, where they can live freely.

It was one of my most difficult tasks and eventually also my most satisfying contribution to the women of the CRPF.

* * *

I also had some novel experiences in the CRPF, vastly different from our routine responsibilities. In the police and paramilitary, Raising Day—the day a force or battalion was founded—is marked with great enthusiasm and ceremony every year. I used to always feel that these functions were a waste of manpower, effort and money. Now I understand why they had to be done. The men and women are so enthusiastic about marching in the Raising Day parade, it lifts their morale, renews their sense of loyalty and deepens their commitment to the force.

The CRPF was raised in 1939. In 1999, for the sixtieth anniversary, the then PM, Atal Behari Vajpayee, had been invited to take the salute at the GC in Jharoda Kalan, about 35 kilometres from Delhi. All IGs were invited to be present as it was a great occasion for the CRPF. I came from Mt Abu.

It was a cold December day. The parade had assembled by 9 a.m. We all had our eyes glued to the sky to spot the PM's helicopter. But that morning there was so much fog in Delhi that the helicopter could not take off. The PM undertook the long journey by road, reaching Jharoda Kalan only after 11 a.m. The entire two hours the force stood still on the parade ground with their rifles, the bitter cold notwithstanding. That day I saw the CRPF's mettle—their discipline, their mental strength and the pride they took in their ceremonies.

The following year, as IG, northern sector, it was my good fortune to organize the Raising Day parade. What a massive exercise it was; an entire township had to be set up at Jharoda Kalan with the whole team working day and night to put up a good show. DIG Mahboob Alam and my staff officer, H.S. Negi, were a great source of strength in this endeavour. In 2000, I also received the DG's disc for my service in the CRPF.

When I was IG, northern sector, the CRPF was tasked with organizing the second All India Police Band competition, where eighteen bands from the states and paramilitary forces were to participate. DG Trinath Mishra always had innovative ideas. He felt the public should be exposed to the beauty and grandeur of police bands, so he advised us to hold the competition at Nehru Park and open it to all. Performing before the public, he felt, would also enthuse the police bands. It turned out to be a beautiful programme and started the tradition of police bands playing in public places in Delhi, which continues to date. I took a personal interest in getting the CRPF band trained by professionals for this competition. To our great joy, they returned with the overall champion trophy and first prize in pipe band.

The CRPF taught me the true nature of loyalty. Rarely have I seen a force that is called upon to sacrifice so much in the name of duty. Yet they exhibit the highest levels of dedication, discipline and respect for authority. They move from one end of the country to the other, handling everything from dangerous counter-insurgency operations to tedious elections, popular agitations to law-and-order problems. When the orders come, they have to move at short notice, often with no idea of what transport or accommodation will be available to them. They just pitch their tents and start functioning, sometimes in the harshest of conditions. Yet they do it all with equanimity.

Even when there are deaths in the force, they go out the very next day, ready to perform whatever duty has been assigned to them. It is truly an extraordinarily selfless service to the nation, for which I feel we should all be grateful.

21

A New State

In Bihar, the demand for a separate state for the tribal populations of Chhotanagpur and Santhal Pargana had been brewing ever since the day India declared her independence in 1947. The Jharkhand Mukti Morcha (JMM) launched a concerted agitation, which led the government to establish the Jharkhand Area Autonomous Council in 1995 and, finally, a full-fledged state in 2000.

Now, the entire civil service cadres of Bihar had to be divided between the two states. This, of course, gave rise to intense speculation about who would go where. Many were hoping to be allotted to Jharkhand; they wanted to get out of Lalu Prasad Yadav's political regime that, they felt, had led to the stagnation of Bihar. Jharkhand looked more promising, with cities like Ranchi, Jamshedpur, Bokaro and Dhanbad showing great potential for progress.

The government of India had laid down clear policies for cadre bifurcation—officers would be allotted on the basis of where they were domiciled. For married couples, the rule book said that the cadre of the senior spouse would apply to both.

Our cadre allotment orders reached us in Delhi on 14 November 2000, a day before the creation of the state of Jharkhand. Rakesh belonged to Jamshedpur, so he was allotted Jharkhand and because he had *inter se* seniority, I too went to Jharkhand. We were happy, thinking that we would finish our central deputation in two years, then go and work in the new state.

In the meantime, our family situation was changing rapidly. After finishing his engineering at Manipal, Tushar wanted to go abroad for further studies in 2001. But where that would be, was the big question. The same year, Anshuman took his class 12 board exams. Since he had no interest in engineering, we were also wondering which stream would be suitable for him. Four-year law courses had just been introduced in India. Anshuman took the admission test to join Symbiosis Law School, Pune.

In my life, certain days have turned out to be life-changing. One day, in May 2001, I came home for lunch to find that a letter had been pushed under the door of our Bharti Nagar flat in Delhi. Tushar had been accepted at the University of Pennsylvania for a master's in engineering and telecommunications. It is an Ivy League university, one where my brother, Samir, had studied. I had visited the campus and had even wished that I could have been a student there. Now, my son was going to UPenn and I was delighted for him!

Then, Rakesh came home for lunch and announced that Anshuman had made it to Symbiosis Law School. As parents, it was a big day for us. Both our children had done well. Yet, it was a moment tinged with sadness. While one would go far away to America, the younger one too would leave home now.

In the afternoon, I had a meeting at the MHA. As soon as I sat across him, joint secretary O.P. Arya handed me a sheet of paper, 'See, this has come.'

It was a note signed by Home Minister L.K. Advani, saying that Babulal Marandi, the CM of Jharkhand, had requested for five officers from the government of India to be repatriated at once as the new state needed them. I saw both Rakesh's and my name on the list. The joint secretary added, 'We are issuing orders for your repatriation.'

I went home in a state of agitation; there was still an entire year left for our central deputation to end. I thought things were going well, and I was enjoying my work in the CRPF. Moreover, hardly anyone ever went back without completing their tenure of deputation! But Rakesh took a philosophical view.

'No, I think we *should* go. We came on central deputation for a purpose—to give the children better educational opportunities. That has been accomplished and they are both charting their own courses now. Our work is done and we should go back. The new state needs us,' Rakesh said. My husband is a firm believer in 'putting yourself in the palm of His hand'.

We got busy arranging funds for Tushar's course, and Rakesh decided to take Anshuman to Pune to take admission at Symbiosis. Earlier, Anshuman's friends had also advised him to take the entrance exam for the National Law Institute University (NLIU) in Bhopal, which he had done. A day before they were to leave for Pune, he received a letter of acceptance from NLIU, Bhopal.

The family was now faced with a dilemma. I consulted Professor Madhav Menon, the founder of the first National Law School in Bangalore. I knew him ever since he came to the NPA to teach law and he also wrote articles for the NPA magazine that I had edited. His advice was unequivocal—send him to Bhopal. It is always good to study law in a university that is solely dedicated to legal studies, he added. We decided to heed his counsel. I went to Bhopal to help Anshuman settle into the NLIU campus. Then Tushar left for the US.

Rakesh was repatriated before me. Trinath Mishra, the DG, CRPF, said he would release me only after finding a substitute. He even laid down a condition. 'I will release you the day you get us the land for the officers' mess,' he smiled.

The CRPF lacked an officers' mess in Delhi, which was a hardship for any officer transiting or visiting the capital. A small plot in Nehru Nagar, in the heart of Delhi, had been identified by the government for us, where we had planned to build an officers' mess. This had been pending for ages. I had smiled at the DG's words. The land transfer was not in my hands, but in the few weeks left, I worked hard with commandant Ravideep Sahi and we managed to get the land. Eventually an officers' mess called 'Vishranti' came up at Nehru Nagar, much to the relief of the CRPF officers.

I was released by the government of India on 31 October 2001 to go to my new cadre—Jharkhand.

* * *

I arrived in Ranchi, the capital of Jharkhand, a year after its creation. We had heard good things were happening in the state—roads were being laid and electricity connections set up . . . I was excited to be a part of this growth story.

Administratively, Jharkhand was in good hands. CM Babulal Marandi had been a minister of state for forests and environment at the Centre, and a very competent minister at that. Both the chief secretary, V.S. Dubey, and DG, T.P. Sinha, were forward-looking, decisive individuals who wanted to lay a solid foundation for the new state. They worked well as a team, with a good understanding between them. This is critical when building something new.

Rakesh had already joined as IG, training and modernization. When a state is created, rules have to be formulated, training procedures laid down, promotions granted and recruitment boards set up. Rakesh had always been interested in matters of training and modernization, and plunged into his new role with great enthusiasm.

Although the CM wanted me to take charge as a zonal IG, the DG felt that my paramilitary experience would be better utilized in reorganizing the armed police. As soon as I began taking stock of Jharkhand armed police (JAP), I appreciated the DG's foresight.

Just as the paramilitary forces are maintained by the government of India, armed police battalions are maintained by the states as reserves. They are deployed to assist the district police whenever there is a special need. The armed police are organized into compact battalions, expected to always be in a state of operational efficiency and readiness.

JAP had been created by splitting the Bihar military police in half. Seven battalions, whose headquarters were in Jharkhand, were allotted to the new state. I soon discovered that the battalions had not been transferred with their full strength, with several men still stuck all over Bihar. We needed to consolidate the battalions urgently and trace our people.

At the JAP headquarters, all I had was one assistant, Mr Jaishankar. Looking at the volume of work before us, I managed to get another assistant and from the companies that had come to Jharkhand, I asked for a few constables who were better educated to be sent to my office.

We started work by first spreading newspapers in the corridor outside my office and arranging all the files that had come from Bihar. It still amuses me to remember those days, this motley group of policemen and I, sitting in the corridor and poring over files, trying to fathom where to begin. But we were not alone in this peculiar situation; even the DG did not have a regular office to begin with, and had been working out of the police mess initially!

Tracing people was a massive task, with SPs in Bihar reluctant to let go of manpower. Fortunately, in all the battalions, we had competent commandants and DySPs. Thanks to their teamwork, gradually we managed to get our people to come and join us. Some were not willing to relocate as their homes were in Bihar. We had to make them come, insisting that they would not get paid unless they joined their battalions in Jharkhand.

Because of my stint in the paramilitary forces from 1994 to 2001, I knew exactly what JAP needed from me. I enjoyed the challenges that came up every day, requiring all of us to think outside the box to come up with innovative solutions. Knowing that the state government would back us all the way energized us even further.

* * *

One of the key functions of our battalions was assisting the district police in tackling Naxalism, which had grown into a huge menace by 2001. The hilly, inaccessible jungle terrain and crippling poverty in the tribal lands made this a ripe ground for Naxalites to prosper.

I realized with shock that there were no proper standard operating procedures (SOPs) about how our men should venture into these dangerous zones. I had seen how, in the CRPF, certain SOPs had become second nature, for example, when marching to any sensitive location, the force would never return by the same route. Or crossing a *kutcha* (unmetalled) road on foot to avoid being blown up if their vehicles went over a landmine, as Naxalites often placed landmines under unpaved roads and covered them with rubble. Or walking in arrow formation to minimize loss of life and limb if a mine exploded. We began formulating these basic SOPs to train and educate the force.

One night we received information that a large team of district police and JAP had been ambushed in Chaibasa, with as many as thirty-nine casualties on our side. The mukhiya of a village had been killed. This was a common modus operandi of the Naxalites. They would kill a civilian—often a village functionary—and when the police went to retrieve the body or while they were retreating, they would be attacked.

After receiving news of the mukhiya's murder, the SDPO (sub-divisional police officer), who was a DySP-rank officer, rushed to the area with a strong contingent of local police and JAP. By the time they managed to retrieve the body, it was dusk. The DySP made the mistake of deciding to return in the dark on the same route and paid for it dearly. As the force was passing through the Saranda forest, they were ambushed and all of them were killed, including the DySP.

We received the information late in the evening and the DG, other officers and I left for the spot immediately. Even though it was dangerous to travel in pitch darkness, we wanted to bring back the bodies of our men right away. We saw that the Naxalites had burnt our vehicles and looted all the firearms. It was a ghastly scene.

The next day, the martyred policemen were given a proper police funeral with a guard of honour; the CM himself came to pay his respects and stand with the force. I was deeply affected by the loss of so many men from JAP.

I used to cross the lush, green Saranda forest on my way to the Kiriburu and Meghahatuburu mines in my CISF days. While we were returning by daylight a few hours later, I noticed how the forest cover had thinned. Earlier, the canopy was so thick that sunlight could not penetrate it, making the surroundings dark even during the day. Now, so many trees had been felled that the forest was awash with sunlight. The depletion made me sad.

* * *

There was an acute shortage of police personnel in the new state and an urgent need to recruit, but we ran into the issue of domicile. The tribal population said they were the rightful people of the land and that only they should be given jobs. But the non-tribals who had lived all their life in Jharkhand mounted a massive protest, saying that they too were domiciled. There was an impasse; no recruitments could be done.

In JAP, we could only recruit for the Gorkha battalions since it was restricted to Gorkhas. Two new companies were sanctioned by the state's home department and we immediately began recruitment. The Gorkhas are traditionally adept in combat situations. With the Naxalite menace so rampant, I felt that we should give them specialized training so they could be immediately deployed for anti-Naxal operations. It struck me that the army had a significant presence in Ranchi. Why not seek their help? When I spoke to Major-General

Thomas Matthews, he readily agreed, and I convinced the DG to allow this.

Our men learnt about all kinds of firearms, jungle warfare and counter-insurgency tactics during their training with the army. I also selected a band of trainers from other JAP battalions and sent them to be trained by the army so that they could in turn train our personnel.

Another innovative practice I borrowed from the paramilitary was the handing over of retirement benefits to our personnel on their day of retirement itself. DG R.K. Sharma had started this practice in the CISF and it had brought great relief to those leaving the force.

But getting the pension papers ready on time was a big task. We discovered that people had not been paid for years post their retirement from Bihar military police. They had been running from pillar to post, with the bifurcation of the force greatly compounding their woes. Struggling to pay for a child's education or medical expenses, they would come to my office to plead their case. Moved by their plight, I went to Patna and met R.K. Verma, the accountant-general of Bihar. Surprised to see an IG so concerned about the pension benefits of constables when no other senior officer seemed bothered about it, he said he would designate a person in his office to sort out the retirement papers. By October 2002, pension started getting disbursed on the day of retirement in JAP, much to the surprise of the men.

Compensation for personnel killed on duty also had to be handled with alacrity. In Bihar, the administrative lethargy had affected the police morale and counter-insurgency response as well. But in Jharkhand we could not afford laxity; we needed our men to be in top form to handle the Naxalite menace. To motivate them to go out and put their lives at risk on a daily basis, we needed to assure them that their families would get proper compensation in a timely manner if anything happened to them in the line of duty. Jharkhand had the best compensation package, but there used to be a delay. I knew things could be sped up as I had seen it in the paramilitary.

The men killed in Chaibasa were from JAP-4, the Bokaro battalion. I ensured that we processed the compensation papers of all thirty-nine slain men on priority and requested the DG to distribute it to the families on the Raising Day of JAP-4. Widows, children, old parents came and broke down while receiving the compensation. It was also an emotional, cathartic moment for us. There was not a single dry eye that day.

The speedy disbursal of compensation had a salutary effect on the force; it gave them an impetus to keep doing their duty.

We launched into welfare activities with the same enthusiasm, starting with health check-ups for the families. I decided to set up eye check-up camps for the wives of the JAP personnel and used our welfare funds to buy spectacles for them. This was hugely appreciated as this was the first time that something was being done for the womenfolk.

When we asked our men what facilities they wanted, they said they wanted to learn how to use the computer. There were ample welfare funds with which we bought computers and engaged professionals to come and train our men. In the evening, the same was offered to their children and wives. We also opened bank accounts for the men where their salaries would be directly deposited, while the wives were given debit cards to withdraw the money. I had seen this in the paramilitary; it cut down on the unnecessary movement of men, who would travel to their villages every month to reach the money, often through Naxalite-infested terrain which was dangerous. We had lost a few men in this way.

Sometimes, we had to resort to innovative means when it came to the welfare of the force. JAP-1, the Gorkha battalion, was stationed in the heart of Ranchi. There was an acute water shortage. When the Indian Oil Corporation approached me to open a petrol pump on our land, I immediately spotted an opportunity. Although it is a Herculean task to get government land on lease, I managed to convince the home secretary to allow us to lease the land to Indian Oil. Here the Kukhri service station came up. With the funds, we started sinking handpumps in the JAP-1 headquarters. I also convinced the Indian Oil authorities to let the wives of the Gorkhas run the petrol pump as it would generate extra income for the families.

* * *

When Bihar police was split, its sports teams and police bands were also broken up. We started holding inter-battalion football, volleyball and hockey matches so that Jharkhand police could start building its teams and compete in national tournaments.

Drawing on my CRPF experience, I tried to build back the Gorkha battalion's pipe band, which was their pride. The JAP-1 band soon started participating in the All India Band Competition. In 2003, they won the third prize among sixteen states. It was quite a feat for a newly raised state, and a big morale booster for all of us.

The Gorkhas were also good shooters. To encourage them and help them improve their aim, I brought in my yoga instructor to teach them concentration exercises. A couple of months after I left Jharkhand, a havildar of the Gorkha battalion did us proud, bagging the gold medal for revolver shooting at the All India Police Shooting Competition.

Our aim was to standardize practices within JAP, which would hold it in good stead even after we were not around. The high level of training, operational efficiency and ceremonial activities inspired by my central paramilitary experience brought a certain glamour and elan to Jharkhand armed police. Be it Raising Day celebrations, inter-battalion tournaments or parades, it gave me great satisfaction to be able to start healthy traditions in the JAP.

From a fragmented force, the men were now fully energized to work for the new state.

* * *

On the home front, Rakesh and I were well-settled in Ranchi. Our children were away pursuing higher studies, and it was just Rakesh's mother and the two of us at home. We made some very good friends and had a good social life.

But things were about to change drastically.

Right after Tushar went to the US for his master's at UPenn in 2001, the 9/11 terrorist attacks happened. The economy was hit, and by the time he finished a double master's, there were no jobs. In March 2004, I went to the US to see him and my sister, Reshma. Although Tushar did get a job eventually, his American visa expired and he decided he would come back home. I left for India in early April, and he was to follow a few weeks later.

When I landed in Delhi, CISF commandant Y.N. Sharma met me at the airport with a message from Rakesh. 'Sir has said you should not return to Ranchi, you should first call him.'

Wondering about this cryptic message, I telephoned my husband to learn that he had been diagnosed with 'retina detachment' in one eye. I was confused, not knowing what it meant. The doctor had advised him to immediately go to Sankara Nethralaya in Chennai for treatment. Rakesh asked me to stay on in Delhi as he would come there. But it took him two days just to reach Delhi because of VIP movement and another day for us to get to Chennai. I was worried sick by the delay.

Retinal detachment expert Dr Prateek Sen advised immediate surgery. I had never seen anyone in my family undergo an eye operation, and I was scared. But I knew Rakesh could not have been in better hands.

The surgery was successful and we all heaved a sigh of relief, although there was going to be a prolonged period of post-operative care. While Rakesh was still in hospital, I received a call from an unknown number. It turned out to be K.M. Singh, the DG, CISF. He said he had heard about my work in the CISF from the officers and asked me whether I would like to join the force again.

I was so surprised! I did not know Mr Singh beyond one short meeting in Srinagar during my CRPF days. I told him where I was and he was most understanding, saying he would ring later.

In June, my father suffered a fall that left him with black bruises on his face. My brother discovered this when he visited our parents for his birthday and asked me to come to Patna at once. My father did not look well at all, and he had to be hospitalized. Tushar was in Bombay interviewing for a job. I asked him to come to Patna as he and my father were very attached to each other.

When his condition stabilized a bit, we brought Babuji home, and Samir left for Delhi. Tushar was to join his new job, so we too left for Ranchi by train. But as soon as we boarded I started getting calls from my mother, asking us to get off. I called my father's doctor and he confirmed my worst fears—Babuji had passed away. By then, the train had picked up speed; I was in tears. I wanted to pull the chain for it to halt but the travelling ticket examiner (TTE) pointed out that the train would stop in the middle of paddy fields. 'How will you get down and make your way back?'

I turned to Tushar. Having him beside me was a source of comfort. Although bewildered by the sudden turn of events himself, my son stepped up and tried to keep me calm. As we helplessly waited for the train to reach the next station, I understood the power of the mobile phone. My mother was alone at home, so I called up my cousins in Patna to ask them to go to our house. My siblings and I were constantly in touch, crying, finding solace in one another's voice. Samir was frantically trying to get a plane ticket out of Delhi, but there were none. I called up some colleagues in the CISF and requested them to arrange a ticket. In those moments of panic and pain, this little device was all we had!

The train stopped at Tarengana station—the same station I had visited while investigating the bus dacoity case as ASP, Danapur. Police work was, however, far from my mind at that moment. I was just an anguished daughter desperate to return home. But it was my police family that came to my rescue.

Tushar and I had alighted right in front of a Bihar military police post. Just as we were wondering what to do, one havildar recognized me as the former DIG, Patna, and they immediately swung into action. I realized anew just how devoted and resourceful our men are! They arranged a car and, within thirty minutes, we were on our way.

Back home, we learnt that Babuji had passed away in his own bed, like he had always said he wanted to. He had asked my mother to switch on the *Ramayana* on television and read the *Sundarkaand* to him. He then passed away peacefully. The whole family gathered in Patna to be together in this moment of grief. We could not imagine our life at home without Babuji.

It was the end of an era for us.

During the thirteen-day mourning period, I again got a call from K.M. Singh. 'Have you considered my request? We want you to come,' he said.

I said yes, I would go.

There was a reason I agreed to leave Jharkhand and go back to the CISF. When Rakesh and I had come to Jharkhand in 2001, we had been looking forward to working in a new state, to help build the foundations of a new police force. We had no intention of leaving, we thought we would retire from Jharkhand police. Ranchi was a good place to live in and we were happy to be there.

But Rakesh's eye condition hit me hard. His doctor had told us that the eyes and ears are very 'sympathetic' to each other. If anything happens in one eye or ear, it is likely to happen in the other too. 'Expect a retinal detachment in the other eye any time,' he had warned us. I became acutely aware that Ranchi did not have an eye specialist. For any critical health concern, we would always have to look outside the state. Even getting to Chennai meant a detour via Delhi. What if there was no time to lose the next time this happened?

Now I understand why civil servants never want to stay in remote postings, be it the North-east or Tier-II and III towns, and why they are always itching to be transferred out. With no facilities for health or education, it is extremely hard to invest your life in these places.

So, when the DG, CISF, rang me a second time, I did not hesitate.

There was another reason as well. Babulal Marandi had suddenly been removed as CM for political reasons. This was extremely unfortunate for Jharkhand. The CMs who succeeded him had neither his vision nor his dynamism. Nothing seemed to be happening. The State Service Commission could not recruit anyone. There was a shortage of DySPs and the Naxalite problem was growing. The state was stuck in a limbo. After the first couple of years Jharkhand did not take off. All this had left me quite dejected. Losing my father felt like the closing of another chapter in my life, and I decided to go to Delhi.

Coming to work in a state when it is in its infancy was a great experience, as everything had to be built up from scratch. With what enthusiasm had Rakesh and I started in Jharkhand! Things were being done in record time, decisions were being taken and there was a sense of purpose as well as achievement and pride. But within three years, we had lost all our enthusiasm. The new state was becoming like the old state.

22

Mission Mode

This is how I returned to the CISF in 2004. The next six years were a thrilling journey, where I was part of a senior management team that oversaw a spectacular turnaround in the size and stature of the force.

The CISF is a need-based force. Raised in 1969, primarily to protect PSUs, the CISF became an armed force in 1983. Whenever the need arises, a survey is conducted, based on which the manpower is sanctioned. This could be as small as twenty-one personnel or in the thousands. In comparison, when the strength of the CRPF or ITBP (Indo-Tibetan Border Police) has to be increased, an entire battalion needs to be raised. This makes the CISF a flexible force, well suited for guarding various kinds of entities. It is also a compensatory cost force, which means the cost of maintenance is borne by the undertakings it secures and not the MHA, which it reports to.

When I joined the CISF as DIG, Bokaro Steel Plant, in 1994, PSUs were its most prestigious charges. But with the liberalization of the economy, the importance of the public sector somewhat diminished. By the end of the 1990s, a sense of stagnation had descended on the force.

On 24 December 1999, Indian Airlines flight IC-814 was hijacked on its way from Kathmandu to Delhi by alleged members of the Harkat-ul-Mujahideen terrorist outfit, to secure the release of terrorists lodged in Indian jails. After briefly landing in Amritsar, Lahore and Dubai, the hijackers took the flight to Kandahar airport in Afghanistan, which was under Taliban control.

The unpreparedness of our airports to handle a crisis of this magnitude became painfully apparent when the pilot managed to land the plane in Amritsar airport for refuelling, but IC-814 was allowed to leave Indian airspace after thirty minutes, without refuelling.

After this incident, the CISF was inducted into airport security in February 2000, starting with Jaipur airport, which had been found to be most vulnerable. Until then, airport security was handled by the local police, for whom this was not a priority area. Over the next few years, the CISF was inducted into all the airports, except Srinagar, which was covered by the CRPF. Today, the CISF handles the security at sixty-five key airports across the country, including Srinagar.

On 13 December 2001, the Indian Parliament was attacked by terrorists. Suddenly, the threat perception for government buildings changed; there was a heightened awareness that Delhi would be attacked again. The CISF was inducted into the North Block, South Block, Central Government Offices (CGO) complex and other critical buildings in the capital. The CISF was no longer a PSU-centric organization.

When K.M. Singh, the DG, had asked me to return to the CISF as IG, he had a specific purpose in mind. He wanted me to work on a long-pending cadre restructuring that had been stuck in the GoI for years.

Despite the expansion, no new posts had been sanctioned. In fact, the DIG (operations), who handled all operational matters of the CISF, was also looking after the airports with just two constables to assist him! This was an untenable situation, especially for a sensitive charge like airports. Every day an incident needed attention. There would be a security alert in one part of the country or another. One or more units would need immediate direction from HQ or there would be complaints from the public that had to be addressed. We needed an entire wing with senior officers who would handle airport operations on a daily, even hourly, basis across the country.

The DG handed me a report for the restructuring of the CISF prepared by M.K. Narayanan, who later became the national security adviser (NSA), and asked me to start working on it immediately. This involved pursuing the matter in the ministries of home and finance, which I did relentlessly. The sanctions came from the government in March 2005, creating 259 posts in the CISF across ranks, including an IG (airports) and two DIG (airports) posts for Delhi and Bombay. My own post, IG (HQ), was also created.

Thereafter, my batchmate, M.S. Bali, as IG (airports), undertook the mammoth task of formulating rules and regulations of airport management. He and I worked very closely, handpicking officers for the airports, seeing their importance for the CISF.

The historic cadre restructuring had far-reaching consequences for the CISF in terms of expansion, recruitment and promotion. The DG congratulated my team and me, saying that our endeavour would impact the CISF for the next twenty years. It was a matter of satisfaction to be able to live up to the faith he had reposed in me while bringing me to the CISF and entrusting me with this critical task.

Mr Singh had given me full freedom to work but he also told me that I should not hesitate to ask him for help. 'I will talk to anyone in the government if it helps our cause,' the DG had told me.

We were incredibly lucky to have S.I.S. Ahmed as the DG after Mr Singh, who enabled us to take the CISF forward, encouraging and guiding us at every step. On 7 July 2005, the London underground was attacked by terrorists, which immediately enhanced the threat perception for Delhi metro. This turned out to be another watershed moment for our force. The government wanted to beef up security in what was becoming the lifeline of Delhi's public transport system. But E. Sreedharan, the MD of the Delhi Metro Rail Corporation (DMRC), was firmly opposed to the idea, as he felt that airport-like checks would cause unnecessary delays for a fast-moving mass transit system, and he refused to bear the cost of the CISF.

But the MHA was steadfast in its decision. It fell upon Mr Ahmed to formulate a strategy of minimum deployment for maximum effect. Together with DIG M.K. Jha, the DG plotted the CISF's deployment in the Delhi metro, point by point, and the force was inducted into the DMRC in 2006.

The same year, a VIP security wing was sanctioned. The intelligence bureau (IB) had reported a spike in the security risk of VIPs, but the government had been struggling to provide security cover to all those in need of protection. So, once again, the CISF was called upon since it could be deployed in smaller formations. These were prestigious assignments that enhanced the status of the CISF. The new inductions also led to massive promotions and recruitments. S.C. Gambhir, an old hand in the CISF, handled all inductions to new units. It was a painstaking job but he took it up with gusto and performed it meticulously.

I feel we could accomplish all this because Mr Ahmed, with his background in the BSF, was well versed in the ways of the paramilitary. He trusted his team, yet he was involved in every aspect of the force and was a bold decision-maker. He was just the leader we needed at that particular juncture of tremendous expansion and diversification.

He trusted my judgement, allowing me to pick my team. I asked my NPA probationer, Taj Hassan, who was now DIG, CISF, north zone, to come join us at HQ. Our team, comprising Taj, AIGs K.B.P. Sharma, N.G. Gupta and myself, coordinated with the MHA and the UPSC to push through the promotions necessitated by the sanction of new posts.

After the 26/11 Mumbai terror attacks of 2008 and intelligence reports of enhanced threat perception to India's information technology (IT) sector, N.R. Narayana Murthy, the co-founder of Infosys, and other corporate leaders requested Home Minister P. Chidambaram to provide CISF cover for the corporate sector.

However, the CISF Act, 1968, allowed it to provide security only to PSUs, and the inherent nature of its charge would have to be changed by an amendment by Parliament. The CISF Act was amended in early 2009 and we entered the private sector that July, providing highly trained armed personnel adept in tactical deployment, to handle terror attacks and enhance the private security hired by corporates. We started with the Infosys campuses in Bangalore and Pune, where the induction was led by R.K. Mishra, IG, western sector. This was followed by our expansion into Electronic City, Bangalore, and several other corporate campuses.

All these important assignments gave the CISF a new lease of life, a huge improvement from the stagnation the force had been facing merely a decade ago.

* * *

Sometimes I look back at my last few years of service with wonder. How enthused we all were, forming teams and launching into one mission after another, each having far-reaching consequences for forces across the country!

The Sixth Central Pay Commission was instituted in October 2006. As I was IG (personnel) in the CISF, I had to pilot their representation before the commission. At the same time as secretary of the Central IPS Association, I was required to also present the representation of IPS officers.

There was a large volume of work to be done, collecting and collating data from everywhere. R.K. Mishra, whom I considered an outstanding officer from his probationer days, had joined me at HQ as DIG (admin.) from CISF, Mumbai, albeit rather reluctantly. I had, in fact, convinced him to come using the same line—*Jungle mein mor nacha, kisne dekha*. But as soon as he got there, he assisted me throughout as I worked day and night to put together the CISF presentation, highlighting the needs of the force before the commission.

On behalf of the police association, our primary request was to get the apex scale of Rs 80,000 for the chiefs of police and DGs in the states. We also wanted to do away with the post of DIG as it was creating problems of parity with the IAS.

On the day the association delegation was supposed to present before the commission, we had hoped that several senior officers would accompany us to bolster our case. Unfortunately, many of them backed out, even citing wafer-thin excuses like, 'I cannot come with you as I have a sore throat.'

I realized that they did not want to be seen on the wrong side of the powers-that-be. Eventually, only two senior officers accompanied us: S.I.S. Ahmed, DG, CISF, and Kuldeep Khoda, DG, J&K.

When the commission's report came out, we were disheartened to see that the apex scale had been extended only to DGs of forces like BSF, IB or CBI, but not the DGs of the state police. We did not lose hope. We renewed our efforts during the review process with help and guidance from M.K. Narayanan, the NSA, P.C. Haldar, the director of IB, and K.C. Verma, special secretary (security).

I also received tremendous support from E.S.L. Narasimhan, a former IPS officer who was then the governor of Chhattisgarh, A.N. Roy, the DG of Maharashtra police, S.S.P. Yadav, the DG of Andhra Pradesh police, and Ranjit Sinha, the DG of the Railway Protection Force.

The association made presentations before several dignitaries, including Shivraj Patil, the home minister, and Sonia Gandhi, the UPA chairperson. My batchmate B.V. Wanchoo, who was the director of the SPG, had arranged for the meeting with Mrs Gandhi. When we presented our case, she responded very positively, saying that policemen were losing their lives in Naxalite operations and something indeed had to be done for them. But the biggest help came from my old CM boss, Lalu Prasad, then the railway minister in the Union government.

He gave us time and several IPS officers went to meet him, including Rakesh and I. During this time, I would often meet Lalu Prasad at events in Delhi and he would say half-seriously, 'Why did you leave Bihar? Why have you gone to Jharkhand cadre, you should return to Bihar.'

At the meeting, he asked me directly, 'What is bothering you?'

When I explained our grievance, he said that it was an important issue. 'I am going to press for this at the cabinet meeting today. If they do not listen, I will leave the meeting!' He asked me to write down our request, and I jotted down the gist of our argument on a slip of paper in Hindi. I handed it to him, and he immediately left for the cabinet meeting.

We later heard that he really did push for the apex scale for state DGs and made it happen, despite severe opposition from his cabinet colleagues.

One person even remembered his wordplay. '*Malai mein makhhi kyun dal diya?*' he asked the cabinet in his characteristic style, hinting that when the government was doing so much for the police, why was it blemishing the good work with a minor caveat.

It was a major achievement for the association that would affect the police in every state, and I was glad all our hard work had eventually paid off.

Another pet project of mine was getting land for the CISF in Jharkhand. When I began working to get posts sanctioned, I realized that one of the reasons the ministry was reluctant to give us more posts was because collecting dues from the PSUs in lieu of deployment was a huge problem. When Mr Ahmed came as the DG, he understood this problem, and helped us launch a dues-collection drive. Our strategy was to start communicating with the top management of the PSUs, not just their accounts departments, and it yielded extremely positive results. That year we redeemed a record amount in arrears, which boded very well for the force.

But Heavy Engineering Corporation (HEC) in Ranchi, which owed the CISF several crores of rupees, was unable to pay the dues as that PSU had turned 'sick'. HEC came under the ministry of heavy industries, where I had managed to establish a rapport with the joint secretary, M.K. Singh, from the UP cadre. He came up with an interesting idea—why don't we transfer you land instead of money?

The more I thought about this innovative solution, the better it looked. Many people within the CISF did not share my views, they wanted the CISF to recover its money. But backed by the DG, we set the ball rolling. HEC had some prime land in Ranchi. Finally, after many liaisons, the ministries of home and heavy industries came to an agreement.

However, when the CISF tried to take possession, the local tribals staged a dharna on the land. I arrived at the site in Ranchi to find a full-fledged agitation—with flags, tents and shouting of slogans. We could not take possession.

When N.R. Das took over as DG, I convinced him to meet Jharkhand CM Shibu Soren once. If Mr Soren saw reason in our claim, we could get the land, I argued. Because I came from the Jharkhand cadre, Mr Das trusted my judgement and readily accompanied me to Ranchi. When we met the CM, all it took was a few minutes.

'Yes, yes, the land will be yours,' Mr Soren assured us, and that was that.

The CISF managed to acquire fifty-eight acres of prime land in a state capital.

The CISF campus in Ranchi was inaugurated on 8 January 2017 by Rajnath Singh, the home minister. It houses the office of the IG, eastern sector, the office of the senior commandant, a reserve battalion, a dog-training school and a training campus. On the day this campus was inaugurated, I received a call from K. Vijay Kumar, the celebrated IPS officer who is well-known for his role in the elimination of the dreaded sandalwood mafia led by Veerappan. Mr Kumar had accompanied the home minister to the inauguration of the CISF campus. When he was told how I had pushed for getting this land for the force, he telephoned me to say, 'You acquired this land, today a huge campus is being inaugurated. I must congratulate you.' I was very touched by his kind gesture.

The reason I had been so keen on getting the land despite opposition from almost every quarter is because I had a vision, inspired by Trinath Mishra, the former DG, CRPF. He would always say that, in the years to come, there will be shortage of land for raising battalions and building headquarters.

'Whichever government is offering you land, acquire it, even if you are not able to put up anything immediately,' he would advise.

So, acquiring HEC land in lieu of dues made perfect sense to me. The Ranchi campus has become a huge asset for the CISF as well as for Jharkhand. I had thought having a CISF facility in Jharkhand was a win-win for both the force and the new state, especially one increasingly affected by Naxalism. A paramilitary campus would mean construction contracts, new schools, a hospital and all kinds of ancillary activities, leading to economic growth. With this larger picture in mind, I was able to convince the state officers not to raise impediments. It felt good, too, to be able to do something for my home state.

The last DG I worked under was N.R. Das, with whom I had a good understanding going back to my DIG, Bokaro, days, when he was DIG, Rourkela Steel Plant. Since he had been in the force earlier and handled many difficult situations, it did not take him long to realize what was required to be done. A decision-maker by nature, he was receptive to new ideas.

Soon after he took over, I was promoted as additional DG, and he entrusted me with the task of selecting a suitable replacement for myself. I picked Swaraj Bir Singh as IG (personnel) from Meghalaya. Now our team comprising Prashant Kumar as DIG (personnel), with two AIGs—T. Selvan and K.B.P. Sharma—worked hard to find ways to tide over the shortage of gazetted ranks. The DG, being an experienced officer in the CISF, was quick to approve our suggestion of giving 'local ranks' and accelerated promotions—using the Limited Departmental Competitive Examination (LDCE) scheme—to personnel already in service. This led to massive promotions across all ranks.

Along with this, we also created a separate recruitment cell under Ratandeep Joshi, a very bright CISF officer who had an MSc from IIT. He did a commendable job in laying down new guidelines and professional methods of recruitment, making the whole process transparent and foolproof. Thus, we were able to carry out recruitments in all ranks during Mr Das's time, and not a single one was challenged at any stage.

All this consolidated the CISF further, helping us meet the new requirements, including the opening of the massive T3 terminal at Delhi airport and the 2010 Commonwealth Games.

* * *

When we moved to Delhi in 2004, Rakesh and I had ended up renovating my parents' flat in Vasant Kunj and making it our home, instead of taking up government accommodation. Rakesh had joined the BPR&D as a director, while Tushar got a good break in Genpact in Gurgaon and moved back from Mumbai. We were delighted to have our son staying with us again.

Anshuman, meanwhile, got a job with ICICI Bank in Mumbai during campus placements at NLIU, Bhopal. He was very excited to be the first one to be placed. We were also happy that he had gotten such a good job on his own merit.

In 2006, the family faced a tragedy. My mother-in-law, who had been living with us, suffered a fall and broke her femur. When we took her to AIIMS, the doctor said that all she needed was a simple surgery, as she did not have any significant health issues. But it had to be postponed by a week as her doctor was called away on some work.

In one week, her health deteriorated to such an extent that she had to be put on a ventilator and was then shifted to the ICU. It was traumatic for Rakesh, Tushar and me to see her, for she never came out of the ICU. One thing led to another and, battling multiple complications, she passed away a month after her fall. We just could not believe how a simple fall had led to this. In the last days, just like my father-in-law, she would tell Rakesh, 'My time has come, you should allow me to go.' She was eighty-one.

Around 2007, we started talking about Tushar's marriage. Several proposals were coming in for him; we asked him if he had anyone in mind. But he said he was open to meeting someone we might find for him. We received a proposal from a Patna family that was known to us. Meghna was a very accomplished girl and I knew Tushar wanted to marry a working woman. We also liked her very much. But the choice was theirs to make, we could only introduce them. When they agreed to the match, we were all delighted. The wedding, however, had to be postponed by a few months because Tushar got admission to pursue an MBA at the Kellogg School of Management in the US.

They got married in November 2008. I was excited because there would now be a girl in the family for the first time. Sometimes the in-laws, especially mothers, feel jealous of a woman coming into their son's life. But that thought never crossed my mind. I had always hoped that my sons found partners they really liked and not just marry their parents' choice. I was also happy that Meghna would be going to the US with Tushar, as I felt it would be a good period for them to bond, away from everything, to understand each other.

23

The End: A New Beginning

I retired from the IPS on 31 October 2010. It was the end of an era, my last day on duty.

The past few years had been full, both professionally and personally. In 2009, when I was promoted as ADG—with a solemn pipping ceremony in the office of the DG, N.R. Das—I had thought it was time to move to another force since the CISF did not have the post of ADG. But Mr Das insisted that I stay on, saying he would ensure that my post was upgraded. In April 2010, I became special DG in the CISF.

This was how I ended up spending six long years in the CISF, a force I had initially joined only to enrol my children in a good school in Bokaro! I now see the merits of a continuous posting, especially in senior positions. I worked with four DGs over six years, providing a certain continuity during this period of massive expansion and restructuring. The CISF felt like home now; there was little I did not know about the force.

Donning my uniform for the very last time, I asked myself whether I was sad to leave a service where I had spent thirty-four years and discovered, to my surprise, that I was not. I was, in fact, happy to be ending on such a good note. There was satisfaction that I had been able to achieve so much, that people respected me, that I had built such strong bonds. These things matter to me.

Were there regrets? Well, my retirement came up before I could head an organization as DG. This missed opportunity rankles a bit only when I think back to the year I lost when my grandmother made me repeat class 1, never dreaming that this slip of a girl would one day have a career and so much would hang in the balance for that one year, besides the years lost later in my life.

But forward-looking by nature, I was already excited about what lay ahead. Whenever people asked me about life after retirement, I would say, 'I will continue to work,' although I did not yet know where.

The DG and other officers gave me a very fond farewell, saying I would always be in their hearts. This, of course, moved me to tears, which I blinked back.

* * *

People presumed I would seek an assignment with the government, but I was loath to ask. Ever since my SP, Bokaro, days, I have never had to lobby for a posting, so now I did not want to go back to the government and ask for a job. I had seen some very senior officers running from pillar to post in the corridors of power asking for a post-retirement position; I did not want to do that.

'Start looking for a job as soon as you retire; you should not sit back thinking something will come to me,' advised my former DG, S.I.S. Ahmed. So, I created a profile on LinkedIn, the employment-oriented networking site, and spoke to my brother Samir, who works in the corporate sector.

In December, I got a call from Julio Ribeiro. 'You have retired? You didn't tell me!'

'What is there to announce, Sir? Yes, I have retired,' I replied with a laugh.

He said he had something for me. 'We have an office in Delhi, somebody will get in touch with you,' he said without divulging anything more. Rakesh and I were most curious about what the job could be. Soon enough, a gentleman telephoned me.

'We have been instructed by Mr Ribeiro to show you our office in Nizamuddin. When can you come over, ma'am?'

Unable to bear the suspense any longer, I asked him, 'Where are you calling from, what office is this?'

He said he was calling from the Indian Music Industry. I was stumped. I had no idea about music or its industry; my last association with music was when my cousin Ranjana and I had managed to shoo off our singing teacher in our teens!

The following day I went to Nizamuddin to find a small, compact office. I learnt the Indian Music Industry (IMI) is engaged in protecting, preserving and developing the copyright of the recorded music industry, with teams in every state. They also told me that, previously, former IPS officers J.N. Saxena and Prakash Singh had headed the IMI, working to curb piracy of music and to protect copyrights. Finally, it all began to make sense.

After a few weeks, Mr Ribeiro asked me to meet him in Mumbai. Before leaving, Rakesh and I speculated what the work might be. We both felt that working for Mr Ribeiro would be a tremendous experience. '*Jo bhi* job *kahenge karne ke liye* (Whatever job he asks me to do), I will do it,' I declared.

Mr Ribeiro offered me the position of chief coordinator, IMI. Working out of the Delhi office, the work involved building and managing teams all over the country. After joining, I began by streamlining the operations of IMI and reorganizing the teams in several states.

As I was returning from Mumbai after meeting Mr Ribeiro, I received another call. To my great surprise, it was the former CBI director, R.K. Raghavan.

While in service, I had been deputed by the DG, CISF, to speak at the Chamber of Commerce in Chennai on coastal security. The request for a speaker had come from Dr Raghavan, who, after the panel discussion, had exchanged a few words with me regarding my plans after retirement. I had told him, too, that I wanted to work, but that I would not be seeking an appointment from the government.

Now, Dr Raghavan was in Delhi for a day and wanted to meet me. When I told him that I was on my way back from Mumbai, he asked me to land and proceed to the departure area of Delhi airport, he would meet me there before boarding his flight back to Chennai. We met for merely five minutes, where he simply said, 'We would like you to join Tata Consultancy Services (TCS) as an adviser on homeland security.'

Two assignments came to me on the same day from two completely unexpected quarters—reinforcing my belief that certain days have marked the turning points in my life. It was quite thrilling.

At TCS, it was a pleasure to work with Dr Raghavan, D. Sivanandhan, my batchmate and the former DGP, Maharashtra police, and Brigadier G.S. Sisodia, who had retired from NSG.

In the course of our work, I was happy to interact with S. Ramadorai, the famed TCS leader who had transformed the IT company into the global behemoth it is today, offering software services across forty-two countries and employing 4,53,000 people. Special attention needed to be paid to the safety and security of such a large and diverse workforce. We would have regular meetings with N. Chandrasekaran, the then CEO of TCS and currently the chairman of the Tata Group, where every time I would marvel at his deep concern for staff welfare. I also saw the kind of faith the employees reposed in him, always believing that if an issue raised by them reached 'Chandra', he would do something about it.

Women make up one-third of the TCS staff strength; I soon found myself working with particular focus on their safety and security needs. It is a young workforce and many of these girls are working for the first time, living away from family and negotiating life in big cities. Being able to utilize my mentoring and police experiences to advise TCS associates in Chennai, Calcutta, Lucknow and Delhi on a host of issues is extremely fulfilling. At the same time, it has brought me in direct contact with today's youngsters and their unique problems, as well as the norms of corporate life. Coming from a career in the government, I have had to relearn certain aspects of professional life, which I have found very enriching.

The job offers, however, had not ended at two. Samir had referred my name to the Novo Nordisk Foundation, who asked me to head a mass diabetes-testing programme in Bihar. This was my home ground and I was always happy to work there. We signed a memorandum of understanding (MoU) with the health department of Bihar and launched a massive drive in every district.

On the request of the Federation of Indian Chambers of Commerce and Industry (FICCI), TCS nominated me to their homeland security vertical. It turned out to be a very active, interesting assignment. Thereafter, when FICCI started a private security vertical, they asked me to head it, given my long years in the CISF. I continue to work as an adviser on this vertical.

The diverse nature of post-retirement work that came my way was a pleasant surprise and keeps me energized.

* * *

Working on women's issues continues to be a passion for me. Since my retirement, there has been a steady stream of speaking engagements at colleges, schools, institutions and corporate offices. On 8 March, International Women's Day, my diary is always packed! In fact, that entire month I receive invitations for seminar and panels on women's issues, women's rights and legal awareness. However busy I am, I try to accept as many as I can because I believe in sharing my experiences and doing whatever little I can to help the cause of women's empowerment.

It has also been my lifelong endeavour to encourage more women to join the uniformed services. My mentoring and advocacy-related work continues after retirement.

One of my most interesting assignments was visiting Kabul in 2014 along with the late Kanchan Choudhary Bhattacharya, the former DG of Uttarakhand police. We visited the war-torn country on the invitation of the international non-profit organization, Oxfam, to interact with Afghan women police.

The purpose was to exchange ideas to help bring about improvements in their women police force and professionalize them. Given the turbulent situation in Afghanistan, my family was not too comfortable about this visit, but I was very keen because it was an opportunity to do something to further the cause of uplifting women.

Situated amid stunning mountains that reminded me of Kashmir and ringed in by armed security personnel at every corner, Kabul was a revelation. Apart from the restrictions on movement and a long list of 'don'ts' that were read out to us by our hosts, what struck me was the number of international non-governmental organizations (NGO) and aid agencies working in Afghanistan to improve the position of women.

We were horrified to witness the condition of their women police. Unlike in India, the women police enjoyed neither status nor respect, be it within the force or in society. As a result, women with education or status were not willing to join, and only those with no jobs or prospects were ending up in the police. While interacting with young women recruits through an interpreter, we were shocked to learn that women police were so looked down upon that some of them felt ashamed and unsafe to go home in uniform.

This was in stark contrast to our experience in India, where it is the uniform that affords us status and a sense of safety.

As soon as they were recruited, they received perfunctory training and ended up doing menial tasks, which led to further marginalization within the force and outside. We met the lone woman officer in the rank of SP. She had been given the charge of a district in Kabul, but we came to know that she was never really allowed to do any police work. Even the men assigned to her security were disdainful of her.

But the government was trying to improve the condition of the women police in all sincerity. Ministry officials, NGOs and advocacy groups were all very keen to understand what we were doing in India. We shared with them how women at every level of police in India were recruited through a common competitive exam and then underwent completely professional training on a par with men. We tried to impress upon them that the way to improve the status of their women police was to mainstream them, and also give them the wherewithal to carry out actual policing duties, not just menial or clerical work.

We came back with a somewhat heavy heart, hoping that our suggestions would help the women police become professional and gain the respect and status they so deserved. Sadly, nothing has changed.

* * *

Personally, the last few years have brought Rakesh and I a new kind of joy—becoming grandparents.

After Tushar finished his MBA, he moved to Hong Kong with a job, then to London and, finally, to our delight, came back to Delhi. He and Meghna had a boy, Kian, and then a girl, Syra. Having them close by has been the greatest pleasure, although we miss Anshuman and his family, who have settled in Mumbai.

Anshuman also went to UPenn to study for a master's degree in law. We then started looking for a match for him, and introduced him to Apeksha, the daughter of a close family friend in the police, an engineer herself who was working in digital advertising. We were very happy when they decided to marry. The wedding was held in a beautiful ceremony in Baroda in 2016. In January 2020, they were blessed with a baby girl, Tanishka.

I had always craved a daughter myself, so the birth of my granddaughters were momentous occasions for me personally.

Being a grandparent is one of the best feelings in the world. With my own children I was always pressed for time, but now I have the luxury to watch my grandchildren grow up every day—participating in their little games, listening to their chatter and telling them stories.

I pamper them in ways I would never have indulged my sons and, in me, I now see my parents, especially remembering the sweet bond my father shared with my sons.

As a career woman, I have great aspirations for my granddaughters. Be it my daughters-in-law or my granddaughters, I never want them to feel hindered in any way from taking up a career. I feel they should have the freedom to choose and be happy in their chosen professional paths.

I was incredibly lucky to be able to pursue an exciting career. More than ten years since I retired, I continue to work with as much positivity as my first day on the job.

24

A (Woman) Police Officer

How do I look back at my 34-year service? As an IPS officer, or as a *woman* IPS officer? In an ideal world, I would simply have been an IPS officer. The reality is that the 'woman' prefix was as much a part of my professional journey as the stars on my epaulettes.

Although all I wanted was to be treated on a par with everyone else—right from our training days at the NPA—I soon learnt to wear this difference as a badge of honour. I realized that instead of being gender-blind in the name of equality, I was in a position to bring a feminine touch to my profession and open up the force for more women. I was the first woman IPS officer in Bihar police. It was my privilege *and* duty to uphold this unique distinction. Thus, at every posting, I tried to sensitize the force to the needs of women, be it within our own ranks or among the public.

I have always felt that women in our country are scared of police stations. They perceive them as hostile places, and will never, *ever* go to a police station alone if they can help it. Yet, if we want to curb crimes against women, we need to make our police stations safe spaces for women. Two incidents early in my career highlighted this dire need.

When I was ASP, Danapur, one afternoon I entered Bihta police station to find a woman in a white sari, sitting huddled in a corner of the veranda. She was so tiny, for a moment I thought it was just a bundle of cloth. When I asked the OIC why she was sitting there, he made a noncommittal remark. So, I asked her myself.

Tears streaming down her face, she said her son had been killed and she wanted to record an FIR. But she had been kept waiting since morning because there was no paper in the police station! The officers had asked her to go buy the stationery if she wanted to lodge a report, but she had no money.

Livid at the insensitivity of the officers, I ticked off the OIC for mistreating a bereaved mother. 'But Madam Sir, we have no paper!' he protested. I told him it was *his* duty to procure the paper, not hers, and instructed him to register the FIR immediately.

I had thought that only poor rural women hesitated to go to a police station, but that misconception was shattered right in my own home.

I was away from Patna when my mother telephoned me one day in great distress to say that an elderly relative had gone missing from the house. She was frantic with worry. I was caught up in a critical case, so I told her, 'Why don't you go to the police station next door and register a missing person's report? I will look into it as soon as I get back.' My mother was horrified. She got really upset with me for even suggesting that she go to a police station all by herself.

I realized that, even though her own daughter was a police officer, my mother did not have the confidence to visit a police station. She felt inhibited. Sadly, this continues to be the prevalent perception among most women in India even today.

But the problem is not just with the police's public interface. When I joined the service, I was accompanying DIG L.V. Singh for an inspection of the police lines in Patna when suddenly he said, '*Yeh bahut bara paap hai* (This is a great sin),' and stormed out.

Following his line of sight, I saw a woman in a white sari carrying a tray of used teacups; she was the widow of a constable who had died on duty and she had been given a compassionate appointment in the police. Mr Singh said it was very demotivating for any policeman to know that if something happened to him, this was the fate awaiting his wife. Although employed as a constable, the men would only give her menial jobs like serving tea or cooking for the officers.

After I gained some seniority, widows of slain policemen became one of my priorities. I would leverage my position as a woman officer to motivate them to take up the jobs being offered, trying to give them the confidence that they could do police work. Sometimes, I also used my authority to secure the future of widowed girls.

On one occasion, a constable had died soon after his wedding. The family came to me to request that the compassionate posting be given to the deceased man's younger brother, who they said would take care of his brother's widow. I met the girl; she was very young, probably still in her teens. I was glad the family was not sending her back to her parents', which was often the case.

But I asked them, 'Why can't the brother marry her?' I insisted that if they were married, I would bend the rules and give the job to the brother. Perhaps it was none of my business, but I kept worrying about the future of this girl.

The family returned after a few days with photographs of the second wedding; I then met the widowed girl and assured myself that her brother-in-law had indeed married her.

In the aftermath of the anti-Sikh riots of 1984, I tried to make sure that all the widows in Bokaro were rehabilitated. I had recommended that every widow be given a job, whether by the Bokaro Steel Plant, the ancillary industries, the police or the government. Although I had left by the time this happened, I was pleased to know that my recommendation had been accepted. I had also spent hours with the women who had lost husbands and fathers and sons, convincing them to take up the jobs being offered.

I feel that only a job secures a woman's future in our society, especially a widow's.

During my last few years in the CISF, there had been a Naxalite attack on one of our units in Damanjodi in Odisha, which had resulted in heavy casualties on our side. One of the widows was so traumatized that she refused to take up the job being offered, nor did her family want her to work in the CISF. When she came to Delhi, I sat with her and her parents for a long time and convinced them to not let go of this opportunity. The DG, N.R. Das, was quite overwhelmed that I had managed to make her see the prudence of accepting the job. He said he had seen a new side of my character that day.

As someone who was in a position to effect change, while the welfare of the force was always my priority, I did keep an eye out to help women personnel whenever I could.

The CISF headquarters had many women in the clerical departments, as well as women constables. When I was DIG (admin.), one day, they came to meet me with a simple request. The building was five storeys high, but the ladies' toilet was located only on the ground floor. Whether pregnant or on their period, they had no option but trudge to the ground floor every time they wanted to use a washroom.

I decided to divide each of the men's toilets, which were large enough, and get women's toilets built on every floor. The move was resented by the men, but it provided great relief to the women.

The issue is not about toilets but about acceptance. In every office that I had worked in at the beginning of my career, even the CID or the Patna headquarters—let alone the districts—we women would have to use common facilities. This was the case even in an elite institution like the NPA, while we were probationers. When I returned to the campus as an AD, I insisted on getting washrooms made for ladies in the main building. Mr Ali, of course, fully supported this effort.

* * *

The management of mahila battalions in the paramilitary required special attention. I have already mentioned the problems we faced with the 88 (M) B in the CRPF in a previous chapter. It was a big learning. When we were laying the foundations of Jharkhand police, I advocated for raising a mahila battalion in Jharkhand armed police. Every battalion has a particular structure based on which the personnel are recruited. I asked for the structure of the 88 M (Bn) from the CRPF and used it as the blueprint to create a structure for the JAP mahila battalion. Keeping our experience at Jharoda Kalan in mind, I insisted that right from the beginning we should have a separate campus for the women.

With a massive expansion in its duties, the CISF began feeling the need for women personnel in large numbers by the mid-2000s. But the commandants were opposed to the idea; they kept saying how difficult it was to handle women or to get work out of them. They were also reluctant to create the separate infrastructure that was needed for inducting women personnel.

I convinced the DG, N.R. Das, of the urgent need to recruit more women. Then the commandants started asking, 'Where will they get trained? What about their barracks? Who will train them? We have no women trainers.' Despite the opposition, I insisted on recruiting women in large numbers. 'I was trained by men, so will they,' I argued.

Again, going by my experience in the CRPF, when the CISF started training women recruits in the regional training centres at Barwaha in Madhya Pradesh and Bhilai in Chhattisgarh, we cordoned off their living quarters so that there was no trouble with the men. During several of their passing out parades, I would be invited as the chief guest by the CISF. How thrilled the women were to see a lady IPS officer! I was delighted as well to see how well the women had taken to their new life in uniform.

The commandants had initially written this off as a fad of mine. It was only much later they realized that, given their increased public interface, the CISF could not have functioned without a professionally trained woman contingent. It was the need of the hour, and I am glad I was in the right place at the right time to oversee their recruitment and training.

Across the paramilitary forces, women have traditionally done very well. The CRPF women had been sent to Liberia for peacekeeping duties under the United Nations and earned a lot of respect for their good work, making the country proud.

I have tried to mentor lady officers wherever I was posted. Sometimes senior officers would try to be over-protective about lady officers and would not give them the tough duty points or exempt them from night rounds. But I did not encourage this and insisted that they be posted at par and perform all the duties expected of them. 'That is how I was trained, that is how I have worked, and they will do the same,' I would say.

I did not approve of women seeking undue benefits because of their gender either. Although sympathetic in certain cases, if they were trying to take advantage of the system, I was strict with them. I would tell them, in no uncertain terms, that they could not refuse postings all the time citing family concerns. The DGs would always consult me while shaping the transfer and other policies for women.

Just because I am a woman, I did not push for unnecessary leeway, yet I also did not become blind to women's needs. I hope I have always given a balanced view.

* * *

Crimes against women and children have always moved me, sometimes to tears, which I saw no point in hiding. Why is it wrong to have empathy as a police officer? I showed no leniency towards the perpetrators, even if sometimes my colleagues belittled my efforts, saying that I was acting out of 'emotion'.

When I started out, there was little we could do in the anti-dowry cell of the CID to prosecute cases of domestic violence and dowry-related deaths because the Dowry Prohibition Act lacked teeth. Even if we made arrests, the accused would get bail soon after. In 1983, Prime Minister Indira Gandhi pushed through the inclusion of Section 498A in the Indian Penal Code, which made matrimonial cruelty a non-bailable, non-compoundable and cognizable offence. We could finally start taking action.

If a father came and reported that his daughter was being tortured, we would immediately swing into action and pick up the husband and in-laws. This started having a salutary effect. I think only a woman prime minister could have ushered in an act like 498A. Although there have been instances of the law being misused by women, having seen the good it has done, I feel Mrs Gandhi did a great service to the country by bringing about this change.

As SP, Bokaro, I once got a chilling phone call from a woman. 'I am being tortured, my daughter has been scalded with hot water, please help us!' I immediately asked the DySP (town) to go to her house, where he discovered their two-year-old daughter had been pushed into a tub of hot water and had red marks all over her tiny body. He arrested the husband.

This case became a big one. The husband happened to be from my community, so fellow members of the community started putting pressure on me to not take action against him. I did not budge, the wife had given a statement and there was clear evidence of torture on the girl child. The wife also accused him of domestic abuse and demands for dowry.

I started getting calls from our HQ in Patna that I was being too emotional about this case because I was a woman. My seniors even insinuated that I was being harsh on the husband because of my history of a failed marriage. I refused to let the loose talk rankle and just followed the law.

Years later, at a wedding in Patna, the same woman came up to me. The man accompanying her said gratefully, 'You saved her life. They would have killed her and her child, but you saved her.' I realized that she had later married this nice man, and was really happy to see things had eventually worked out for her.

* * *

Another landmark development was the adoption of the Vishakha Guidelines in 1997, which covered prevention of sexual harassment at all workplaces. I was part of several such inquiries in the paramilitary.

During my tenure as ADG, CISF, the MHA had asked me to inquire into a case in the CRPF in Tamil Nadu. A junior doctor had accused a DIG of making sexually coloured remarks. There were no eyewitnesses. It was her word against his.

Whoever I interviewed spoke in favour of the accused DIG, although they also said the lady doctor was competent and sincere in her work. Some people also mentioned that she was a 'divorcee', as if that had any bearing on the case! It would have been useful to speak to her reporting authority, but the senior doctor was recuperating from a bypass surgery. I made several trips to the CRPF unit but could make no headway. After months, I managed to speak to him over the phone. 'Yes, something must have happened that day; she came and told my wife that the DIG had misbehaved with her, she was very upset.' I recorded his statement and forwarded my findings to the ministry that the allegation was true, after which the ministry compulsorily retired the DIG.

Unfortunately, like with the domestic violence law, women sometimes misuse this law, doing a great disservice to genuine victims. If I found a case to be false, I did not spare the woman complainant.

Once there was an allegation of sexual harassment against a doctor by a junior lady doctor in the CRPF in Nagpur. I knew him earlier when he had been posted under me. He was a competent doctor with a good reputation. My opinion of him notwithstanding, I decided to look into the case with an open mind. When I visited the clinic that was the PO and tried to recreate the chain of events as reported by the victim,

I found holes in her testimony. Further inquiries revealed that this officer and her husband, both working in the CRPF, were preparing to take the civil service exams, because of which they had been refusing duties outside the GC.

Based on all the evidence, we were able to establish that it was an ill-motivated case. She had filed the allegation against her senior to pre-empt any punitive action against herself because of indiscipline. The Vishakha Guidelines mandated that a committee be formed, which included a member of a local NGO. The representative from the NGO concurred with my findings and we turned the case false. I recommended very strongly that the complainant be dismissed from service as she was not fit to continue. It was a horrendous accusation to make against a fellow human being and a gross misuse of the legal remedies available to her.

In another case, a deputy commandant in a CISF unit in Maharashtra had asked a lady constable to vacate an official residence as per rules and was slapped with a harassment charge for it. The case turned extremely vexing because the inquiry officer, a lady commandant, sided with the lady constable without even examining any witnesses. Things were not adding up, so the officers placed the file before me to take a decision. I ordered a thorough 'de novo inquiry' (further inquiry), after which the deputy commandant was found not guilty. The complainant was eventually dismissed from service. When I asked the lady commandant why she had gone along with the false allegation, she said it would have been difficult for her to go against another woman in the force. I was very disturbed by this clique-like behaviour.

Such cases become a huge hindrance in integrating women in our uniformed forces on a par with men. Even the DGs are not immune to the implications. I have had women officers come and say ruefully to me that whenever they go to the DG's room to discuss a matter, the DG makes sure to keep the door open, which they never do for male officers. I have even heard some senior officers say that they never receive a woman officer alone in their office, they ask their PA to be present. This is very demeaning for woman officers, and I feel seniors should refrain from doing this.

Alienating one part of the force is never the answer to any problem.

* * *

Over these pages, I have dwelt at length on my life as a woman police officer. But what about my life as a woman?

At the beginning of our careers, when Rakesh returned to Patna on promotion as SP rural, he was entitled to an earmarked house. All my life, I had wanted a home and a family. This was it. I purchased furniture and lovingly decorated our drawing room, dining room and bedroom. I also organized the kitchen and Tushar's playroom. I love cooking, and it was a pleasure to see Rakesh polishing off the food I would prepare. Looking after Rakesh and the boys has always been very fulfilling.

I feel one can be a devoted wife, a doting mother and a good officer; there is no contradiction in these roles. Throughout my service, I have always tried to balance my home and job, never wanting to give up one for the other. Be it helping Rakesh get his sisters married, looking after my in-laws or my own parents, bringing up my children or caring for my nieces, nephews and cousins, I feel a woman can give so much selfless love to the people who are with her.

As a woman IPS officer or, for that matter, as a woman, you must always preserve the core of your femininity. It is a rare gift that should not be circumscribed by ephemeral circumstances.

In conclusion, having relived my entire journey in the course of writing this memoir, I feel blessed to have been given the opportunity to be the first woman IPS officer of Bihar police. I hope I was able to do justice to this extraordinary life.

I would, however, not be doing justice to my story if I did not end with the story of a woman who made it all possible.

25

The Gift of Freedom

When I moved to Bokaro as SP in May 1983, soon after the birth of my second child, I initially left baby Anshuman in my family's care in Patna and took Tushar with me. My mother had sent an old family maid, Pachia, to help me.

At the SP's bungalow in Bokaro, I noticed a tall, dark-skinned woman, dressed in a black, glass-nylon sari standing in the kitchen, a baby tied to her back with a long piece of cloth. She was so thin she looked emaciated.

'Who is she?' I asked the sergeant major. He said her name was Agnes. She used to look after the two boys of the previous SP—the one who had been hastily transferred because of trouble in the police lines. Since they did not take her along, she was hoping the new SP would keep her. But I had brought my staff with me, and I did not want more help. In fact, I needed her to vacate the outhouse so that Pachia could stay there.

Agnes was looking at me with frightened eyes although she did not say a word. The sergeant major pleaded her case. 'Madam, just keep her. She does not have a husband. Where will she go? She won't demand much. Just Rs 30 a month and food from your kitchen.'

I was in a hurry to take charge in the SP's office, so the matter remained unresolved. When I returned, I saw that she was still in the house. I was in a fix. What would I do with her? I got busy with work and almost forgot about her for the next few days. A couple of weeks later, I brought Anshuman to Bokaro. With the boys being a handful, I noticed Agnes coming forward and trying to help. Her habits were extremely clean; she would wash the milk bottles very well and handle Anshuman deftly. She was even able to rock him to sleep, which is a boon for any mother!

I started taking an interest in this strange woman who had quietly joined my household. She shared her life story with me. Agnes came from Longa, a tribal village near Bokaro in the district of Gumla. She had been married very young, and had lost her husband suddenly to a stomach ailment after two years, leaving her with a son. She started living with her parents, with no livelihood or prospects. Looking at her pitiable condition, her sister, Mary, who was a constable posted in Bokaro, brought Agnes to the city.

Leaving her son with her mother in the village, Agnes came to work in Bokaro. She said she was exploited and gave birth to a daughter. This was the baby I had seen tied to her back. She started working for the SP's family but, when they left, she did not know where to go.

What kind of a life would this woman have with a young son in the village and a baby daughter in her arms? What would be the future of these children? My heart filled with compassion for this helpless young woman, and I felt almost compelled to do something for her.

One evening, we were all out in my jeep. I was sitting beside the driver, and Agnes was in the back seat with the children. Suddenly, there was an urgent call from one of the police stations. I asked the driver to take us to the thana concerned and told Agnes to wait in the vehicle with the boys, so that I could go in and attend to some work.

When I returned, I saw Agnes looking at me strangely. 'You went into a *police station*? I don't even know what a police station looks like,' she said, her eyes round with awe. She was fascinated that a woman had walked into a police station with so much authority. I think she began to see me in a new light that day.

I asked Agnes if she was educated. 'Yes, I am second-pass,' she replied proudly. But she was not really literate. As SP, I had started a system of training women as home guards, which is a reserve force called upon to assist the police when there is need for manpower in law-and-order or bandobast duty.

'Why don't you undergo the home-guard training?' I suggested to Agnes. I do not think she understood what it meant, but went nevertheless because I had asked her to.

Then, a remarkable thing happened. Just like the IPS uniform had given me a new identity when I wore it for the first time at the NPA, I saw how the home guard's uniform transformed Agnes. Probably for the first time in her life, she started feeling empowered. She was in uniform; she was marching; she even received some firearm training. Her demeanour and body language started changing. She became smarter, more articulate, livelier. She was also financially better off, as the home guards receive a fixed pay.

If we could teach her to write her name, we could open a bank account for her, I realized. So, I asked a constable to teach her to read and write a little. Although it was difficult for her, eventually she learnt to write her full name—Agnes Bilung.

Thus, we opened a bank account for her so she could save her salary. This was the beginning of our journey together.

* * *

When Rakesh and I got posted to Hyderabad in 1986, we were feeling a little lost, because Pachia wanted to go back to the village as she had two daughters to marry off. It was true that our old maid had left her own girls with her mother to come and look after us. Now, it was time to let her go back home.

But what would happen to our boys? Rakesh and I were mulling this problem when Agnes came up to me and said, 'I will come with you to Hyderabad.'

I was quite taken aback at her decision. She said she had thought it through; she would send her daughter to her mother, so she could continue working for me. I could see she was taking charge of her life. We were, of course, delighted. By then, Agnes was indispensable in my house, carrying Anshuman tied to her back, and looking after everything. He was extremely attached to her as well.

Since we were leaving Bihar, she could only come with us in a private capacity. Although it was a little expensive for us, I decided to continue paying her the home guard's salary because I did not want to diminish her income. She would save and send money to her village every month.

In Hyderabad, Agnes really flowered and came into her own. Gone was the mute, timid woman of the village. With no orderlies or the usual trappings that come with a senior officer's accommodation, she became the main person running our home at the NPA. She would help us haul buckets of water, manage the kitchen and look after the children.

Just as we were expanding our horizons through our interactions with IPS officers from different states and our children were all growing up together, I saw how Agnes had begun to interact with the staff of other officers and explore the campus on her own. It was a secure place, so I was not worried.

From then on, wherever I was posted, Agnes was my constant companion—Patna, Bokaro, Delhi, Ranchi. We could not imagine our home without her; Agnes had become family. Our friends and extended clan also became very fond of her. She knew everything about them—who liked coffee, who took sugar in their tea and how much, which nephew liked cheese toast and which niece wanted an omelette for breakfast. Whenever our parents stayed with us, Agnes would take great care of them as well.

She was an honest woman, I do not ever remember locking anything up. She never asked me for anything except one request—getting her only brother a job in the police, as her family was always pressurizing her. I was able to help her brother get recruited as a follower in Bihar military police, which made Agnes very happy.

By the time I was posted to Jharkhand, her son Iranius had come of age, and now she wanted me to find him a police job too. He had not studied much and was living off his mother, frequently turning up at our house to demand money from her.

Jharkhand police was recruiting in big numbers and there were reservations for tribal candidates, yet Iranius could not get selected as a constable because of his short height. But Agnes kept up the pressure on me. She had been a second mother to my sons and even if I found her son annoying, I wanted to do something for her.

There is always a shortage of cooks in the police, so I asked my driver to fix Iranius up with a local dhaba, where he would work without pay and learn the basics of cooking. My relatives were amused to see what I was getting myself into, but the boy toiled for six months and managed to get selected as a police cook. Agnes felt at peace as a mother, for she had gotten her son a job.

When Agnes's daughter, Scholastica, finished school, I helped her get into an ITI, and later got her enrolled in a college for a bachelor's degree.

* * *

After our retirement, we stayed on in Delhi. I realized that we were all getting old, I would get another girl to help out in the house but kept Agnes with me.

In November 2013, Rakesh and I had gone to Sankara Nethralaya in Chennai for his eye surgery. When we returned, Agnes said she was not feeling well and was unable to eat. As she took off her shawl, I was shocked to see her stomach looking bloated and worried whether it was a tumour. I sent her to the local doctor. An X-ray and ultrasound revealed an accumulation of water in the abdomen.

I took her to Rockland Hospital, a private hospital close to our house, where the doctors drained out the liquid and sent it for tests. When the reports came, we were asked to meet Dr Arun Kumar of the oncology department. The doctor diagnosed Agnes with third-stage ovarian cancer. Sitting beside me, Agnes did not even understand the prognosis, but seeing my expression, she started asking me with urgency, '*Yeh kya bol rahein hain* (What is he saying)?'

I was so pained, I could not bring myself to talk.

The doctor said she needed immediate surgery, the cost of which would run into several lakhs of rupees. Money is a universal language, and Agnes understood what was being said. She looked at me in panic, 'Memsahib, *mere paas toh itna paisa hi nahin hai*, operation *kaise hoga* (Madam, I do not have so much money, how will I get the operation done)?'

Choking back tears, I told her not to worry about money, that she was family and we would pay for her treatment.

The doctor told me that, even with surgery, Agnes had another two and a half years to live at best, which I did not tell her. I returned home broken although I tried not to show it. But she knew me too well and would keep asking me, 'Why are you looking so sad?'

Agnes went through multiple surgeries and several rounds of chemotherapy. The treatment left her in tremendous pain and low spirits. Sometimes she would be crying in agony through the night, with Rakesh making her hot water bottles, me rubbing her back. We nearly turned the house into a cancer-care ward, nursing her along with other household help. Later, her sister, Albesia, started staying with us because Agnes now needed round-the-clock care. But whenever she felt a little better, Agnes would try to start working around the house. I would try to tell her not to worry about money, to eat fresh fruit and take rest.

Everyone in the family, including my sisters and my sons, pitched in, and over the next sixteen months we did whatever we could for her treatment.

Dr Kumar was extremely surprised. 'I can't believe it. Cancer treatment is so expensive. People abandon their own relatives, and you are paying so much for a maid?'

His words really affected me. I thought Agnes had done so much for us, she had raised our children, taught them values, loved and cared for all of us. If she was not family, then who was?

In December 2014, some friends suggested we take her to Shanti Avedna Sadan, a hospice that provides palliative care for terminally ill cancer patients. It was around Christmas, so Agnes was happy to go. The nuns there put them through prayer in a fresh, clean and festive atmosphere. The nuns are remarkable; I have so much admiration for the service they are providing. They do not charge any fee for this selfless service of providing succour to the dying. Anshuman came from Chennai to be with Agnes for her last Christmas. Tushar, who was visiting from London, also had a tearful meeting with Agnes.

The bonding between Anshuman and Agnes was of pure love. Whenever he would come home from hostel or work, he would hug her. And Agnes pampered him without end. She was never too tired to cook something for Anshuman, be it an odd time of the day or night. Two days before she died, Rakesh gave her a couple of photographs of Anshuman. In one of them she was carrying him tied to her back. She smiled and placed the pictures on her heart. Rakesh knew she was in communion with him and was wishing him all the best in life.

I have not known a gentler soul.

I went to see Agnes before going to Patna to bring my mother to Delhi. She was fading in and out. 'Hold on, Agnes, I will come back and take you home,' I said. Upon my return, when I landed at Delhi airport and switched on my phone, I learnt that Agnes had passed away fifteen minutes ago. Rakesh said that, like every mother, Agnes had been waiting to see her son one last time, clinging to life until she saw him. Finally, Iranius came, and within two to three days Agnes passed away. We arranged for her body to be taken to her native village in Gumla for the burial.

Every year, Rakesh and I make a donation to the hospice on Agnes's death anniversary. She had left instructions that her savings be used for her daughter's wedding. We ensured this was done, and all of us from the family also pitched in when Scholastica got married. Agnes's family has kept in touch with us over the years.

I always say that I was successful outside the home only because Agnes was in my home.

Given the kind of family life I had led, with a constant stream of guests and relatives, family commitments, old parents and little children in the house, I would not have been able to pursue my career with such focus had I been constantly between home and work.

Agnes allowed me to be the officer and homemaker I always wanted to be.

All I did was spend ten minutes with her every morning discussing the needs of the household, then I could head to work, knowing that everything would be taken care of. Not just that, Agnes took great care of me too. When I came home, my clothes would be ironed, the geyser would be on and coffee would be ready.

At the organizational behaviour course in Australia, they taught us that a good personal assistant helps an executive achieve all his goals. I feel that for a working woman—who is an executive both in the office and at home—an efficient, trustworthy help at home is just as important.

A few months after we lost Agnes, Rakesh and I went to Jerusalem. Rakesh had carried a picture of her and, while he held it in his hand, we prayed for her eternal peace at the Church of the Holy Sepulchre, where Jesus was buried.

If my husband Rakesh was the wind beneath my wings, this waif-like, barely literate, tribal girl was the backbone of my career. If my uniform gave me status, Agnes gave me the freedom to wear it. There is not a single day that I do not think of Agnes with gratitude or miss her presence in our family.

Epilogue

Before I could complete this book, I lost my mother. How innocuous is this word 'lost'! From the time I opened my eyes, she was always there, for seventy-one years of my life. A mother, a sister too, a consoler, a nurse, an adviser, a helper, a doer, an epitome of values and elegance, an eternal believer in my capability . . .

Gracious Amma,

Fate made me a helpless spectator as you slipped away from us. Your love and kindness will comfort me for the remaining years I am without you. All that you taught me remains with me. My success was possible because of your constant support and abiding trust in me.

I owe so much of who I am to you.

I miss you, Amma.